Commensality

Commensality

From Everyday Food to Feast

Edited by
Susanne Kerner, Cynthia Chou, and Morten Warmind

Bloomsbury Academic
An imprint of Bloomsbury Publishing Plc

B L O O M S B U R Y
LONDON • NEW DELHI • NEW YORK • SYDNEY

Bloomsbury Academic
An imprint of Bloomsbury Publishing Plc

50 Bedford Square	1385 Broadway
London	New York
WC1B 3DP	NY 10018
UK	USA

www.bloomsbury.com

BLOOMSBURY and the Diana logo are trademarks of Bloomsbury Publishing Plc

First published 2015

British Library Cataloguing-in-Publication Data
A catalogue record for this book is available from the British Library.

ISBN: HB: 978-0-8578-5680-7
PB: 978-0-8578-5736-1
ePDF: 978-0-8578-5729-3
ePub: 978-0-8578-5719-4

Library of Congress Cataloging-in-Publication Data
A catalog record for this book is available from the Library of Congress.

Typeset by Fakenham Prepress Solutions, Fakenham, Norfolk NR21 8NN
Printed and bound in India

Contents

List of Illustrations

Notes on Contributors

Boris Andersen (M.A. in Media Sociology and Literature, University of Copenhagen) is a Ph.D. fellow at Aalborg University, associated with the research group Foodscapes, Innovation, and Network. His present research is focused on young people's food habits, commensality, and cooking skills. Other research interests include health in meal communities, youth and foodblogs, as well as the relationship between young people's interest in cooking and food manners during education in home economics and the environment.

Stuart Campbell is professor of Near Eastern Archaeology at the University of Manchester. He has directed and co-directed the Domuztepe Project since 1995, and has worked previously on prehistoric sites in Iraq and at the Bronze Age site of Jerablus Tahtani in Syria. His research has involved a wide range of approaches to understanding prehistoric societies, including symbolism and use of ceramics, funerary practices and the ways in which the past was remembered in prehistoric societies. He also has methodological interests in chronologies, site formation processes and archaeological practice.

Cynthia Chou is Associate Professor of Southeast Asian Studies at the Department of Cross-cultural and Regional Studies at the University of Copenhagen. Her research focuses on center–periphery relations, indigenous communities, and the relationship between movement and identity constructions in Island Southeast Asia. Her publications include "Agriculture and the End of Farming in Singapore," in *Nature Contained: Environmental Histories of Singapore*, ed. Timothy P. Barnard (Singapore: NUS Press, 2014) and *The Orang Suku Laut of Riau, Indonesia: The Inalienable Gift of Territory* (London and New York: Routledge, 2010).

Maria Bianca D'Anna studied Near Eastern prehistory at the Sapienza University (Rome) and is now working on her Ph.D. dissertation on the Arslantepe period VI A pottery at Eberhard Karls University (Tübingen). She has worked at Arslantepe since 1996 and took part in excavations and surveys in Turkey, Syria, and Azerbaijan. One of her research interests is the role of food politics and commensality in early complex societies.

Alexandra Fletcher is the Raymond and Beverly Sackler curator of the Ancient Near East at the British Museum, with special responsibilities for the prehistoric collections within the department of the Middle East. She has been part of the Domuztepe project team from 1996 and managed the excavation's program of ceramic research. Her research deals with aspects of identity, social development and the study of social information contained within material culture, particularly objects associated with food and drink.

Paul Freedman is a Professor of History at Yale University in the U.S.A. His fields are medieval history and the history of food. He has written extensively on Catalan society in the Middle Ages. He is also the author of a book that considers the demand for spices. Freedman edited *Food: The History of Taste*, a volume of essays that consider food from prehistory to the present. It has been translated into ten languages.

Carolin Jauss studied archaeology and languages of ancient Western Asia, Middle Eastern Studies and Anthropology at the Albert-Ludwigs-Universität Freiburg im Breisgau and the University of Arizona, Tucson. After a stay at UNESCO's headquarters in Paris, she worked as assistant at the Free University Berlin. She is a member of the project "Commensality and Shared Space in the Context of Early State and Urban Development in Mesopotamia and Southwest Iran" that is part of the Excellence Cluster Topoi at the Free University Berlin.

Susanne Kerner (M.A. and Dr. Phil, Free University Berlin, Germany) is Associate Professor of Near Eastern Archaeology at the Department of Cross-cultural and Regional Studies. She has been directing the German Institute for Archaeology of the Holy Land in Amman as well as leading several excavations in Jordan. Her research interests include the development of social structure and hierarchy, food and its social relations, and gender archaeology. She has written on specialization and social dimensions of pottery, and her latest edited publication is *Climate and Ancient Society* (2014).

Yvonne le Grand, while doing research for a project on the politics of cooking, became interested in the political economy of the global food system. Currently she is pursuing a Ph.D. in social and cultural anthropology on the conflicting beliefs and ideologies in the genetically modified food debate in Portugal at the Institute of Social Sciences of the University of Lisbon.

Astrid Møller-Olsen holds a Master's degree in Comparative Literature from the University of Copenhagen. She studied Chinese as her minor, including half a year at Beijing University. Her publications include articles on Ah Cheng's material Daoism and Lu Xun's use of cannibalism as a literary theme. On her blog (http://www.writingchina.wordpress.com) she writes about food, drink, and the body in Chinese literature.

Cornelia A. Nell, after her undergraduate degree at the National University of Ireland NUI Maynooth in Anthropology and English, lived in Bolivia for some time. She returned to Europe in 2007 in order to take up a Ph.D. in Social Anthropology with Amerindian Studies at the University of St. Andrews in Scotland. Her work is based on fieldwork in the Bolivian Andes in 2008/9.

Hanne Nymann is a historian, currently working as project manager as well as historical researcher for the Qatar Islamic Archaeology and Heritage Project (University of Copenhagen). Her academic interest lies within the topics of historical food and consumption studies, working from both textual and archaeological sources, with a particular interest in the culinary cultures of the pre-modern period of the Persian Gulf.

Jordan D. Rosenblum is Belzer Associate Professor of Classical Judaism at the University of Wisconsin-Madison. He received his Ph.D. in Religious Studies from Brown University (2008). He is the author of *Food and Identity in Early Rabbinic Judaism* (Cambridge: Cambridge University Press, 2010).

Ingvild Sælid Gilhus is Professor of Religion at the University of Bergen, Norway. She works in the areas of religion in late antiquity and new religious movements. Main publications include *Laughing Gods, Weeping Virgins: Laughter in the History of Religions* (1997) and *Animals, Gods and Humans: Changing Attitudes to Animals in Greek, Roman and Early Christian Ideas* (2006). She is the book review editor of *Numen* and an editorial board member of *Temenos*.

Tan Chee-Beng, who is from Malaysia, has taught at several universities and is currently Distinguished Professor at the Department of Anthropology, Sun Yat-sen University. His major areas of interest have been cultural change, ethnicity, and ethnic relations, Chinese overseas, religion, anthropology of food, indigenous peoples, and development, and his research areas include Southeast Asia and China. His recent publications include *Chinese Overseas: Comparative Cultural Issues* (2004), as editor, *Chinese Transnational Networks* (2007), *Chinese Food and Foodways in Southeast Asia and Beyond* (2011), and, as co-editor, *Food and Foodways in Asia* (2007), *The World of Soy* (2008).

Katheryn C. Twiss is Associate Professor of Anthropology at Stony Brook University in New York. She co-leads the faunal analysis team at the Neolithic site of Çatalhöyük in Turkey. Her research interests include ancient food production, preparation, and consumption; human-animal relationships; and the origins of village life.

Penny Van Esterik (B.A., University of Toronto, M.A. and Ph.D., University of Illinois, Urbana) is Professor of Anthropology at York University, Toronto, where she teaches nutritional anthropology, advocacy anthropology, and feminist theory. She works primarily in Southeast Asia. Her research interests include food and colonialism in Southeast Asia, women's health advocacy, breastfeeding, and maternal and child nutrition.

Morten Warmind is Associate Professor for the Sociology of Religion at the Department of Cross-cultural and Regional Studies at the University of Copenhagen. His interests include pre-Christian north-European religious tradition, religious change, and food habits in the Classical world. He is the author of several studies on Celtic religion and society, modern religious importance and the role of early Christianity.

1

Introduction

Susanne Kerner and Cynthia Chou

Food and the consumption of food are very much a part of everyday discourse, and innumerable questions about them are discussed in public media, academic conversations, and over private dinners. A main concern in many of these discussions revolves around the elements connecting food with health: what kind of food is healthy (official suggestions keep changing),[1] and why do nearly one billion people go hungry, while at the same time many Western and increasingly Middle Eastern countries have considerable problems with obesity?[2] Today, European countries run large state supported research projects on food behavior in order to solve the problem of ever increasing health costs resulting from "wrong" eating habits. Food is one of the essential elements of human life without which survival is not possible, yet it is much more than simple biological nutrition. This book therefore deals with the cultural aspects of food and food consumption.

Commensality literally means eating at the same table (*mensa*). In its broader general meaning, it describes eating and drinking together in a common physical or social setting. Eating is, in all cultures, a social activity and commensality is undeniably one of the most important articulations of human sociality (Fischler, 2011: 529). As Freud (1918: 174) observed: "To eat and drink with someone was at the same time a symbol and a confirmation of social community and of the assumption of mutual obligations." Food is tasty only because of the pleasure derived from eating it with good company or of knowing that eating with the right company confers social distinction (Freedman, 2007: 15). To put it in a nutshell, commensality is the essence of food, and commensal acts are essential for the integration of a society. Moreover, these are acts that must be continually reinforced through practice. Commensality is about creating and reinforcing social relations (Bourdieu, 1984). As the chapters in this volume demonstrate quite clearly, the question of who takes part in commensal occasions is highly significant. Whereas daily meals may form around a relatively stable core of participants, special commensal occasions encompass persons who do not usually eat or drink together. Widening the social circle (or commensal circles as Van Esterik calls it in her chapter in this volume) brings forth a variety of other effects.

1

Early treatises on commensality focused largely on issues pertaining to obligatory or prohibited commensalism as a social and psychological functional bond, uniting or separating social groups. For Robertson Smith (1889 [1957]), Marcel Mauss (1954) and Emile Durkheim (1981 [1894]), commensalism forged shared identities. Explorations into commensal totem-taboos that impacted upon the degree of internal group social distinctions and the intensities of group divisions between insiders and outsiders were further explored by Levi-Strauss (1963), and developed by Mary Douglas (1966) in her groundbreaking work on *Purity and Danger*. To this day, these works continue to be the foundations in our understandings of how commensality serves as a medium for shared cognitive taboos in boundary-maintaining mechanisms. In the realm of these studies, the concentration has been on the religious, ritualistic, and sacrificial aspects of commensality. What was overlooked was the fundamental dimension of everyday commensalism.

From as early as 1910, attempts were made by Georg Simmel to analyze commensality beyond the formal feast. He placed his primary emphasis on discussing the establishment of social bonds through the common or mundane meal. In "Die Soziologie der Mahlzeit" (Sociology of the Meal), he was eloquent on the subject of how "the exclusive selfishness of eating" is transformed into a habit of gathering together "such as is seldom attainable on occasions of a higher and intellectual order. Persons who in no way share any special interest can get together at the common meal ... There lies the immeasurable sociological significance of the meal" (Simmel, 1997 [1910]: 130). Commensality, he stressed, was not only to be understood within the context of ceremonial feasts. It was specifically also a part of the sharing of the common everyday meal. It is through the sharing of the common meal that a person's biological and "exclusive selfishness of eating" is transformed into a collective social experience (*ibid.*: 130). In Audrey Richards' (2004 [1932]) study of the Bemba of Zambia, she argued how the biological determinants of appetite and diet are molded by particular systems of human relationships and different cultural traditions as well as customs. According to her, "It is for want of this concrete data that Durkheim and his followers of the French sociological school have given a misleading account of this question. Like Robertson Smith, they have emphasized that eating is a social activity, rather than an individual physiological process, but in their hands this sociological aspect of nutrition has developed into a positive apotheosis of the ceremonial meal" (Richards, 2004 [1932]: 180).

Following these theories about the important sociological aspects of commensality, many volumes have very fruitfully studied the political, social, and ritual importance of one particular kind of commensality: that is, the feast (e.g. Bray, 2003a; Dietler and Hayden, 2001a). While many of these studies are archaeological, they draw on the work of cultural anthropologists and historians, including particularly Douglas (1966) and Appadurai (1981).

In this volume, our locus of analysis is that eating and the sharing of both the formal and common meal constitute, to borrow Marcel Mauss's (1954) classic concept, a "total social fact." That is to say, they are occasions which simultaneously embody and present all aspects of society: the economic, jural, political, religious, aesthetics, moral, etc. It follows then that the contributions in this volume will analyze commensality in all its forms. Special emphasis is given to the sharing of mundane meals as a key domain for understanding the praxis of commensality. Such habitual forms of interaction allow people to "read" and understand each other. Understanding does not come automatically; it needs to be reinforced. Everyday commensality has an important role in this reinforcement as it consists of the sharing of food, conversation, and exchange of body-language between the participants. People do not just feast; they also—and much more frequently—take part in everyday meals that are eaten in the company of particular sets of commensal partners. In mundane meals, as well as in special meals, the politics of inclusion and exclusion—the "gastropolitics"—play a central, if often masked, role (Pollock, 2012a). Here Foucault's (1977) notion of the relations between power and body, expressed in his ideas of biopolitics, becomes important. The political dimensions of commensality encompass first the inclusion–exclusion aspect of it, which is so important in structuring a society in past as well as present societies (e.g. not being able to eat pork can work very much as an exclusion in a pork eating society) and both in the private as well as the public sector; second, the socio-political motives for a particular public commensal action in societal power plays that also touches upon inclusion; and, third, the interest of modern (and past) states in the health (and thus body) of their citizens.

So far, food studies have tended to focus on extremes, say, to concentrate on attitudes about food and commensality in countries or cultures categorized as "Western" and "modern" versus "tribal"; or types of meals such as "feasts" versus "common meals." The point we want to make in this volume is, however, that not all peoples in the world eat around a table or a common hearth—in fact, there are insurmountable variations of all kinds. We shall demonstrate that all cultures have ideas and rules governing commensal behavior. Exclusion from and inclusion in commensal events need not be absolute categories, that is to say, it does not necessarily mean total exclusion or total inclusion per se. People might be partially included or partially excluded. They may, for instance, be able to see, smell, and hear the sounds of a feast while having only limited access to the food and drink that are partaken by others. Furthermore, whereas daily meals may form around a relatively stable core of participants, special commensal occasions encompass persons who do not usually eat or drink together. On such occasions, widening the social circle inevitably brings with it a variety of other effects. A holistic or multifaceted approach to the study of commensality has therefore been adopted in the selection of contributions to this volume. The result is that the essays, taken together, present a worldwide and historical scope to the study of human commensal behavior. The essays represent studies in several European countries, the U.S.A., China, Bolivia, Southeast Asia, Turkey, and the Near East, spreading across a time span from the Late Neolithic period (sixth millennium BCE), through the Medieval period to the present day. This volume is a celebration of the varieties of people that make up our world and the wealth of human experience. We take up the challenge to "take commensality seriously" (Hirschman 1996) and fully explore the concept in its various dimensions and operations.

In addition to this Introduction, there are 16 chapters in this volume. Each of these can be read and understood on its own. However, they have also been arranged in an order that effectively connects and unifies them under three common themes: namely, everyday commensality, special commensality, and the role of commensality in identity formation and its role as a social and political tool.

The first part of this volume comprises of Chapters 2 to 6. It deals explicitly with everyday commensality and the fundamental social importance of including and excluding members of a society to reinforce important relationships. Co-presence is allowing the sharing of food as integral parts of social behavior. Everyday commensality is a habitual form of being gathered together, and forms a base for trust and also a routine that allows the minimization of conflicts in daily life. Food and foodways are traditionally objects of archaeological research, often in connection with the development of food production during the Neolithic.

C. B. Tan's chapter begins the section on everyday commensality. Tan discusses the various forms of commensality with emphasis on commensality as a human social institution that expresses the value of hospitality, which is crucial for cultivating social relations. The concept is explored through the categories of "domestic commensality," "kin and communal commensality," "ceremonial and religious commensality," "political commensality," and "hospitality commensality." Each category is exemplified and discussed on the basis of data derived from extensive fieldwork in Southeast Asia. Tan demonstrates how the different categories of commensality differ and interplay. He also shows how commensality provides the embodied experience of social relations with people, and that the concept does not just denote the simple fact of eating together, but may also function as a lens to study culture and social relations also.

In Chapter 3, Penny Van Esterik looks at the most fundamental of commensal actions: the sharing of food between mother and child. This particular form of food sharing is discussed as a practice that begins *in utero* and stretches back to our evolutionary and ontogenetic pasts. While most studies of commensality consider the food sharing practices of adults, this chapter draws attention to infant and child feeding, thus revealing new dimensions of commensality. It is argued that breastfeeding is at the conceptual core of human commensality, and models food sharing for all humans. Without being fed by someone, a newborn dies. The commensal relation created by the first paradigmatic act of food sharing involves reciprocity, intimacy, and nurturance, and can be analyzed by reference to commensal circles. The commensal circle is a space where people share food, eat together, and feed each other. Commensal circles expand from feeding *in utero*, to include breastfeeding and related practices, siblings, other household members, community members, and strangers. Commensal circles may also include ancestors or spirits who are fed along with human family members.

The ongoing debate about the importance of commensality for contemporary societies and their health is the background for Chapter 4 by Boris Andersen. The relation between commensality and obesity among young Danes is discussed here. The research is based on Danish youth under 28 years old and their habits of commensal eating (or not). The importance of commensality as a means to curb obesity epidemics is discussed, as well as the different conceptions of food as a possible contributing factor of obesity. The influence of physical frameworks is studied in contrasting the American lifestyle (very health oriented but eat alone) with the French lifestyle (where food plays a large role and people eat together).

Chapter 5, by Yve le Grand, presents another specific aspect of everyday commensality. The discussion is based on fieldwork undertaken with an environmental activist group based in Lisbon, Portugal. The commensal food studied is the *Jantar Popular* (JP) that Grupo de Acção e Intervenção Ambiental (GAIA), an environmental non-governmental organization (NGO), facilitates every Thursday of the week. The JP is a vegan dinner made with organic, genetically modified organism (GMO) free, locally produced, and socially just ingredients. This dinner is organized by volunteers, from planning the menu to cleaning up the space(s) at the end of the evening. Without volunteers there would be no dinner. Commensality becomes an ideal tool for putting environmental food politics into practice through "just" eating in commensal surroundings. Simultaneously, the JP turns into a Temporary Vegan Zone, in the vein of Turner's (1969) "communitas," as it becomes a temporary place where people can transcend their everyday experience of food.

In Chapter 6, Maria Bianca D'Anna and Carolin Jauss report their findings from their studies of cooking practices during the second half of the fourth millennium BCE in southwestern Iran (Chogha Mish) and northeastern Anatolia (Arslantepe), to gain information about past commensal events and the role of food in society. Like food consumption, cooking can take place in various social contexts, and how, where, when, and by whom food is cooked plays an important role in commensal practices. D'Anna and Jauss attempt to trace the interplay between material culture, people, and the different roles of cooking practices within the two communities under study. Through the analysis of vessels according to their shape, capacity, and use-wear traces, insight is gained into everyday as well as out-of-the-ordinary meal preparation. The two case studies show that cooking touched multiple spheres of life, and the labor organization connected with cooking had many facets. Food cooked to be consumed on the spot and secondary products that could be stored played possible different roles in both communities. This does not only imply a diverse spatial and temporal proximity of the two activities, but it seems also to be related to different social contexts.

The second part of this volume, comprising Chapters 7 to 10, examines different forms of special commensality, spanning from identifying elements of commensality in archaeological contexts to specific examples of medieval banquets. Special commensality serves various purposes: providing crucial periodic reaffirmation of social groups, establishing power relations that are central to the maintenance of community and political organization, and providing necessary communal labor (Halstead, 2012). Different kinds of foods may mark feasts as distinct from daily meals, such as large portions of meat or culturally unusual foods; special sets of drinking vessels or eating equipment might also be an element.

Katheryn Twiss opens the discussion on special commensality in Chapter 7 by examining the core concerns in the archaeology of food, and, more specifically, the special events in commensality. Three key methodological issues affecting archaeologists are identified. First is the fact that different food-related data sets have different relationships with human activity, so the findings, for example of animal bones and cereals, have to be interpreted in their contextual meaning. Second is the fact that the context and character of a sample determines its interpretative utility. Third is that full integration of multiple data sets remains a challenge, and is more than just looking at all available material. Twiss also delves into the definitions of food and feasting as used in archaeology, and their possible meaning for commensal acts.

In Chapter 8, Paul Freedman, provides the historical approach to the question. Banquets across different time periods in European and American history are studied as complicated forms of commensality, especially in connection with excess and hierarchy. This chapter thus deals with the less comfortable elements also expressed through commensality. Particular medieval banquets were rich on excess, where several hours of dining over dozens of courses were not unusual. More contemporary forms of commensality have a less gregarious character, the question of hierarchy, however, remains to be an important topic in banquets, expressed in the seating order of the medieval banquet as much as in the inaugural dinner of the recent American president. The rules of what has to be included in a successful banquet are discussed as well.

In Chapter 9, Alexandra Fletcher and Stuart Campbell bring into focus ritual feasting which constitutes another kind of special commensality. They maintain that, from a modern Western viewpoint, ritual is traditionally defined as something extraordinary that happens beyond the limits of the everyday with special people, places, and material culture. This has created challenges for the interpretation of prehistoric archaeology, as such a definitive separation of the sacred and everyday is not the norm for all societies. It is argued here, therefore, that the challenges facing archaeologists in identifying and interpreting prehistoric commensality, ritual, and domestic activities cannot be considered in isolation from each other. With this in mind, the mortuary and feasting practices at the Late Neolithic (c. 6200–5400 cal. BCE) site of Domuztepe, southeast Turkey, are re-examined in order to identify those elements, which constitute the ritualization of everyday activities and objects.

In Chapter 10, Susanne Kerner discusses the role of drinking vessels from the Late Chalcolithic Southern Levant (4500–3800 BCE) in the negotiation of identity (on different levels) during special commensal activities. The Late Chalcolithic period of the Southern Levant shows a remarkable amount of individual drinking vessels, more than known from any time period before. The individual drinking vessels are characterized by their small size and shape (chalices and cornet shaped). Individual eating vessels also increase, but not to the same amount. This phenomenon of change in the material culture is interpreted here in connection with a change in social structure. The growing complexity of the social-political organization of the Late Chalcolithic required commensal occasions, where questions of identity (those of a person, a family, and larger social groups such as kin groups) as well as the hierarchical order needed for both to be negotiated and re-stated. Commensal drinking played an essential role during these occasions.

The third part of this volume, comprising Chapters 11 to 17, focuses on the role of commensality in identity formation as well as its role as a social and political tool. It begins with considerations of the importance of food in national contexts, both on a private (Chou) and public level (Nyman), that explore aspects previously discussed by Appadurai (1981). The more private identity negotiations in a modern community (Nell) and in literature (Møller-Olsen) illustrate standpoints as explicated by Douglas (1966). The following three chapters discuss commensality in decidedly religious contexts, all concerned in different ways with boundary creating, moving from inside considerations (Rosenblum), prejudices (Warmind), to the creation of ritual and mythological prototypes in the process (Gilhus).

Cynthia Chou, in Chapter 11, considers the role of food in a wider national context. In focus here is the role of "iconic" food in practicing, performing, and "concretizing" national identity in a non-religious context. Eating holds a community together and "iconic" dishes play a role in this. This chapter examines the socio-cultural ideas of contemporary Singaporean national identity expressed by the consumption of the humble dish, chicken rice. It explores the implicit and complex ways by which this dish has taken part in developing Singaporean cultural identity and nationalism, and how this has developed historically. In terms of an "imagined communities" cum food commensality analytical framework, this dish serves as an important means for expressing a national identity.

In Chapter 12, Hanne Nyman uses an example of cuneiform texts to show how the king publicly declared certain food preferences in order to construct a nomadic identity, and through that maintain his authority over this particular group of his subjects—groups of nomadic people. The cuneiform archive from the palace at Mari (modern Syria) contains records of more than 1,300 communal meals mainly from the eighteenth-century BCE ruler Zimri-Lim. These documents not only describe a highly developed palatial cuisine but also illuminate the importance of commensality in forging alliances and maintaining political authority. Besides the usual administrative tablets, letters are also available, some of which report on the king's demand for various foodstuffs. This offers access to an elusive subject in ancient history: that of culinary preferences. It is suggested here that certain foodstuff, such as locusts and truffles, were not the demands of a gourmet king as usually interpreted. Zimri-Lim ruled a complex political landscape consisting of both settled and mobile people. By serving and eating locusts and truffles, integral parts of a nomadic cuisine, the king sought to construct a nomadic identity to maintain his sovereignty.

In Chapter 13, the identity creating role of food is studied by Cornelia Nell, based on fieldwork in the small Andean community of Cabreca in Bolivia. Food and cooking are central to everyday life, and nourishment constituted an important sign of status. This ethnographic chapter describes the ways in which the inhabitants use food as a medium to confirm and challenge relationships. Social networks are negotiated through foodways and sharing. As the allocators of food, women play an important role in this. They prepare the meals and serve them. Although there are certain rules that they must follow, they decide what and how much food everybody receives, and thus rework and restructure human relationships.

In an even more "mundane" context, Astrid Møller-Olsen, in Chapter 14, studies the effect of commensal as well as purposeful solitary drinking and its social consequences in contemporary China, in the novel *Liquorland*, written by the 2012 Nobel prize winner for literature Mo Yan. Alcohol is, among other things, used here as a symbol of involvement in life. Rules and regulations for drinking alcohol as part of commensality are numerous in the modern Chinese context. Being part of, as well as standing outside of, commensal drinking can be a powerful tool in constructing and expressing identity; and one's inability to conform to the norms of alcohol consumption can have severe social consequences. This chapter presents some examples of culturally significant drinking cultures found in Chinese literary history, creating different identities, with the aim of investigating how *Liquorland* relates to, and is critical of, these. Through a thematic analysis of the novel, however, it becomes apparent that alcohol is more than an ideological institution: it is a productive, material stimulant, and a symbol of involvement in life.

The inside look is studied by Jordan Rosenblum in Chapter 15. A culture's own justifications for foodways are too often ignored in the academic study of commensality. In seeking to understand how a particular group constructs the rules around the table—what, how, and with whom one will or will not eat—the rationales for these rules must be factored into any scholarly analysis. In this chapter, examples of ancient Jewish apologies for the kosher laws are used to demonstrate the considerations and methods used in the construction of such justifications, in order to remind scholars of the importance of this consideration. To outsiders, the laws might be explained as ethical; inside the rabbinic tradition, close textual analysis was often required to understand, that is to justify, the prohibitions.

Another inside view of religious practices of food behavior is presented in Chapter 16, by Morten Warmind. The Christianization process of the Roman Empire was accomplished gradually over several centuries. Exploring this process from the point of view of commensality seems obvious, as Christians were noticeable to outsiders in at least two ways: They would not eat sacrificial meat and were participating in communal meals in secret. Further, denial of food by Christian ascetics in Syria and Egypt at the end of the third century was well known, and used as a tool in creating hierarchical relationships. Different authorities expressed different views on commensality of Christians and non-Christians, first allowing, then strictly forbidding, the eating of sacrificial meat. The latter separated Christians from what was considered then polite society. Worse, a (mis)understanding of the commensality of Christian brothers and sisters consuming together the body of Christ, was probably behind charges of incest and cannibalism.

In Chapter 17, Ingvild S. Gilhus takes up a number of points made in Freedman's Chapter 8 to illustrate the centrality of commensality for religious meals. This chapter considers ritual meals in three religious societies as well as in the traditional Greco-Roman religion. A banquet is usually the last step in a sacrifice where one or more animals are slaughtered; the cult room of the adherents of Mithras was a dining room; the Eucharist was a key ritual in Christianity; and one of the most prestigious rituals of the Manicheans took place at the banquet table. It is shown how the ritual meal may be thought to promote mundane and extra-mundane prosperity, and to connect past, present, and future by means of mythological prototypes. Special emphasis is placed on the ways the religious identities are created and sustained and both internal and external boundaries are defined through the meals.

Acknowledgment

The volume is based on selected peer-reviewed papers presented at a workshop held in October 2011 that was financed by the Institute for Cross-Cultural and Regional Studies (ToRS) of the University of Copenhagen. The editors would like to express their gratitude to the Internationalization Committee of the institute as well as the institute director, Ingolf Thuesen, for the financial support and help given. We would also like to thank Anna Haldrup for her opening speech and the following students for their help: Nikoline, Salwa, Dyveke, Marc, Maria, Jeanet, Kristoffer, Ann-Sofie, Rasmus, Rikke, Nora, Ole, Kim, Pia, Marie, Mads, and particularly Marie Devald.

Part I
Everyday Commensality

2

Commensality and the Organization of Social Relations

Tan Chee-Beng

Introduction

The earliest serious discussion of commensality can be traced to W. Robertson Smith, who, in his study of the religion of the Semites, discusses the god and his worshippers in a sacrifice as 'commensals' (Smith, 1957 [1889]: 260). While his focus is on religion and eating together on occasions of sacrifices, he points out that "those who eat and drink together are by this very act tied to one another by a bond of friendship and mutual obligation" (Smith, 1957 [1889]: 265). In today's social science rhetoric, this means that commensality is not just a biological act of consuming food; it is also a communicative act which has the significance of social relations. It is relevant to the study of social organization, which when perceived broadly includes political organization. Since eating together is a social act that has communicative significance, it involves rules of hierarchy and solidarity, boundary making as well as symbolic expression. All these have implications for the organization of social relations. While some social anthropologists have in their writings mentioned commensality,[1] most have taken it for granted, as when they write about communal celebration and feasts; only a few such as Anigbo (1987, 1996) have made commensality the focus of their study. However, feasts have long attracted the attention of anthropologists, historians, and archaeologists; and feasts are associated with commensality, which historians and anthropologists, including ethnologists and archaeologists, are now paying attention to (cf. Dietler and Hayden, 2001a).

According to the *Merriam-Webster's Dictionary* (2014), the word commensal, meaning one who eats at the same table, is derived from the Latin word *com* (together) and *mensalis* (of the table). In Latin, table is *mensa*. Thus commensality may be understood simply as eating together. Not all languages have a specific term for this, but the same phenomenon is understood and may be described in different ways. I learned from my first anthropological fieldwork in 1972, then as an undergraduate student, among a Malaysian aboriginal community (known as Orang

Asli), a very simple Malay term that gave me the first lesson of commensality and boundary making. These Orang Asli often used the Malay term *tak sama makan* (not eating together) to draw the line between them and the Malays who were Muslims, and usually declined the invitation of the Orang Asli to eat together at their home. Similarly, when they wanted to emphasize solidarity with the Chinese, who were not Muslims, they used the term *sama makan* (eat together or can eat together). Thus *sama makan* and *tak sama makan* indicate commensality and non-commensality: a way of describing social and ethnic relations through the metaphor of food. Years later, in my research in Sarawak in East Malaysia, I found the terms are also used by other non-Muslim indigenous peoples in relation to Muslims.

Grignon (2001) has used the terms domestic commensality, institutional commensality, everyday commensality, exceptional commensality, segregative commensality, etc. These are convenient usages that may be adopted, but it is better to group the types of commensality into a few broad categories. In this chapter I will discuss domestic commensality, kin and communal commensality, ceremonial and religious commensality, political commensality, and hospitality commensality. While domestic commensality is the most basic human experience of commensality, commensality beyond the family must have grown out of the human experience of eating together as the most effective and welcome way of getting people together and to have fun. Conviviality through eating together is the basis of commensality.

In this chapter I will first discuss the various forms of commensality and the significance of commensality in human social interaction, with the focus on organizing social relations.[2] Jack Goody, in his discussion of the anthropological theoretical approaches to the study of food, begins with a discussion of the study of commensality, in particular Robertson Smith's view of commensalism and maintenance of social relations, thus the functional approach (Goody, 1982: 13). We need not be concerned with fitting the discussion into any theoretical approach. I shall discuss various forms of commensality with some emphasis on commensality as a human social institution that expresses the value of hospitality, which is significant for cultivating social relations. This is a kind of commensality, which may be called hospitality commensality. There is hospitality in commensality but commensal hospitality can be very instrumental for attaining certain aims, and in this respect all commensality beyond the domestic sphere is political. Hospitality commensality may express symbolic capital and cultivate social relation, but the immediate aim is really to celebrate a social relation and to give hospitality and show friendship.

Domestic commensality

Domestic commensality may be considered the most basic form of commensality. This is despite the fact that Smith (1957 [1889]: 279) had warned about assuming commensality as an extension of the family meal, since in some cultures men do not eat with their wives and children. But this is due to rules of commensality in a family or kin group because of gender hierarchy or other considerations. Nevertheless, eating as members of a family, even if not all the members are at the same table due to rules of hierarchy based on age or gender, must be an important experience and adaptation in human evolution. Here there is also the sharing of food acquired or produced by one or more members of the family. In fact historically the primary bond between the mother and the child is the bond of mother giving her breast milk to the child. After the child is able to take solid food there is the experience of the child eating with the mother and other members of the family. Sharing food with family members is a very basic experience within the family and this cultivates a deep bond over the years. It is the most primary form of commensality. Domestic commensality begins with parents providing food for their children. Thus in the parents–children commensality, there is the commensalism that biologists are familiar with, which exists between two kinds of organism in which one obtains food and offers protection for the other. Indeed commensalism does exist in many kinds of human commensality, in the form of one person or one party providing food for the commensals.

Ethnographic evidence today shows that there are different expectations of domestic commensality. Some, such as the Italians that Carole Counihan has studied, regard family meals as strictly for family members except when specially invited, and members of the family are expected to eat together. Outsiders and even relatives who are not members of domestic commensality are expected to leave when a family is about to have their meal, as indicated by the setting of a tablecloth (Counihan, 2004: 118). Cultural diversity aside, there is also the class factor. Generally poor families may not always insist on eating at the same table. In China, workers and peasants are often seen eating alone and even roaming about while eating, carrying the bowl that contains rice and some cooked food. In a rural village in Yongchun, Fujian in China, where I have studied, I often saw individual villagers carrying their rice and dishes in a bowl in the left hand and handling the chopsticks in the right hand, and roaming to a neighbor's house to eat in order to join a conversation, especially when there was a visitor; now and then going back to his or her house to get more rice or dishes. I call this roaming eating (Tan, 2003). This does not mean there is no domestic commensality, for most of the time the members of the family do eat together, or they are the members who are "legitimate" to eat together as a household. In fact, in the kind of roaming eating that I have just described, individuals may be eating at the same time with other members of their family, but may just wander off with their bowl of rice and dishes. Anyway, it is convenient to eat together to share whatever food a domestic group has. In modern affluent families, it is obviously convenient for the preparation of food and cleaning up if all eat at the same time.

The Kelabit in Sarawak, Malaysia, have a similar way of bringing food to eat with a neighbor but it is not roaming eating. In May 1990 I stayed for a short period of time with a family in Arur Dalan in Bario, the present Kelabit homeland in Sarawak. I had meals with the family. A neighbor whom I got to know quite well often joined us for dinner. However, he always brought his own plate of rice and dishes to join us, although he also ate some of the dishes cooked by the family I stayed with. My point is that there are different arrangements and expectations of commensality, and anthropologists should pay attention to this.

Among some peoples, such as the Yi and the Ersu in Sichuan in China and the Kelabit in Sarawak, the fireplace is symbolic of domestic commensality. In the case of the Yi and Ersu, the fireplace is in fact made in the living room of a traditional Yi or Ersu house, where family members gather and guests are entertained. Of course the fireplace is not only used for cooking, the heat from the fire also provides warmth in cold weather. What is significant is that the fireplace is made in the living room. It is also here that guests are received and where hospitality commensality (see Figure 2.1) is arranged.

Domestic commensality is the most basic form of commensality that grows out of the convenience of members of a closely related family eating together. These family

Figure 2.1   Esru fireplace (photo: Tan Chee-Beng)

members, which normally constitute a household, are entitled or expected to share the food resources. The anthropological definition of a household is based on a unit that shares cooking and, if possible, daily domestic commensality. Family division into separate households is marked by separate cooking and separate domestic commensality, and in this respect domestic commensality can be political, too. But domestic commensality is generally characterized by the expectation of care and sharing. This assumes special significance on festive occasions when the union of the family is emphasized. The Chinese New Year eve reunion dinner and the American Christmas dinner are obvious examples. Because of the care and warmth in domestic commensality, inviting a friend to join a family meal is a very warm gesture, and so hospitality commensality that is extended from domestic commensality is a very special kind of commensality.

Kin and communal commensality

Kin or members of a community need to get together every so often to celebrate, to grieve or to perform communal religious rites. Such celebrations call for conviviality and feasting, or some form of eating together. Thus it is common to have commensality for such life crisis celebrations as births and weddings as well as for other kin or communal gatherings, including funerals in some cultures. Kin and communal commensality expresses and reinforces social relations within a social group. Some smaller celebrations may involve family members, while others involve a wider circle of kin and friends or a local community. Communal commensality is often religious and so overlaps with religious commensality celebrated by a local community.

A very common kind of kin commensality is on the occasion of a wedding feast. Wedding feasts are an important event in most communities. Nowadays such feasts are mainly held at restaurants, but before this modern way of holding wedding feasts, people generally held them at home or in a local community. The Chinese in Malaysia, for example, nowadays generally hold the wedding feast at a restaurant as it is considered more prestigious to do so, but in the past, such as in the 1950s, it was common to have wedding feasts at home. This involved relatives coming to the house to prepare food before the wedding, and it was a joyous occasion, with much opportunity for kin to show support by contributing labor and all kinds of assistance, even if the main cooks were hired. In February 1983 I attended a Chinese undergraduate student's wedding at his home in a village in Kelantan, Malaysia (see Figure 2.2). The occasion and the feast brought his relatives together, no doubt reinforcing kin solidarity. Interestingly, among the Malays many in the cities still conduct wedding *kenduri* (feasts) at home. It is not uncommon to find a street in a housing area blocked by tables and chairs under a canvas cover in front of a house. People in Malaysia understand that this is for a Malay wedding feast and drivers will simply drive to another street to find access to one's destination.

Figure 2.2   Chinese wedding. Kelatan, February 1983 (photo: Tan Chee-Beng)

A wedding feast held at home allows much more kin participation. Not all food for a wedding feast held at home need be cooked in the groom's or bride's house. There are many ways of organizing a wedding feast and this is where ethnography can enlighten us. In the case of the Badeng Kenyah in Sarawak, Malaysia, for instance, an important item for wedding commensality or other communal commensality is rice wrapped in a kind of long broad leaf from the plant called *tarit*. As a wedding feast involves a whole community eating together, female relatives organize themselves to make such rice packages in different homes. These are then brought to the longhouse or apartment of the groom and, together with other dishes, are laid out neatly in rows on mats, and the people sit in rows on the floor to eat together. There is much kin and communal participation in a Badeng wedding (see Figure 2.3).

Anthropologists can study how a local community prepares a feast or organizes commensality. The rural Chinese in the New Territories of Hong Kong have an interesting practice that is now well known in anthropological literature. This is *sikh puhn*, which in Cantonese literally means "eating basin," that is, eating from a common pot. This culinary custom was first made well known in anthropology with the publication of an article by James L. Watson in *Anthropos* in 1987 (Watson, 1987), and since then a number of local anthropologists have written about it, too (Cheung, 2005; Chan, S., 2010; Chan, K. S., 2007). Each village in the rural New Territories belongs to a major lineage (bearing a particular surname) the members of

Figure 2.3 Badeng feast. Data Kakus, June 1992 (photo: Tan Chee-Beng)

which organize village banquets on such occasions as weddings and lineage ancestor worship, by having *sikh puhn* commensality. People at each table share a big basin of cooked food comprising of pork, pig skin, chicken, duck, squid, tofu, bean curd sheets, mushrooms, Chinese radish, taro, etc. The guests take the dishes from this basin to eat with rice. The collective dish is called *puhn choi* or "basin dishes." James Watson argues that this way of eating emphasizes equality, as the villagers or lineage members, despite their social status, all eat from the same pot. Nowadays, *sikh puhn* has been promoted by the tourist industry and the media as a unique Hong Kong foodway, and some urban Hong Kong people find it convenient to order *puhn choi* for the Chinese New Year reunion dinner, so there are restaurants that cash in to cook *puhn choi* for the festive occasion (see Figure 2.4).[3] Others experience eating *puhn choi*, as pointed out by Selina Chan (2010: 212), as tasting "traditional village culture."

For the Chinese, funerals are also occasions for kin to eat together. In the case of the Cantonese in Hong Kong, after a funeral family members and some close relatives go to a restaurant for a meal together before going home. This is called having *gaai wai jau* or "expelling pollution wine." As the name indicates, it is for symbolically expelling the funeral pollution but it also serves to have the close relatives (siblings, patrilateral uncles and aunts, etc.) together, to console one another, before they

Figure 2.4   Puhn choi. Ping Shan, April 2007 (photo: Tan Chee-Beng)

return to their respective home. Despite the name, the commensals do not necessarily have an alcoholic drink. It is such a standard practice in Hong Kong that restaurants usually have standard sets of menus for such a meal. Cantonese migrants and their descendants in America continue to observe this practice together with its symbolism. In San Francisco, for example, after a funeral the Chinese family and friends go to Chinatown to have such a meal (Crowder, 2005: 217–18).

In the case of the Babas, who conduct funeral rituals at home, the funeral usually takes place on the third day, although it can also be later on the fifth day. During these days, relatives and friends come to express their condolences and, in the evening, pork flavored rice porridge (*bah-be*) is served. On the day of the funeral, if it takes place in the early afternoon, a lunch is served. If the deceased dies of old age, a noodle dish flavored with *sambal nanas* or "pineapple chili salad" is served. The cooked fresh noodles symbolize long life. The salad is made of raw cucumber and pineapple cubes, flavored by a culinary paste made by pounding together some candle nuts (*buah keras*), shrimp paste (*belacan*), red chilies, and salt. Eating with relatives and friends is thus an essential part of such a Chinese funeral.

We note from the above discussion that restaurants have become important sites for organizing commensality. In the modern era, restaurants are common, where food is professionally prepared by chefs. The wealth and status expressed through lavish feasts in the past can today be easily arranged by choosing a particular class of restaurant (such as a famous one in a five-star hotel) and expensive food served. Thus in many cultures all around the world, wedding feasts and many other kinds of celebrations are increasingly being held in restaurants. It is convenient to do so and is even perceived as prestigious. There is also the practical problem of space in urban living. Nevertheless, as we have seen, there are some families in the city that still prefer to organize wedding feasts at home.

Last we need to note that kin and communal commensality is not always viewed positively. Some individuals may see it as an obligation because attendance or non-attendance is usually viewed as a measure of one's commitment to the kin group or community. Thus not all commensals are willing participants; they attend so as not to be misunderstood as not valuing a relationship or commitment to a group. Maurice Bloch (1999) describes this as a "test" among the Zafimaniry of Madagascar. Among these people there is also the fear of poisoning, and it is advisable to bring a magical antidote to poison when visiting a foreign village (p. 144). Today, in modern societies where there is a strong legal system the fear of attending a commensal meal, if any, is not poisoning by people but food poisoning; that is, it is a health issue. For the Chinese there is always the health issue in a feast when people use their own chopsticks to take food from a common plate or bowl. There have been attempts to encourage the use of *gongkuai*, or serving chopsticks, rather than one's chopsticks to pick food from a common plate. In Hong Kong, as a result of the SARS outbreak in 2003, the use of serving chopsticks has become popular in restaurants and public eating, so much so that it is now an etiquette not to use one's own set of chopsticks to pick food from a common plate. At high-end Chinese restaurants, a diner may even be provided with two sets of chopsticks: one for eating one's food and the other, the *gongkuai*, for picking food from a serving plate or bowl.

Ceremonial and religious commensality

Robertson Smith analyzed feasting in relation to sacrifice and the worship of gods. Whether "the god and his worshippers are commensals" is a matter of perception and context, since in the Chinese worship of deities and ancestors, for instance, the worshippers eat only after the spirits have symbolically eaten. Nevertheless such religious feasting is done to honor the gods, and what is socially significant is that the feasting brings a relevant group of kin or worshippers together. Religion provides the fellowship, which is reinforced by religious commensality. Religious commensality is not only rich in symbolism but also promotes fellowship. Perhaps the most powerful image of such commensality is the Last Supper Jesus Christ had with his disciples. The Christian communion today symbolically stages this commensal union with God. For Muslims everywhere, Id al-Adha or the Feast of Sacrifice, which falls on the tenth day of Dhu-al-Hijja, the twelfth and last month of the Muslim calendar, is celebrated with prayer in the mosque and the feasting of food from the animals sacrificed, usually mutton or beef. As it is also the celebration at the end of the annual pilgrimage to Mecca, this is known in the Malay world as Hari Raya Haji, *hari raya* being the Malay word for festival. In China this is known as Guerbang Jie, a term that was derived from Persia and the original Arabic *qurban* for "sacrifice." For the small community of Chinese Muslims in Hong Kong, on which I have done some research, the Muslim festivals like the Mawlid (Prophet Mohammad's birthday, called *Maulud* in Malaysia), the Id al-Adha and the Id al-Fitr (celebration at the end of the fasting month, called *Hari Raya* in Malaysia), are important occasions of commensality and fellowship at their own place of worship.

Among the Chinese in Malaysia, Chinese popular religious practices are both a matter of private and communal worship. In Bukit Rambai village in Malacca, where in 1977 I began my study of the localized Malay-speaking Chinese called "Baba," both the Baba and the non-Baba Chinese in the village honor the Chinese Earth God known locally as *Toa Peh Kong* (literally Big Uncle God) at his communal shrine on the second of the second moon. After all the religious rites have been performed, a feast is held in the afternoon for all members of the religious community. It is a commensality that annually brings the ritual community together. The other communal feast that is organized for religious commensality is that organized in the seventh moon for the celebration of Zhongyuan, which is popularly called the Hungry Ghost Festival.

The Hungry Ghost Festival is known in the Minnan (Hokkien) language as *poodoo* or *pudu* in Mandarin, also known by the Buddhist term *yulan shenghui*. This is an important occasion for communal worship; both in rural communities and in urban wards, to placate the ghosts (the deceased) said to be released from purgatory during the Chinese seventh moon. In Malaysia each Chinese settlement or the Chinese business people in a quarter of an urban center celebrate the occasion on a fixed day in the seventh moon, when the wandering ghosts and the "King of Hell" (*Da Shiye*) are placated and a communal feast is held. The commensality makes the local Chinese organizational structure obvious and reinforces the solidarity of the ritual community. In Quanzhou, Fujian, however, no communal feast is organized after a *pudu* worship, instead each household performs the *pudu* worship separately but at around the same time in each ritual community (based generally on an urban ward). After the worship, some relatives and friends are invited to eat the *pudu* meal together. This kind of commensality is called in Minnan *ziah poodoo* or "eat poodoo."

Commensality is an essential part of celebrations. Different cultures have their respective ceremonial commensalities associated with religious observations, which anthropologists can study and describe. The Javanese, for example, are known for their *slamentan*, which Clifford Geertz describes as "perhaps the world's most common religious ritual, the communal feast" (Geertz, 1960: 11). The *slamentan*, small and big, are held for all kinds of life-crisis celebrations, memorial services, and religious celebrations (cf. Koentjaraningrat, 1985: 546). The ceremonial and religious commensality serves to bring people together as a community, and symbolizes communal and/or religious identification. There are of course overlaps with kin and communal commensality, since many of the latter involve religious rites, too.

Political commensality

Commensality can be organized for a political purpose, and the politics of commensality has been important in human history. In this respect the term "commensal politics" (Dietler, 1996) is useful. It takes little imagination to organize feasts for political purposes, and both histories and fictions have stories of kings and even ordinary people inviting rivals to a meal or feast to have them arrested or poisoned. Rulers had organized feasts to award officials, celebrate victories, or promote alliances. Jacob Wright, in his study of the politics of commensality in ancient Western Asia, shows how rulers used commensality "as one of the most popular means to promote internal social cohesion and forge external alliances" (Wright, 2010a: 212).[4] This was also true of imperial China, with differences of course; as Yü (1977: 62–70) points out, Han mural paintings contain many feast scenes, including those held in a governor's mansion for his subordinates. There were of course many feasts in the imperial palace. Interestingly, in the case of feasts for visiting foreigners including tributary rulers, there were elaborate rules governing the choice of the wine and food during the Tang dynasty, but the emperor did not eat with the guests (Schafer, 1977: 133). The official banquets in imperial China reflected political power, and there were elaborate rules governing the preparation of feasts for different ranks of officials. During the Song dynasty, for example, palace high officials could be served 11 courses. Third ranked officials "had seven dishes, one box of sweet deep-fried food, and five pitchers of wine" (Freeman, 1977: 166).

Meals can be arranged to express social status and hierarchy. Kings and emperors and noble families had long used feasting to express power and class status. Other than imperial banquets, the Romans also regularly held public banquets in the streets for the ordinary people (Strong, 2002: 37). While the rich and the powerful people today do not hold such big feasts as the kings and emperors did, except in some royal weddings and large wedding banquets in restaurants, the "national feast" has remained important in the conduct of foreign affairs, especially in receiving foreign dignitaries. Who is or is not included is significant in the politics of power and influence as well as status. Even the dishes served and the foodways may be significant, as in the case of President Nixon's use of chopsticks in his visit to China in 1972 to officiate the relationship between the U.S.A. and China. In Belize, during Queen Elizabeth's visit in 1985, the local roast *gibnut* (a kind of large rodent) was served at the Queen's banquet, and the dish became a national pride. It became a symbol of Belizean national identity (Wilk, 1999). While national banquets today are not organized so much as to forge state-to-state relations or to show lavishness, as the emperors' did, national banquets are highly symbolic to reflect the level of honor that a visiting head of state is given and thus expresses the relations between states and the status of the host state.

Today it is not uncommon for politicians to organize public eating to rally support. They may even use existing forms of communal or religious celebrations to organize commensal eating. In Malaysia, for example, the *hari raya* open house of the Malays has become important for celebrating social relations among the Malays and non-Malays. *Hari raya* is the Malay term for the celebration of "Id al-Fitri" after the fasting month. On the first and subsequent two days of this celebration, Malays, who are Muslims, welcome neighbors and friends, irrespective of ethnicity and religion, to visit them and eat some sweets specially prepared for the celebration. Politicians have also used this open house concept to open their house or official residence to the public. In fact while doing research in Trengganu, Malaysia, in 1987, I found that a Chinese politician in this predominantly Malay state organized a big *buka puasa* (breaking fast) feast in a community center for the Muslims to break fast during the fasting month which precedes the *hari raya* celebration. Here we see a non-Muslim politician using the Muslim practice of breaking fast commensality to organize a political commensality to enhance his support among the Malays. This is not normally done by the non-Muslim politicians elsewhere in Malaysia.

Commensality can be used politically to include or exclude. We are familiar with the famous example of castes: high caste Hindus do not eat with low caste people. Commensality is here used to draw boundaries and to reinforce existing social stratification. We should, however, note that it is the social structure that defines social relations and limits the range of commensality. Such rules of inclusion and exclusion create commensal circles[5] of people who can eat together. Applied broadly, people of different hierarchy (e.g. social classes) generally have different commensal circles, although the social skill of some individuals allows them to be part of a wide range of commensal circles, such as of both the rich and the poor. In fact commensality can also be used as a political expression to challenge the rule of social exclusion. Such is the case with modern educated Hindu students who wanted to project a modern inclusive Hindu identity by eating together with students of different castes, even as early as the nineteenth century (cf. Roy, 2010: 8). Of course, according to Buddhist accounts, Buddha and his disciples had during their time already challenged the caste stratification by receiving food or having meals with the different castes (Malalasekera and Jayatilleke, 1958). Accepting food and eating together can be a powerful form of resistance to racism and injustice.

Commensality can also be made coercive, and this kind of political commensality is largely ideologically devoid of hospitality. James Watson's discussion of the public mess halls in Maoist China provides a vivid example of this (Watson, 2011). This kind of coercive commensality was not the usual kind of institutional commensality (cf. Grignon, 2001: 25) as found in hospitals, jails, or boarding schools. It was used by the state to mercilessly attack the family as an intimate form of domestic organization. As Watson (2011: 42) points out, while the Israeli kibbutzim and other small groups have also used collective dining to organize social relations with some success, the one promoted in Maoist China was an extreme form of socialism which attacked the family structure that people considered as important to their life. In a sense this is not real commensality, which generally has some form of hospitality even if it is used politically. Collective dining by force needs to be distinguished from commensality that grows out of social convention or which is based on the value of hospitality.

Today political commensality organized by the state is significant more for its symbolic function than for achieving a concrete political end. However political commensality is important and instrumental in social and business relations. For example, providing a good meal for a government official or business partner can be an important way of forging significant *guanxi* (social relations) to get things done in China. Although there is much emphasis to show hospitality, I treat this as political commensality and distinguish it from what I call hospitality commensality, which we shall now turn to.

Hospitality commensality

Eating together, or taking and receiving the food someone provides (like the children receiving food from the parents), cultivates solidarity or feelings of acceptance. This human experience is easily extended to persons outside the family or friends to show friendship and solidarity. Inviting a non-family member to eat with the family is the highest expression of friendship, and an invitation to share one's food or to eat with one's group, which can be one's family or a kin group or circle of friends, is at the minimum a friendly gesture. Smith highlights this very well in his example of the Arabs who fear that a stranger in a desert may be an enemy, but "if I have eaten the smallest morsel of food with a man, I have nothing further to fear from him" (Smith, 1957 [1889]: 270). Treated to food and eating together over time cultivates a moral relationship of solidarity, which the hospitality obliges one to uphold, albeit there may be cases of betrayal. I call this kind of commensality, hospitality commensality, which is largely an extension of domestic commensality. Hospitality commensality has been important in human history and will continue to be important for establishing social relations.

The extension of family meals to friends is an important principle of expressions of friendship and hospitality. This takes the form of joining family members for a meal or entertaining friends and visitors with food normally eaten at home. Some cultural ways of eating are very convenient for arranging hospitality commensality. A good example of this is the Turkish mixed *kebap* (*karişik*; see Figure 2.5) served in a big round container from which guests take the large sheets of bread called *lavash*, pieces of mutton, chicken, baked tomato, vegetables, and baked long green chili. A more traditional dish served this way is *marube*, which is rice mixed with meat and vegetables.[6]

For the Chinese nowadays, whether in Malaysia or China, friends are usually entertained in a restaurant. The class of the restaurant and the expensive dishes ordered indicate the extent that the host considers the *guanxi*, or the nature of the relationship. Eating together is expected in the case of friends that one has not met for some time. In some societies, like in the U.S.A., to be invited to eat at someone's house is an honor. In the case of the Chinese, only close friends or relatives may be invited to eat at home, where home cooking is often referred to humbly as *cucha danfan*, literally plain tea and simple food. Honored guests should be treated in restaurants where the host has to pay; the commercial nature of this treat makes it more prestigious than the homely fare.

However, whether eating together at someone's home or not has political and economic dimensions. In Hong Kong, where most people live in small apartments, it is not a common practice to invite friends to have dinner at home. Even extended family members usually meet at a restaurant to eat together. Having dim sum is thus not just having food, it is an arrangement for parents and, for instance, married daughters, daughters-in-law and their children, to meet, such as on Sundays. It is this

Figure 2.5   Bursa, mixed kebap, July 2011 (photo: Tan Chee-Beng)

social significance as well as its connection with Hong Kong identity that *yumcha*, an occasion for drinking tea and eating dim sum, has been studied anthropologically (Tam, 2001). In Malaysia and mainland China, where most people have fairly spacious houses or apartments, it is not uncommon for good friends to drive to each other's house to socialize over tea or a snack. But having an evening eat-out snack (called *xiaoyue* in Chinese) has become an important way friends eat together and socialize in a relaxed public space.

Ethnographically it is interesting to study how people of different cultures extend domestic commensality to show hospitality to friends and even strangers.

I had an interesting experience when I visited a community of Lun Bawang for the first time. This was in June 1989 when I went with a Lun Bawang student to visit some Lun Bawang communities in Limbang, Sarawak, Malaysia. Limbang neighbors Brunei, and this is where many Lun Bawang in Sarawak are to be found today. Once headhunters and known to earlier English writers as Muruts, the people call themselves Lun Bawang while the similar people in Sabah, the other East Malaysia state, call themselves Lun Dayeh. We first arrived in the evening unannounced at a small longhouse community in Long Meringau, where my student had relatives. The people were pleased to see her, whom they had not seen for some time. We were treated to food in an apartment of the host who was closest in relationship to my student. I was hungry and ate a full meal. My student did not eat much and I thought she was too busy catching up with news with the relatives who gathered around us. After the meal we were invited to a second apartment for another meal, and then another apartment, each of which laid out sumptuous food in their respective longhouse apartment, most of whom obviously had cooked more food after our arrival. I then realized that my student had played a cultural trick on me by not warning me that for the Lun Bawang, kin and honored guests were expected to be served food by each apartment, and the visitors had to accept the hospitality. I was touched but I wished I had been told beforehand as I had to try very hard to eat some food served in each apartment. Fortunately it was a longhouse with a few apartments only. Still it was an unforgettable experience, both the hospitality and the pain of forcing oneself to eat on a full stomach.

As anthropologists have observed, the rules of hospitality commensality differ from people to people. Even among the Chinese there are differences between the Chinese of different places. In mainland China, eating together with visitors and friends often involves drinking *baijiu* or spirit. Among many minority *minzu* (minorities as classified by China), drinking rice wine or other spirits is common. Some, like my experience among the Rungus in Sabah, Malaysia, and the Ersu in Sichuan, China, sing toasting songs. While I have mentioned the element of commensalism in most domestic and hospitality commensality, this is not so in all cases. In Japan, commensality among friends at a restaurant generally involves each sharing the cost of the food. This is unlike the Chinese among whom there is a host to pay for the food.

We have seen that commensality or non-commensality can be a way of drawing boundaries between groups. In the case of *sama makan* and *tak sama makan*, mentioned earlier, this is not so much of using commensality to include or exclude. It is a rhetoric that reflects how food taboo can affect social interaction. The Orang Asli do not use an ideology of commensality to exclude the Malays. It is the Muslim food taboo on pork and the rule of consuming the meat of animals that have been slaughtered according to Muslim law. This makes it difficult for Muslims to eat the food prepared by non-Muslims, especially if the Muslim food taboo is not observed. Nevertheless, Muslims and non-Muslims can still eat together if the Muslim food taboo is taken into account, such as eating in a *halal* restaurant, or at a vegetarian restaurant. Studying commensality in different cultures is not only a lens to see how social relations are conducted and the cultural views involved. It also helps to identify ways to promote intercultural understanding.

Conclusions

The discussion above shows that it is convenient to think of various levels and categories of commensality. Domestic commensality is most basic, and what is called hospitality commensality in social relations may be considered as an extension of domestic commensality. Kin and communal commensality is significant at a communal level, while religious commensality is organized for a local community or religious community. Political commensality is very broad since commensality can be organized by ordinary people and by the state for political purposes. Feasts are important when considering political commensality. They are not only important for communal celebration; they are also useful for forging solidarity and alliances and consolidating power as well as expressing power and status. In this respect, it is useful to note Michael Dietler's analysis of feasts by classifying them into empowering feasts, which emphasizes "the manipulation of commensal hospitality towards the acquisition and maintenance of certain forms of symbolic capital, and sometimes economic capital as well"; patron-client feasts; and diacritical feasts (Dietler, 2001). The latter two feasts seek to maintain existing power relations, with the diacritical feasts using expensive or exotic foods, elaborate serving utensils and distinguished settings to reflect class and aesthetics.

I should like to further discuss hospitality commensality as an institutionalized way of expressing the value of hospitality, because it has been important for organizing human interaction. Hospitality through the medium of food and eating together is a value that is still important for the conduct of social relations with friends and relatives. Given the increasing globalization and global encounters, what I call hospitality commensality is even more important. To have a cross-cultural and cross-national experience in commensality is a very special experience that is both local and cosmopolitan. In fact there is also a need to prepare this kind of commensality experience for tourists and people who wish to be a part of a local community, albeit temporarily as foreign visitors. For example, to eat together with a Turkish host over a large tray of mixed *kebap* is a very special experience that immediately brings foreign visitors close to the Turkish people and local culture, albeit it involves meeting only a few Turkish people. Food and commensality have the immediate effect of bringing the local culture to the visitors. Thus certain local ways of commensality have important potential for organizing tourism and cross cultural contacts.

The significance of commensality, which will continue to be with us into the future, is that it is not just the significance of eating together; it is the expression of the value of hospitality, of expressing care and love or of valuing a relationship. This institution of hospitality has helped in human social evolution in organizing and maintaining social relations beyond the domestic unit or a small human group. It continues to be useful for organizing social relations in this even more globalized and cosmopolitan world. Commensality understood this way is a way of inclusion in a human world that is differentiated by ethnicity, and nationality, religion, and class. Anthropologists inspired by Claude Levi-Strauss have since long paid attention to the function of marriage in promoting alliances. This might be important in past human societies; today few people arrange marriage to promote alliance between human groups, although the kin relations so formed are expressed and reinforced in commensality for in-laws. Hospitality commensality has wider significance for friendship and for establishing as well as maintaining social networks. After all, food rather than sex can be consumed together with a group of people at the same time for promoting friendship and social relations. Commensality provides the embodied experience of social relations with people. Our discussion shows that commensality is not just a simple fact of eating together; it is a lens to study culture and social relations.

3

Commensal Circles and the Common Pot

Penny Van Esterik

Introduction

Eating together, commensality, is the moral core of human society. Feeding and eating teaches us that our relations with others are not optional; we are all connected through food and eating. Most studies of commensality consider the food sharing practices of adults, where the social obligations created by food sharing are usually reciprocal. Breastfed infants and young children are seldom included in discussions of commensality since they are considered to have no independent agency and are passive eaters, having to be fed by others. Scholars in food studies ignore breastfeeding because breastmilk is neither produced agriculturally nor industrially. Breastfeeding doesn't fit. But, in this chapter, I argue that it is an important part of commensality.

Commensality—the act of eating together and sharing food—is a special kind of consumption—one much less explored by economists or nutritionists. The humanities and social sciences are well positioned to undertake the interdisciplinary collaboration necessary to understand and explain the social and emotional context of food sharing. Commensality is one very effective way to understand relatedness. The commensal relation created by food sharing involves intimacy, nurturance, and reciprocity. The intimacy of food sharing is well expressed by Martin Jones, in his book *Feast: How Humans Came to Share Food*, where he points out that, meals, like sex and reproduction, "resist attempts to distance the person and the organism" (2007: 12). But there is a domain that necessitates taking the next analytical step—putting meals, sex and reproduction together. They come together ontologically in feeding the fetus *in utero* and breastfeeding.

Nurturance refers to the capacity to nurture others, to care for them with empathy. This usually involves the provision of food. The activities of caring for others, feeding them, and, most importantly, eating with them are at the heart of nurturing practices. In past theoretical formulations, nurturance was considered a personality trait of women. As attention shifts to the activities of nurturing, it is clear that whoever performs these acts of nurture gets better at them, regardless of gender, although there is usually a wide range of skills exhibited in nurturing behaviors.

Social reciprocity is a basic part of what makes us human. Reciprocity is most apparent when considering food sharing by adults, where there is often a degree of calculation. For example, dinner invitations ensure that invitations to share future meals will follow. However, festive dinner parties often require careful calculations about who to invite and how elaborate the meal should be. Similarly, sharing the cost of rounds of drinks or food requires trust that the next round really will be "on me." The business lunch has developed reciprocal obligations to an art form. Many caring practices are reciprocal, in that they benefit both the giver and the receiver of care, as with breastfeeding or massage, for example. The process of food sharing can become competitive or exclusionary, as competitive feasts such as potlatches on Canada's northwest coast illustrate.

Michael Pollan, in *The Omnivore's Dilemma*, argues that the perfect meal is one that you make yourself, without incurring reciprocal debt (2006: 409). For infant feeding, breastmilk is defined as the perfect food, and women do make it themselves, but in many cases it incurs an explicit debt. For example, many Thai rituals, including ordinations and weddings, begin by reference to paying mothers back for their milk. With infant feeding, adults "pay it forward," explicitly or implicitly, with the expectation that feeding children and sharing food with them will ensure that children will provide them with food in their old age. The reciprocal debts of food sharing can be a burden as well as insurance against future needs.

Infant feeding and commensality

Food sharing is a contemporary practice that begins *in utero* and stretches back to our evolutionary and ontogenetic pasts (cf. Jones, 2007). Studies of food sharing have a long history in anthropology, including the early work of Robertson-Smith (1889) who viewed commensality as the core of religion. Contemporary nutritional anthropologists focus on commensality, but seldom include infant feeding in their studies of diet and food sharing. Breastfeeding is mentioned by Audrey Richards as a part of Bemba diet (1939), but ignored by both Marvin Harris (1898) (who could have used the example to defend materialist theory) and Mary Douglas (1996) (who could have built arguments around the symbolic power of breastmilk and breastfeeding).

Similarly, breastfeeding specialists generally ignore both local and global food issues because of the embodied individual nature of breastmilk production. Infant foods are generally not shared, but are made for one baby, sometimes for only one meal, and, in Euro-American societies, the meal may be thrown out if not finished, as recommended by public health professionals. Infant feeding is even more intimately connected to commensality in the global south where mothers may pre-masticate their own food for an infant, share a bowl with them, or finish their leftovers. By drawing attention to infant and young child feeding, new dimensions of commensality emerge, including the contrast between dependent and independent eating, feeding and eating, and feeding self and others.

In this chapter, I would like to argue that breastfeeding is the conceptual core of human commensality, and models food sharing for all humans. Without being fed by someone, a newborn dies; the act of feeding a newborn sets up a social relationship that can last a lifetime and beyond. In *Feast* (2007), Jones asks how we came to eat together face to face; the answer must begin with the mammalian moments of eating face to breast, the first experience of social meals around the breast/hearth. All social life involves negotiating boundaries between self and other, inside and outside. This play between inside and outside is often disrupted in North American households when parents decide that there will be no more maternal embodied contact with the infant after the birth, and that commercial foods, originating totally outside the maternal body, will build the new infant's constitution. In the global south, this decision may well prove fatal; in the global north, many infants survive without ever receiving breastmilk (myself included).

While adults in some parts of the world survive very poor diets, what a baby consumes during the first year of life shapes subsequent adult health. Williams examines how events at different stages in the lifecycle, including infant feeding, influence an adult's vulnerability to chronic illness like cardiovascular disease and metabolic syndrome (2009: 163). Adults expect and thrive on food diversity and varied diets; infants thrive on a single food—breastmilk or an inferior milk-like substitute. It is adults who try and force food diversity on infants and toddlers, to bring them to the commensal table before they are ready.

Unlike adult diets that are so culturally shaped that it is difficult to establish what could be considered an ideal diet, there are agreed upon standards and policy guidelines about the ideal diet for infants and young children: exclusive breastfeeding for six months followed by local indigenous complementary foods. While cultural factors do affect breastfeeding and young child feeding, breastmilk and breastfeeding is the only example of a universal food and feeding system (cf. Akre, 2009). The problem is in the implementation of that policy; only in Scandinavian countries have policies been implemented that successfully support maternal breastfeeding. The result of this support is that nearly 98 percent of women initiate breastfeeding, and over 50 percent of infants are exclusively breastfed at six months, according to UNICEF statistics.

Let me illustrate my argument by reference to the commensal circle (Figure 3.1), a conceptual tool that has both developmental and cross-cultural implications. I first described circles of commensality for a UNICEF workshop on care held in 1994, and subsequently published (Van Esterik, 1995: 394). The commensal circle is a space where people share food, eat together, and feed each other. These circles are pre-constituted culturally before any individual guest or newborn enters them. Commensal circles may include ancestors or spirits who are fed along with human family members.

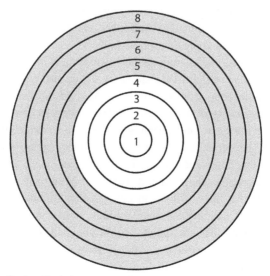

Embodied Commensality
1. *in utero*
2. ritual pre-lacteal feeds
3. breastfeeding/breastmilk substitutes
4. shared breastfeeding/pre-masticated food

Enculturated Commensality
5. sharing food with siblings and other household members
6. sharing food with community members
7. feasts and political commensality
8. sharing food with strangers/food aid

Figure 3.1   Envisioning the commensal circle (drawing: Susanne Kerner)

Embodied commensality

I refer to the period from pregnancy to around six months or whenever household foods are added to an infant's diet, as a period of embodied commensality, when the foods shared are produced within the mother's body; this period is represented by the four innermost circles.

As food passes from outside to inside the pregnant woman's body, it also moves into the fetus, embedded inside the inside. Food that is external to the body becomes internal, and is incorporated into the body—first by the mother, and then by her breastfed child. Maternal food, then, shapes the constitution of the growing fetus; as the infant moves from inside the maternal body to outside, it continues to take its food from the maternal body in the form of colostrum[1] and breastmilk. The first embodied lesson from breastfeeding is that bodies are given over to a shared activity, as an infant latches on to a mother who has already learned her society's embodiment patterns. The embodied intimacy of breastfeeding can be disturbing to some mothers, particularly those without adequate social supports.

Commensal circles expand from feeding *in utero*, to include breastfeeding and practices such as wet nursing and pre-mastication of food. Many groups provide a pre-lacteal food such as honey or ghee in a ritual feeding. This does not constitute the sharing of daily meals, but a ritual feeding of a culturally significant food to the infant that socially acknowledges that the infant is indeed a Lao, or Mexican, or Korean child. The first acts of feeding set up a social relation between an infant and mother, or whoever has the primary responsibility for feeding a newborn. All children move from dependence on maternal nurture in the form of breastfeeding (or substitutes) to the ability to eat independently and eventually feed others. Breastfed infants are not completely passive eaters with no agency; breastfeeding offers the first opportunity to reject foods, an act that may be empowering for infants and frustrating for mothers. For example, infants may bite the nipple if mothers do not pay sufficient attention to them.

Another example of the intensity of the interconnection between mother and infant concerns the shared taste of foods. Colostrum and breastmilk contain the flavors of the maternal diet and act as a "flavor bridge" between the maternal diet and the flavors experienced later in household meals. Recent experiments confirm that dietary learning begins *in utero* and continues through the flavor cues in mothers' milk. Flavors such as vanilla, garlic, carrot, and caraway can be found in breastmilk, and exposure to these and other flavors facilitates the acceptance of novel tastes in complementary foods. Breastfeeding, then, facilitates acceptance of complementary foods after six months through this direct learning of flavors and indirectly through the daily variation in the taste of breastmilk, compared to the stable flavor of commercial infant formula (cf. Hausner et al., 2010). Although the flavors of different foods are transferred through breastmilk selectively and in small amounts, these flavor experiences in infancy track into childhood and adolescence as food preferences (Housner et al., 2008).

Pre-mastication of food is another shared intimate and embodied act of food sharing. Pelto et al. (2010) explain the underreporting of pre-mastication around the world, as well as some potential benefits of the practice, particularly in areas of the world without suitable complementary foods.

After six months, infants need complementary foods—foods that complement breastmilk, and receiving these foods draws infants into broader commensal circles of varying sizes, forms, and complexity. In some parts of the world, infants and children are welcome around the table; in others, they may move to separate commensal circles for males and females, or be fed at different times in the kitchen, for example.

Embodied commensality accomplishes several things. It is in these circles where infants and children are socialized into the taste regimes of their households. It is where they shift from co-regulation of appetite to self-regulation. Embodied commensality sets the emotional tone for eating: is it a time of pleasure? of fear? of abuse? It attunes infants to recognize social and relational cues during feeding. This period shapes the new person's constitution including their gut ecology and potential for future diseases.

Enculturated commensality

Already with the first introduction of food produced outside the body, we begin to see a shift to more enculturated commensality where the foods selected (including pre-lacteal feeds such as ritual food offerings of honey) and the mode of sharing (wet nursing, pre-masticated foods) are more clearly culturally constructed. While embodied commensality is driven primarily by custom—usually transmitted by the practices of women—culture shapes the rules that govern household and community commensal circles, including the foods served, the order of serving, and eating etiquette.

However, when women are gatekeepers of the commensal system, they still adhere to cultural rules that may have them eating least and last, and feeding their boy babies more and better foods (as in much of South Asia.) The papers presented at the workshop on Commensality and Social Organization provide many examples of enculturated commensality.

This process of food socialization involves people moving in and out of a variety of commensal circles, each move creating insiders and outsiders. Pregnant women or the elderly may opt out of particular commensal circles, or be readmitted to others, as, for example, when women elders are welcomed in to male commensal circles. In North America, it is not uncommon for breastfeeding women to be expelled from the commensal table, and expected to eat and feed alone, out of sight of others. Popular media regularly report on complaints that the sight of women breastfeeding in a restaurant makes other people lose their appetites.

In North America, leaving the commensal table was a common punishment for unruly children—expelled from the commensal table where pleasure is found. This punishment is less effective today, when families are invested less in commensal activities such as eating together, and pleasure is found away from the commensal table.

A single household may have multiple commensal circles—one in the kitchen and one in the dining area, one for males and another for females, one for weaned children and another for adults, one for married, another for unmarried; co-wives may each have their own circles with the husband moving between circles in an equitable fashion. Thai and Malay children may practice a form of roaming commensality, taking a bowl of rice from their own household and wandering into other households to see what accompanying dishes they might be offered. Commensal circles that overlap households may be discouraged in other communities.

Meal format and food items also shape commensality. A buffet, a four-course dinner in a French restaurant, pizza, a tuna fish sandwich, a large pot of rice, a cheese fondu or raclette all encourage different patterns of food sharing and turn-taking, and need to be considered in explaining food sharing in household and community settings.

Religion and religious practices shape commensal circles at the household and community levels and continuing up the analytical levels to include feasts and feeding strangers; religion influences the food served, who eats with whom, and the meaning of individual food items. Orthodox Jews' disgust reaction to pork, for example, links them to everyone else in their commensal circle, who also reject pork. This religious-based shared disgust response differs from disgust for a food as an expression of personal preferences based on past experience. Many religions encourage food sharing beyond the household, as seen in the morning alms rounds of Theravada Buddhist monks, soup kitchens, and the shared fasting and feasting of Ramadan.

Feasts are a form of political commensality where questions of hierarchy and trust must be addressed before food can be shared. Feasts usually require an excess of food or the provision of special items not in the usual household meals. Community feasts in upland Southeast Asia, for example, act as food insurance and validate claims to power. Communal feasts reflect their awareness of living in a precarious environment, where unpredictable floods, raids, draught, pests, or disease threaten the community. Feasts may be within clans and lineages, or between them, expressing degrees of competitiveness or solidarity, and often incur reciprocal debts. Upland groups in Southeast Asia report converting to Christianity to avoid the expense involved in competitive feasting which often required killing a large animal such as a water buffalo.

State banquets and large-scale feasts are examples of political commensality, part of the consumption work of creating alliances beyond the immediate family and community group. The state banquet in the texts and films related to *The King and I* provide a complex example of culinary colonialism, as the King of Siam courted the British emissaries from Singapore. In a paper on this event, I argued that the key message should not be, "Shall we dance," but "Shall we dine" (Van Esterik, 2006).

Commensal circles could also be used to examine the involuntary commensality of jails, schools, churches, and monasteries. In these contexts, is it important that everyone in the commensal circle be apportioned the same amount of food to avoid envy or the appearance of inequality. Students and patients in hospitals may try to thwart this institutional commensality by bringing food from home because they do not trust the quality of the food or its halal or kosher designation. Attention to the fluidity of commensal circles reveals some of the predicaments of food sharing, and how to avoid sharing. As an extreme example of the refusal of commensality, restaurants may mix garbage in with their leftover food to make the leftovers inedible for dumpster divers who scrounge in the garbage for free food.

Communist Lao People's Democratic Republic (PDR) is a food-insecure country with strong commensal culture even before socialism provided ideological justification. Extended families and guests sit around the same low bamboo table or mat, select from the same food dishes—even the same spoons, eat at the same time, and interact socially. In rural Lao communities, strangers as guests are easily absorbed into these resource-poor settings; women add more water to soup and take smaller portions, much like the "family hold back" strategies of North American meals when extra unexpected guests arrive.

It is likely that food-insecure communities have more complex commensal strategies. Food aid may well disrupt some of these commensal strategies, particularly when aid is targeted to specific households or vulnerable groups within households. Commensal strategies may result in communities being denied food aid when they strive to appear generous by feeding visiting officials as honored guests, rather than acknowledging their food shortages.

Methodological implications

Working with commensal circles raises new questions that can best be answered by interdisciplinary and ethnographic research in food settings. Much of what we have learned about commensality is about adult males sharing food in the household and beyond. But commensal patterns begin in infancy: infants and young children are important parts of commensal circles. Examination of commensality requires a lifecycle approach that includes careful attention to gender and age differences. How are young children socialized into the food sharing patterns of adult household members? When does an infant enter the commensal circle? When can it self-regulate its food intake?

The challenges and opportunities of interdisciplinary work on commensality are myriad. Archaeologists and historians are particularly sensitive to timeframes and context. How do social anthropologists address the historical development of commensal circles? Has global capitalism shifted the meaning of food sharing away from the idea of shared substance to the person as a rational individual responsible for his/her own food? How do new foods get incorporated into meals? Are they first introduced into the household commensal circle, or in communal feasts? Are social media and information technologies providing opportunities for new kinds of commensality, such as sharing a meal over Skype or Facebook, when what is shared is the setting and appearance of food rather than its taste?

While archaeologists must pay attention to material conditions in the form of artifacts and refuse, other social scientists may become so obsessed with the symbolic meanings of food that they fail to look at material objects, or fail to pay sufficient attention to the spatial and temporal dimensions of commensality. Ethnographic fieldwork provides opportunities to examine how food sharing across the generations has changed. Cookbooks provide some clues as to how items, portion and batch size have changed. Questions to elders about how they were fed, and their memorable meals may shed light on changes in commensal patterns over time.

Kitchens may be constituted as private, gender specific commensal circles, far removed from the public eating taking place in more formal dining areas. This observation could go a long way toward explaining the unequal intra-family food distribution patterns noted in some communities. Who is nibbling, sampling, and cleaning up leftovers in the kitchen? Does eating from the same pot promote a more equitable distribution of food within the household? Studies of intra-family food distribution need to include the informal eating that takes place in these secondary circles.

We also need more careful examination of the material conditions of poverty kitchens in both the global south and global north—kitchens where spices, herbs, condiments, and stores of staples such as sugar, salt, flour, and oil may not be available, and also where there is only one pot for cooking. The manipulations necessary to prepare an appetizing meal under poverty conditions are astounding; preparing special foods for infants and toddlers in such conditions is particularly difficult. Have those concerned with changing food practices paid enough attention to the material conditions necessary to prepare healthier meals?

Finally, do we have adequate interdisciplinary methods for developing comparative, regional approaches to commensality? Anthropologists in particular have lost interest in comparison, but commensality is one domain where regional patterns may be instructive.

Practical implications of commensality

Academic food studies carry no obligation to address food-based problems. Nevertheless, research on commensality has the potential to shed new light on nutritional problems. For example, inequitable patterns of intra-family food distribution can result in serious health problems, particularly when women and children have restricted access to food. More attention to commensal circles might reveal what circles encourage the most equitable division of food to its members, and what circles always favor adult males.

Perhaps commensal circles will provide a new way to understand disordered eating, both obesity and anorexia. What are the implications for obesity if toddlers enter adult commensal circles too soon, or stay too long in circles that give them protected access to special foods? Consider, also, the fact that anorexics actively resist commensality, refusing to eat in others' presence and removing themselves from the commensal table. On the other hand, in North America, many young anorexic women celebrate a shared, ascetic non-eating community on websites that explore anorexia as a lifestyle choice (such as pro-ana-nation.livejournal.com and prettythin.web.com).

The distinction between shared cultural food proscriptions and personal preferences is important to keep in mind as we seek individual and institutional solutions to eating disorders. Does commensality help keep eating in balance, smoothing out some of the extremes of phobic, picky and binge eating? Eating with others may encourage people to eat some things they like but not too much, and eat some of what they are not fond of, for social reasons.

But the act of eating together may also contribute to health problems. Take, for example, the food sharing practices of lowland Lao families. Family members take sticky rice from a common basket and soup from a common soup bowl, with family members having their own spoons, or access to a common spoon. The wide availability of cheap plastic soup bowls, cups, and spoons might discourage the use of shared soup bowls and cutlery, and reduce the incidence and spread of hepatitis A and bacterial infections. Sharing alcoholic beverages from a single glass carries complex meanings that may be more resistant to change. In many festivities I attended in Lao PDR, the rice liquor was provided in a single glass, with the host consuming the first glassful, and refilling it to toast each guest in turn from the same glass. (I remember, with acute embarrassment and shame, my attempt to have my portion poured into my relatively clean travel mug, a serious breach of commensality.)

The availability of small bowls might also make it easier to set aside and process a portion of protein-rich food for a toddler. Southeast Asian meal formats allow people to individualize their food consumption at the level of mouthful, dish or meal by the use of sauces and condiments. This meal format has important implications for feeding toddlers and young children who may eat from common dishes but refrain from adding spicy or bitter sauces and condiments. Lao infants and toddlers can fill themselves with balls of "play-dough-like" sticky rice, before they have the dexterity to take portions of protein-rich dishes (Van Esterik, 2011). Addressing the problem of child malnutrition requires adults to monitor their children's consumption of the protein-rich "with rice" dishes.

It is in the transitions from embodied to enculturated commensality, from internal to external food source, from mother to other as feeder, from custom to culture—where child feeding problems develop. As commensal circles expand and contract to include or exclude siblings, other household members, community members and strangers, infants and young children may lose protected access to their food supply, and face increased risk for malnutrition.

Playing with our food: Theoretical implications of commensality

Commensal circles raise new conceptual and theoretical questions, and may prove useful for examining food sharing cross-culturally. If we pull apart commensality, and deconstruct the commensal elements, we find varying degrees of sharing— shared food, shared spaces or tables, shared time, and shared social interaction. Not all elements are stressed in all commensal events. Looking more closely at the ethnographic evidence, we see cases where people who sit at the same table may be eating different food; they may or may not be eating at the same time. It is common in North America for family members not to eat at the same time. But it is important not to idealize the shared family meal, as the interaction may not always be pleasant, particularly for children.

The food industry has responded to these changed commensal circumstances; Kentucky Fried Chicken (KFC) family buckets of chicken now contain three different kinds of chicken to appeal to family members who might otherwise not eat together and participate in the KFC commensal experience. We have yet to explore how globalization of the food system affects commensality. However, it is likely that fast food restaurants and culinary tourism have profound implications for food sharing practices.

Commensality helps us address paradox, and draws attention to the simultaneity of tensions of inclusion and exclusion that exist at different levels of commensality. The tensions listed below are all interconnected. First is the tension between the universal desire of social primates to share food and the desire to hoard food—to make sure that there will be enough food for you and your family. Do we shrink the commensal circle in times of food insecurity, or expand it to include others? We are social primates who feel empathy for others, and even chimps are ready to share food with those who beg or indicate they are hungry or with those they want to impress. Think of the meals you would serve to your potential in-laws, or potential business partners.

Second is the tension between the relaxed intimacy and cooperation of immediate face-to-face family meals (the inner circles), and the potential risk or coercion implicated in large feasts, and formal state dinners, involving eating with others who may become allies or enemies (the outer circles).

Third is the conceptual and disciplinary tension between the producers and consumers of food, and between the nutritional and the culinary. Nutritionists who view food as fuel and the gastronomes and social scientists who stress food as pleasure often exist in separate disciplinary silos, and more often than not, ignore commensality altogether.

Fourth, the subject of child feeding reveals tensions between our desire for commensality and our fear of food dependency and even the fear of food itself.

Last, is the contrast and tension between food as commodity and food as a human right. In a paper on the right to food (Van Esterik, 1999), I made a distinction between the right to food, which is implemented in emergencies through UN agencies; the right to be fed, which includes provision of food to infants, young children, the sick and elderly; and the right to feed, a right that is virtually ignored, but probably keeps more people fed than the implementation of all other rights.

Many food-related human problems might be solved if we explored the nurturing power of commensality and made food sharing and the right to feed others,[2] rather than the right to food the driving force of global public policy. Recently the U.N. Commission on Human Rights adopted a resolution on the right to food by a vote of 52 for and 1 (the United States) against. It called for collective solutions to global issues of food security in a world of interlinked institutions.

Commensality is not based on the right to food, but on the primate and human impulse to share food. Food sharing as the commensal core of human society shapes the moral economy of communities. That is why everything about food and eating creates such emotional tensions. Limiting solutions to hunger to questions of food security and the right to food, fails to acknowledge and build on the evolutionary and historical strength of the nurturing power of commensality and the relations created through food and eating, explored in this conference.

Acknowledgment

This chapter was developed from ongoing work on a book, *The Dance of Nurture*, co-authored with Richard O'Connor; the argument will be further developed in the book's chapter on commensality with more ethnographic evidence to support the argument. This version of the chapter was revised following suggestions from workshop participants.

4

Commensality between the Young

Boris Andersen

Introduction

The interplay of food, people and meals has in the past ten years attracted special political attention, in view of what has been called the obesity epidemic. This latter notion refers to the fact that we in the Western world are experiencing a dramatic increase in the number of people with life-threatening obesity, including a variety of health-threatening complications as a result. Interest in food and meals thus becomes not only a question of being able to understand and describe, but also a question of being able to provide effective actions that encourage a change in our behavior in dealing with food, which predominantly means to get us to reduce our caloric intake in combination with an increase in physical activity.

If, for a moment, we leave the concern for physical health out of the equation and instead consider the interaction between human beings, our food and meals in the broadest sense—a cultural-historical perspective, covering both the anthropological and the sociological implications—it becomes clear that such campaigns, however powerful they might be, articulate a very specific view on the matter: they encourage and promote a particular relationship between us and the food we eat. This is a relationship that does not leave room for the pleasure-filled taste experience, nor for the meal, the community, a relationship that cannot accommodate the many co-meanings—be they desire- or aversion-related—that our dealings with food, throughout history, have been connected with. There remains only an exclusive individual relation between the food (that is, its nutritional content) and the individual consumer.

Through three examples drawn from current research, this chapter will argue for the appropriateness of including the social environment of our eating—commensality—much more actively in our understanding of what actions to take to restrict the rising obesity levels, rather than maintaining a narrow focus on the food's nutritional content in combination with a demand for individual self-control. In conclusion, the concept of Foodscapes can—as a potentially fruitful analytical perspective with an interdisciplinary approach—embrace a much needed holistic understanding of the interplay between food, people and physical space.[1]

On obesity, food and meal pleasure

In understanding commensality's potential importance to both restricting obesity and to influencing our food and meal habits in general, the French sociologist Claude Fischler's work holds a special status. He and his research team have, for almost a lifetime, been working with food in an intercultural context. He is particularly interested in how people of different countries perceive food and health.

The common denominator for the answers he received from American and British participants in the investigation is that they, to a remarkable degree, associate the term food with nutritional content, and with the food's content, and particularly on the part of the Americans, with a feeling of bad conscience, that one perhaps eats too much or might do so: "In Great Britain, and especially in the United States, food is associated first and foremost with nutrition. In the U.S. there are additional elements—the *responsibility of the individual*—toward his or her body and health, and feelings of *guilt if one hasn't made the 'right choices*" (Fischler, 2008, emphasis added by author).

The study also shows a French and Italian perception of food that is completely different. In these countries, food is associated with culinary experiences and certain dishes, and, not least, with the social community that the meal can give rise to. "For the French and the Italians, *food mainly evokes culinary practices* [...] *Eating means sitting at the table with others*, taking one's time and not doing other things ..." (*ibid.*, emphasis added by author).

Now, one might believe that this southern love of good food must naturally stick to the ribs, and that it must be the Frenchmen that are weighing heavily on the bathroom scales. But, paradoxically enough, that is not the case. Fischler's research team has also investigated how the citizens' body mass index (BMI) has developed, that is to say, the cipher that shows whether a person is underweight, normal, or overweight (BMI is calculated as weight/height × height; for example, a BMI of more than 30 is an expression for severe obesity that can be threatening to one's health).

Here, however, it has been shown that the Americans and British have put on the yellow leader's jersey, while it paradoxically enough is the taste-quality and meal-fixated French who have a much better ability to hold the thin line. How can this be explained? Should not the omnipresent campaigns that are to sharpen our attention on food's nutritional content and fat percent be precisely what makes us hold the course on the thin line's attractive thin tracks? "The general trend does seem to be the same everywhere in the developed world, with average weight and obesity going up. But there does seem *to be a French peculiarity*, with the lowest average

Body Mass Index (BMI) in Europe and the lowest prevalence of obesity (defined as a BMI of 30 or more). In other words, the *steepness of the slope is different*" (*ibid.*, emphasis added by author).

Fischler's study points, however, to yet one more interesting difference between the American–British food culture and the French. For the French also hang out together, both while preparing food for others, and while being mealtime hosts and eating together. This dimension went almost unmentioned by the Americans and British.

In connection to the obesity discussion, it makes sense that we eat differently, when we eat together with others, than when we eat alone. Mealtime community puts a limitation on the potential desire to overeat. However, if we eat alone it becomes solely our own ability for self-control and food conscience that must stand the test, and that battle can seldom be won each and every time.

Fischler himself summarizes his research in a powerful appeal:

> Instead of medicalized views on food warning us against their dangers, we should hear about the taste, history, origin, varieties, and culinary, social and nutritional values of the products [...] Rather than a personalized diet, even based on genetic evidence, we recommend cultivating the social practices of cooking and sharing meal [...] The medical line encourages everyone to 'make the right choices' but what it really does is, it merely reinforces and accelerates a 'disenchantment' (What the German sociologist Max Weber called *Entzauberung*) of the world: the loss of a belief in magic and the supernatural world. (*ibid.*)

He points to the fact that the collective articulation of food as solely a nutrient content also affects the way we think about food and food communities; it is, so to speak, not free of charge.

Although it is obvious that Claude Fischler's research does not in itself give clear answers to the causes of differences in food culture, and although the link between food culture and hyper-eating hardly can be attributed solely to the French priority of common meals and gastronomic experience, he usefully stresses the need to mainstream the meal's sociological and historical perspective, even in research contexts where the interest is otherwise directed at solely specifying paths to a change in our dietary habits towards the lower-fat version.

Along these lines it is noticeable that the World Health Organization's (WHO's) notion of health de facto contains more than a mere physical-corporal dimension, a social dimension and a mental dimension are included as well.

Besides stressing the fact that "feeling well" means more than just not "being sick," but that the wellbeing of individuals has to do with the co-existence with others and the joy one feels in connection to that as well, Fischler's research points to the possibility of there being steady links between the three dimensions. That is the case when, for instance, a negative experience of oneself or of one's life leads to a stressful state (the mental dimension) in which one starts to overeat, or when for instance positive human interactions in relation to the meal (the social dimension) prompt a choice of buying healthy goods.

In the following I will exemplify how the social dimension and the mental dimension should be included, and how we need to expand the use of the notion of "the physical."

The social dimension on commensality: Food as a medium through which we offer community

Now as an example to illuminate the significance of commensality in a specific social context of our meal culture, we will mention the Danish food sociologists Lotte Holm's and Katherine O'Doherty Jensen's work (Holm and Iversen, 1999).

As representatives of the food-sociological research tradition their research gives insights at a micro-sociological level into some of the interpersonal relationships that play a part in our handling of food. These range from parents' frustration (Holm and Iversen, 1999) over not being able to create a good framework for common meals in the family, the man's love of red meat, some women's health-threatening fear of fat, someone's bad conscience about not being able to prepare food from scratch, and, further, to the challenge of making proper food for oneself, and avoiding over-eating, when one eats alone. All of these are factors which must be integrated in a complete understanding of our dealings with food.

Table 4.1 Meals as a medium

The food and the meals are also symbolic forms of nutrition, because the carefully prepared meal expresses care for the ones it is made for. (Holm and Iversen, 1999, author's translation)	In modern family life cooking practice works as a recurring confirmation of the family as a community [...] meals are to be seen as the medium through which the family daily reproduces itself. (Holm and Kristensen, 2012, author's translation)	The fact that young people aim at detaching themselves from the family to establish themselves as independent and individual beings, is also anticipated in the everyday eating and cooking practice. Thus, the meal is not merely a medium for the creation of the family. It is as much the physical and social context in which temporary displacement and absence mark the dissolution of the family-hood, which is necessary for the young people's liberation. (Holm and Iversen, 1999, author's translation)

A model of Holm's and O'Doherty Jensen's conclusions can be synthesized as shown in Table 4.1.

Table 4.1 gives an insight into Western family's everyday meals, viewed from the perspective of the social interactions between the grown-up parents and their teenage children, including the emotions and struggles this entails. But the model also opens up for consideration food and the meal in a perspective that reaches beyond the mere local family context. One such consideration should be mentioned here.

The food—regarded as a medium—conveys a symbolic content, which constitutes an addresser and an addressee. And the addresser can—the food being a medium—seek out to include or exclude the addressee from the commensality, while the addressee, on the other hand, correspondingly is capable of approving or neglecting the invitation.

This chapter does not aim at elaborating on the perspectives for research that this view on commensality invites. This is mentioned as a warning against forgetting the most obvious, when we plan to avoid the obesity epidemics: our relationship with food is not something purely individual, it is always tightly interwoven in our mutual relationships to the people with whom we are commensally grouped.

The mental dimension and commensality: On the importance of having someone to eat with, and the importance of the physical framework of the eating

Turning our attention now to the mental dimension, a 2010 study among young Danes (Forbrugerrådet, 2010) seems particularly relevant: it shows that, next to a lack of money for the purchase of goods, the main reason why young people do not eat self-made food lies in the fact that they have no one to cook for—i.e. they have no one to eat with. It is not surprising that the motivation for preparing meals is linked to having someone to do it for, and taste and share the experience with. Being a part of a group fulfils an individual desire.

My own ongoing analyses of interviews with young people living in Danish student hostels strongly indicates that the potential sharing of a meal (commensality) is the strongest factor for motivating the young people to cook. (It should be mentioned that the joy of cooking together with others is a strongly motivating factor, as well. Proposing a home-grown notion, commensality should be complemented by "commencooking").

Again, we see that the focus on the nutritional quality (or culinary quality for that matter) is not the deciding factor. We emphasize the importance of adding the individuals' interpretations of their own lives, and what motivates them (the mental dimension), onto our research in commensality.

The physical dimension and commensality

Before finishing off by listing my methodological points, the notion of the physical dimension needs elaboration. The WHO's notion of the physical refers to the human body, that is to being sick versus not being sick. But, in a holistic view on commensality, such a notion of the physical dimension is not sufficient. In a holistic view the physical dimension ought to include the material aspect of the location where the commensality takes place.

The relevance of that aspect becomes clear in another Danish study (Engholm, 2010), which points out how the physical environment in student hostels influences the opportunities for—and nature of—commensality. Questions about "community challenges and problems" evoke answers like: "dirty kitchens, because of lack of cleanliness," "the standard is so low that no one feels any responsibility," and that some "chill out in their own rooms and will not participate in the community." As one student said, "it is often so bad in the kitchen that you completely lose the desire for being out there, cooking is indeed out of the question."

Seen in this light, cooking and commensality is suddenly a matter of rules and traditions for cleaning and physical arrangement. It is not a matter that can be solved by pointing a finger at eating too much fat.

Methodological note about the need for a holistic perspective on the interplay between food, people, meals, and physical space

To sum up: with reference to the works of Claude Fischler and his points about there being a problematic link between the joy of food/meals and the notion of being overweight, there is an array of matters that have to be taken into consideration, even on the part of health-centered research, which hitherto has been dominated by a narrow interest in nutritional content and its consequences for our physical wellbeing. We have proposed three dimensions which could be relevant to take into consideration for a more holistic approach:

1 The social dimension: food is a medium through which commensality is encouraged.
2 The mental dimension: the link between the individual's desire for making one's own food and the possibilities for sharing meals with others.
3 The physical dimension: the material framework of commensality is of importance to the establishment of commensality.

In the light of the arguments above, we finally suggest the Foodscape-perspective[2] as being an appropriate holistic, interdisciplinary research mode in the study of commensality, which also includes our attempts to understand and to fight obesity epidemics.

First, because of its linkage between "food" and the physical-spatial-visual suffix "scape," it focuses our attention on the fact that interactions with food and meals always happen in (and should therefore be interpreted in conjunction with) the physical-material context in which we eat: how are we seated, who are the others, how is the light, the colors, the sounds, the time of day, etc.? In other words: commensality cannot simply count as being an inter-subjective and mental phenomenon, but has to be researched as a part of a physical–material context.

Second, it will encourage us to consider commensality from a more practice-theoretical perspective. By one key definition practice is "a routine type of behavior that consists of several interrelated elements: forms of bodily activities, forms of mental activity," things "and their application, background knowledge in the form of comprehension, skills, types of motives and emotional states" (Reckwitz, 2002a). Basically, it is obvious that no one attends "commensal" eating without preconceived knowledge and experience; we are enmeshed in a number of structurally pre-existing conditions for our actions. Those conditions can be of anthropological, ethnographic, discursive or cultural nature. And similarly macro- as well as micro-sociological levels are obviously in play in the complex web of factors that we are influenced by. But it seems obvious that all these factors—despite their forceful explanatory value—would, taken separately, tend to overlook how we, in our dealings with the food and each other, might or might not alter the structural specific framework in which we eat. Therefore the practice-theoretical perspective is important.

The theme of this chapter on commensality and obesity epidemics can be seen as an invitation to further research into a Foodscape perspective.

5

Activism through Commensality: Food and Politics in a Temporary Vegan Zone[1]

Yvonne le Grand

Introduction

Current issues and developments in the global food system of industrial meat production, distribution, and consumption, and their detrimental impact on the environment have led various researchers and institutions to conclude that eating less meat and adopting a vegetarian—or even a vegan—diet would significantly lessen the environmental impact of greenhouse gas (GHG) emissions related to livestock production into the environment (e.g. Goodland and Anhang, 2009; Millstone and Lang 2008; Steinfeld et al., 2006; Pimentel and Pimentel, 2003).

From an anthropological point of view the question of what might be a more sustainable diet for the world at large might seem trifling, as there are so many people with ever so many food habits determined by history, culture, memory, identity and taste, to name but a few influences (Millstone and Lang, 2008; FAO Newsroom, 2006; Myer and Kent, 2003; Holtzman, 2006; Rozin, 1998). This question, however, is not referring to a "world diet": the same food for each and every person anywhere on the globe. It rather addresses the issues of nutritional social justice and sustainable practice in relation to how the rapidly increasing world population as a whole can feed itself without depleting the planet.

Although I was well aware of the dependency of industrial agriculture on the input of fossil fuel, the link between livestock production and GHG emissions came as a surprise to me. All of a sudden supermarket advertisements offering cheap meat did not look innocent any longer. Indeed, how was it possible that a consumer in the developed world could buy a kilo of beef for less than €5? Thus I became interested in the question of what people who had changed their diet for environmental reasons do to express their concern with the environment through food in their daily lives.

The groundwork for this chapter was laid in 2009, during four months of ethnographic fieldwork with GAIA (*Grupo de Acção e Intervenção Ambiental*), an environmental non-governmental organization (ENGO) in Lisbon, Portugal. Its main concern is with protecting the environment and social justice.[2] According to Mara, one of the informants, "GAIA is what the people who are there at the moment want it to be."

Since March 2008, it has organized a weekly vegan dinner called the *Jantar Popular* (JP) that is entirely run by volunteers. I chose the JP as the subject of my research, as it has a clearly observable structure that is independent of who is volunteering. However, without volunteers, there would not be a *Jantar Popular*.

As a participant-observer I did all the chores that a JP volunteer would do: from cleaning the dining spaces at the end of the evening to planning the menu, from shopping for groceries to helping with the formulation of the principles of the JP, from cooking to scrubbing the institutional-sized pans and kitchen utensils. On many occasions I assisted in the kitchen, washing and chopping vegetables, and cleaning the kitchen counters. On two occasions I was the "volunteer chef," the one who has the lead in the kitchen during the preparation of the food. The first time about 180 people came to partake in the dinner—a rather emotional experience for me as the responsible cook. It was an assorted bean dish, a *chili sem carne* (chili without meat), accompanied by plain boiled brown rice and a red cabbage, carrot, and raisin salad with a coriander-lemon dressing topped off with toasted sesame seeds. As a cook I think that nothing is more satisfying than to see people licking their plates clean afterwards, even if that is not a very elegant action. I never served food or collected the money for a dish, because I did not want to be in the spotlight—I thought that would undermine my being there as an observer.

I also conducted semi-structured interviews with people who actively volunteered for the JP—13 informants in total. One thing that all but one of them had in common was that at a certain stage during their lives they had gone abroad to study in a student exchange program. Another thing many people had in common was that they had been vegan at a certain stage in their lives, but later reverted to being vegetarian, or even to eat some meat or dairy products again.

For Sara, another informant, environmental activism is directly linked to food activism as "it is where environmental activism becomes personal." She observed that, in general, activists tend to focus a lot on calling attention to the issues they are concerned with but when it comes to their own eating or consumption habits they are often not aware of any inconsistencies.

The JP can be considered a "consumption ritual," as described by Cele C. Otnes in *The Blackwell Encyclopedia of Sociology*:

> At such events, individuals engage in both consumption and other behaviours with actions that can be characterized as formal, serious and intense. They [the rituals] are distinct from other more mundane consumption laden activities to the extent that *they provide opportunities for individual and social transformations which may be temporary or permanent.* (2007: 753; emphasis added by author)

This chapter deals with the JP as a ritual meal where the food consumed expresses the political and cultural choices in terms of diet of the participants, while building and reinforcing a sense of community of belief among them at the same time.

One thing that struck me from the first time I went to a JP in January 2009 was the sense of excitement that hung in the air. This sense of excitement surrounded not only first-timers, but also the people serving the food and the "regulars", people that come (almost) every Thursday. To me, everybody seemed to function at a higher level of energy. Despite the cold and the rain outside, there were some 60-odd people who were either standing in line for the food—a vegetable stew with seitan—or already seated around the tables that were dwarfed by the high ceilings of the space. As I was there with Virgil, my local host, I was introduced to some of the volunteers of the JP who told me what the JP was and what to do—that I had to wash my own dish and cutlery after I finished, for example.

As the number of eaters was rapidly growing by the week, it became unfeasible for the volunteers of the JP to speak with each and every new person and explain the how and why of the JP. Thus the idea was born to have information posters around on the walls near the food serving and the dish-washing area. Consensus being the *modus operandi* of the group, the wording of the principles and the reasons of the JP took at least a month to compile. Until the handwritten general information board was completed, photocopies of instructional bits and pieces were taped to the wall.

Thus, while people stand in the food queue, they can read about the 'Jantar Pop' on the main information board, strategically located near the serving table, that the JP "(...) is a non-discriminating space, that is open to all people who accept and respect that everybody is different, independent of their ethnicity, creed, nationality, sexual orientation, age or social status" (translated by the author).

In the next section I will focus on the environmental impact of the *Livestock Revolution* and how this came into being, as it is the main reason why the JP is a vegan dinner.

To meat or not to meat, an environmental dilemma

As alimentary diets go, research has shown that there is a tendency for people to eat more meat the moment they have more expendable income (Belasco, 2006; FAO Newsroom, 2006; Myers and Kent, 2003; Tilman et al., 2001; Delgado et al., 1999a, 1999b; Heinz and Lee, 1998; Drewnowski, 1999; Fiddes, 1991; Tannahill, 1988). Meat is considered, in many cultures, to sit at the top of the food chain (e.g. Pimentel et al., 2000).

Historically, meat, due to its scarcity, was considered a luxury and was consumed ostensibly by the secular upper class (Elias, 2000: 100). In a chapter aptly titled "The Mysterious Meanings of Meat," Beardsworth and Keil conclude that there is no real opposition between meat's appeal for consumers and its symbolic significance: "On the one hand, meat's appeal for its human consumers is seen as rooted in its nutritional properties, particularly in its ability to provide a comprehensive range of nutrients. On the other hand, meat's significance is said to reside in its symbolic charge, in its complex meanings relating to power, status, strength and gender which it can be used to convey" (1997: 217). However, as the nutritional and symbolic meanings of meat are intrinsically intertwined and feed on each other, the opposition is false.

Nick Fiddes states that: "Time and again, in different contexts, cultures, social groups, and periods of history, meat is supreme. Within most nations today, the higher the income bracket, the greater the portion of animal products in the diet. (…) Meat is so significant that, all over the world, people describe a 'meat-hunger' that is unlike any other hunger" (1991: 13).

The production of meat is a costly process as it involves many non-renewable natural resources such as land, water, and fossil fuel to produce and process the crops that are needed to feed a rapidly growing number of industrial meat animals or livestock.

For example, Eshel and Martin (2006) examined the respective GHG emissions associated with plant- and animal-based diets and compared the impact of one's dietary choices to those associated with choices concerning one's personal transportation (see also: Leitzman, 2003; Baroni et al., 2006). They concluded that: "For a person consuming a red meat diet an added GHG burden above that of a plant eater equals the difference between driving a Camry and a SUV [sports utility vehicle]. These results clearly demonstrate the primary effect of one's dietary choices on one's planetary footprint, an effect comparable in magnitude to the car one chooses to drive" (2006: 12).

In terms of global food security, the production of meat needs more caloric input than it provides in return: "(…) livestock consume 77 million tonnes of protein contained in foodstuff that could potentially be used on human nutrition, whereas only 58 million tonnes of proteins are contained in food products that livestock supplies" (Steinfeld et al., 2006: 270). In other words: humans and animals are now competing for the same resources, which will drive up food prices, which in turn will put even more stress on the world food system to produce more food, thus putting food security at risk.

The next section will deal with who eats at the JP and how it is presented.

Jantar Popular: public and format

Although anybody can join in a JP, it is probably safe to say that at least half the people at a JP are Erasmus exchange students. Erasmus students come from all over Europe, are usually between 21 and 27 years of age, and spend one to two semesters in Lisbon. The nationalities I encountered most were German, Spanish, Italian, and French, and the odd Scandinavian.

The rest of the people are what I would like to call "friends of GAIA": people who were or are members of GAIA, and the "curious people"—those who have heard about GAIA and want to learn more about the organization, and/or those who are curious to experience eating vegan food.

How to describe the non-Erasmus people? Their ages are more diverse, from parents and their young or teenage children, to Portuguese students. From "30- and 40-somethings" to people in their 50s or 60s. Interestingly enough, many people in the over 30 age bracket are foreigners—long-time residents in Lisbon, who might have been alternative or even hippies back in the days. In general, I think that the eaters as a whole are quite a cosmopolitan group, people with tertiary education and qualifications, coming from an urban middle-class background.

In his article in *Food and the City in Europe since 1800*, Alain Drouard remarks on reforming diets in, for example, Germany, at the end of the nineteenth century, that:

> In reaction to the traditional diet as well as the food industry, several initiatives, theoretical and practical, came into existence for the promotion of alternative forms of diet in German cities between 1880 and 1930. ... The advocates of natural methods and reform were neither marginal nor sectarian. They were recruited in Germany among the urban middle class, i.e. among people with high levels of education and qualifications ...
>
> Finally, vegetarianism appeared as a global project of reforming conditions of existence, based on the quest for a 'natural' way of life unfolding not only in a diet but also in health and medicine. As for naturism, it seemed to crystallize the anguish of declining, falling, parting from original harmony, generated by the speed of progress, urbanization and industrialization. ... Blaming the industrialization of agriculture and its harmful effects, the diet reformers anticipated the concerns of modern diet and ecology. (2007: 220, 224)

Reformists in the nineteenth century usually came from a middle-class background. This is still the case today when it comes to activists. According to Anthony Giddens, new social movement (NSM) activists come from: "the 'new' middle class that works in the post-1945 welfare state bureaucracies, creative fields, and artistic fields [*including many students*]. This finding led some to describe NSM as a form of 'middle-class radicalism' ..." (2009: 1018; emphasis added by author). The tradition of social activism coming from within the middle classes is reflected within GAIA and the JP—without exception everybody I have interviewed has been or still goes to university, and all of them were born in an urban environment.

GAIA and their environmental activism act like a filter that attracts like-minded people. Two more of the things my informants have in common are that they have done at least part of their studies abroad, and that somehow food plays an important role in their lives. Being abroad exposed them to realities different from those in Portugal, or in Julian's case, different from the United States of America where he was born and raised, although his father is Portuguese.

I asked him how he had discovered GAIA, as he is not frequenting Erasmus or other exchange students circles and GAIA do not advertise the JP. Julian answered that he was looking for "something social, something radical to do with food." He heard about GAIA during his Portuguese language course but did not follow up the lead and check out the JP because he found "the 'hood' [the neighborhood where the JP takes place] rather intimidating." When Julian finally overcame his resistance and braved the neighborhood, he felt he had arrived: "I thought the people looked interesting. I also found them, the people, attractive and beautiful, both mentally and physically."

Although cooking is not his passion, he volunteers with the *Hare Krishna* on Mondays as well. Julian has come to the conclusion that food groups are the best way to tackle a new social environment:

Food groups are the most generic, radically oriented groups of people. So I always end up searching them out when I get to a new place. I moved a lot around after I left home and had to make new friends all the time. Looking for people I can relate to, I search out food groups because generally they exist more often than other kinds of radical groups. By radical I mean socially radical, outside of conventional politics. (Julian, April 17, 2009)

To give an idea of the quantities for the JP of March 12, 2009, anticipating 150 to 160, we bought:

9 kg beans (a mixture of chick peas, red kidney, white mungo, pinto, black, and azuki beans, chicheros, and lentils)
6 kg Hokkaido pumpkins
5 kg red cabbage
3 kg red onions
garlic
1 kg grapes
8.5 kg brown rice
2 liters of *Risca Grande* olive oil (voted the best organic olive oil of Portugal in 2009)
1 kg lemons
5 kg carrots
3 kg tomatoes
bunches of fresh parsley and coriander

In the end 180 people ate the food prepared by five people.

While one group of the volunteers prepare the food in the kitchen, others prepare the pre-dinner activities that can take the form of a film or documentary projection, after which the issues are discussed by the public and the person(s) who proposed the topic. Sometimes specialists are invited to share their knowledge and experience with the audience. The audience is expected to participate actively in the ensuing debate.

Whatever the topic, from permaculture to guerrilla gardening, from suburbs to peak oil, or from the "one straw revolution" to the future of food, all topics follow a common thread: that humanity in the developed world should consume less and live more sustainably as there are no additional planets to help sustain humanity as a whole at the consumption level of the developed world.

After the political program, people line up for the food. They can read the menu on a handwritten blackboard that also gives an estimate of how much of the food is organic. They pay €3, pick up a plate and cutlery, and are served. While waiting in the queue, people can browse and buy libertarian literature that is on display on the table adjacent to the serving table.

A table with books, magazines, and pamphlets on anarchism and animal welfare and rights next to the food serving table is no coincidence. When eating at the JP, eaters consume both food for subsistence *and* food for thought—the symbolism is hard to miss.

After people collect their food, they look for a place to eat. Sitting down or standing up, the talking and drinking are animated. It usually feels like there is a party in progress because of a "buzz" in the air, a certain excited energy.

In the following section I will concentrate on what the concept of commensality—literally meaning: eating with others around a table—implied at different moments in time and place. Next, I will analyze the JP through the concept of temporary autonomous zones (TAZs) and develop the relationship between commensality, activism, and a vegan TAZ.

Commensality as a social interface

In *Cooking, Cuisine and Class*, Jack Goody points out that early anthropological research on food "examined the links between the offering of food to supernatural agencies and other aspects of social organization" (1982: 11). He mentions *The Religion of the Semites* (Smith, 1997 [1889]) as one of the earliest studies on how commensality—the sharing of food around a table—has a beneficial influence on both establishing and maintaining social relationships among people. Robertson Smith observed in Lecture VII that: "(...) the act of eating and drinking together is the solemn and stated expression of the fact that all those who share the meal are brethren, and that all the duties of friendship and brotherhood are implicitly acknowledged in their common act" (1997 [1889]: 247; Goody, 1982: 12).

In early Christianity, women were mainly absent from the dinner table (Bellan-Boyer, 2003). When commensality was in fact only open to a certain group of men, it is perhaps easy to understand why the open, communal meals, as encouraged and practiced by Jesus as described in the Gospel of Thomas, were considered a scandal in the social context at the time:

If one actually brought in anyone off the street, one could, in such a situation, have classes, sexes, and ranks all mixed together. Anyone could be reclining next to anyone else, female next to male, free next to slave, socially high next to socially low, and ritually pure next to ritually impure. And a short detour through the cross-cultural anthropology of food and eating underlines what a societal nightmare that would be.

> ... not just of eating together, of simple table fellowship, but what anthropologists call "commensality"—from *mensa*, the Latin word for "table." It means the rules of tabling and eating as miniature models for the rules of association and socialization. It means table fellowship as a map of economic discrimination, social hierarchy, and political differentiation. What Jesus' parable advocates, therefore, is an open commensality, an eating together without using table as a miniature map of society's vertical discriminations and lateral separations. The social challenge of such equal and egalitarian commensality is the parable's most fundamental danger and most radical threat. It is only a story, of course, but it is one that focuses its egalitarian challenge on society's miniature mirror, the table, as the place where bodies meet to eat. (Crossan, 1994: 74ff.)

In *The Sociology of the Meal*, Georg Simmel observed that everybody has a physiological need to eat and drink. Unlike the sharing of, for example, thoughts, Simmel writes in the essay: "what a single individual eats can under no circumstances be eaten by another. (...) The sociological structure of the meal emerges, which links precisely the exclusive selfishness of eating with a frequency of being together, with a habit of being gathered such as is seldom attainable on occasions of a higher intellectual order" (1997: 130).

In other words, the commensal intake of food forms a bridge between the sphere of the selfish individual and the social collective.

In "Melding the Public and Private Spheres: Taking Commensality Seriously," Albert Hirschman analyzes the evolution of the Greek banquet in ancient times and he:

> feels tempted to suggest that a direct link exists between the banquet and the emergence of Athenian democracy, that towering political invention of the Greeks. ... It would seem that Simmel was right: if Athenian democracy was one of its externalities or side effects, the sociological-political significance of the meal or banquet was truly immense. (1996: 543, 545)

Hirschman concludes that, from a purely biological point of view, eating is the self-centered and private activity of satiation—the physiological process during a meal to (eventually) stop eating when feeling satisfied. But when the eating is done in common, it goes together with many and diverse public or collective activities, such as eaters engaging in conversations or discussions, exchanging information, learning table manners, telling stories, and so on. Thus, the social, political, and cultural consequences of the common meal are manifold and varied.

In this light, the JP can be seen as a radical event as the JP is an open invitation: anybody can go there and share in the meal. There is no need to book a place and there is no obligation to volunteer, although it is made very clear that without volunteers there is no JP.

So what kind of commensality are we dealing with in the context of the JP? Based on the essay on the typology of commensality as proposed by Claude Grignon (2001), I would like to describe the commensality of the JP as an "intentional form" of the commensal encounter—a form of commensality that is neither a result nor a manifestation of a pre-existing social group:

> We probably have to consider separately the special case where the guest group does not emanate from a pre-existent group, but is by itself its own purpose and its own expression. This is the case at encounter commensalities, extemporaneous, short-lived or at least temporary (which, however, do not gather completely at random), like the company at table during a package tour, for example, the company of travellers at dinner around an inn's common table (table d'hôte), or, more or less stable but more lasting, the informal groups of regular attendants who meet at the café, the restaurant or the bar. These forms of commensality have in common that they occur on the fringe of habitual social life, within its parentheses and its interstices. (Grignon, 2001: 24)

At this point it is important to bear in mind the difference between commensality as an *expression* of identity and community, and commensality as an *interface* for exchanging ideas, opinions, stories, etc.

The JP is the weekly manifestation of a direct action, in which GAIA functions as a facilitator that provides JP volunteers with kitchen space and equipment, budget, and location, "independent of what GAIA is at that moment."

When I set out to research how people who had turned vegetarian or vegan for environmental reasons put their changed food habits into practice in the public realm, I thought initially that the JP was an act of consumer resistance in which mindful consumers took a stance on what they ate, and showed it to the world—their mindfulness was based on new insights into the workings of the global food system. As a consequence, these mindful consumers turned their insights into practice by organizing a weekly vegan dinner to spread new ideas, demonstrating to people who were not vegetarian or vegan that a meatless meal is nevertheless a meal.

However, the two most important aspects I encountered that I could not tie in with the scholarly literature on consumer resistance were the emphasis by the informants on the horizontal, non-hierarchical organizational structure in GAIA and the consensus decision making this implies, and the buzz in the air when the JP is going on, as if a party were in progress. It is here where the concept of temporary autonomous zones comes in, which will be explained in the next section.

The temporary vegan zone

In the article "Food Choice, Symbolism, and Identity: Bread-and-Butter Issues for Folklorists and Nutrition Studies," Michael Owen Jones (2007) argues that in nutritional studies the main emphasis is on diet and health, without taking into account what the symbolic aspects of food in people's everyday life mean to them (Jones, 2007: 162). While reading, I scribbled *"eating as activism???"* in the margin.

Rereading the scribble a year later, I suddenly remembered Hakim Bey's book *T.A.Z. The Temporary Autonomous Zone, Ontological Anarchy, Poetic Terrorism* (2003). The book consists of three parts, of which Part 3, about the temporary autonomous zone (TAZ) is relevant for analyzing the JP.

In sum, Hakim Bey, a.k.a. Peter Lamborn Wilson, an American anarchist, poet, and philosopher, argues that the creation of temporary spaces is a social/political tactic. Bey, in the role of prophet for building an alternative society, observes that in the formation of a TAZ, these temporary spaces elude formal structures of control. The TAZ is not an end in itself but a tool to think with and act through.

Bey was inspired by the idea of "Pirate Utopias" in the Caribbean in the eighteenth century. He describes a scattering of remote islands that formed an information network where pirates could hide, repair their ships, take in water and food, and trade objects. On these islands, mini-societies lived consciously outside the law for as long as they could hold out against the (colonizing European) authorities. The people on these islands lived as "intentional communities." Bey conceptualized the TAZ in 1985, without giving an exact definition of the TAZ, as a TAZ is undefined by its very nature and can only be understood in action.

> History says the Revolution attains "permanence", or at least duration, while the uprising is "temporary". In this sense an uprising is like a "peak experience" as opposed to a standard of "ordinary" consciousness and experience. Like festivals, uprisings cannot happen every day—otherwise they would not be "non-ordinary". But such moments of intensity give shape and meaning to the entirety of a life. … things have changed, shifts and integrations have occurred—a difference is made. (Bey 2003: 98)

In the above context, it does not matter that the JP is a recurring weekly happening—same event, same place, same time. The fact *that* every week, the JP needs to be constructed by volunteers—from planning the menu, till cleaning up the rooms at the end of the evening—contributes to the intention of creating a *place* where temporarily something is about to happen.

According to Bey each TAZ begins with its realization. As the TAZ is a simulation of the "anarchist dream" of free culture, it can operate invisibly in the cracks and crevices of "state omnipresence." The State, plotting out the territory, seemingly makes the map of the territory become the territory, a closed situation. However, as no map can ever be 1:1, where the map is different from the territory, the TAZ can take place, opening up the territory.

These invisible cracks in a system of state power are reminiscent of what James C. Scott describes in *Domination and the Arts of Resistance* (1992) as "public" transcripts and "hidden" transcripts, the crack being the equivalent of a hidden transcript.

I shall use the term public[3] transcript as a shorthand way of describing the open inter-action between subordinates and those who dominate …

If subordinate discourse in the presence of the dominant is a public transcript, I shall use the term hidden transcript to characterize discourse that takes place 'offstage', beyond direct observation by power holders. (Scott, 1990: 2, 4)

On Thursday evenings the JP becomes a safe haven for practicing the "arts of resistance," through intentionally eating vegan food. "Whether open only to a few friends, like a dinner party, or to thousands of celebrants, like a Be-in, the party is always 'open' because it is not 'ordered'; it may be planned, but unless it 'happens' it's a failure. The element of spontaneity is crucial" (Bey, 2003: 102–3).

The JP is an open invitation that extends to everybody and anybody, even to those without money, as in exchange they can participate in the preparation or the cleaning up of the JP. As a weekly recurring event, the JP is planned. It becomes a kind of TAZ where a certain kind of food, namely vegan food, is intentionally eaten in common. Therefore I think of the JP as a *temporary vegan zone* (TVZ), "in which all structure of authority dissolves in conviviality and celebration" (Bey, 2003: 102), and where "private and public spheres melds" as "the common meal leads to individual satiation and, as a result of commensality, has important social and public effects" (Hirschman, 1996: 533).

In the TVZ each person can directly experience food coming from a different food production system, while eating in common. The food is not just any kind of food, but a specific kind of food that is considered environmentally and socially just by the organizers of the JP.

In the TVZ, eating turns into a political act as commensality performs the double role of being both the action *and* the tool for transmitting the ideas behind the eating of vegan food. Thus, commensality is not only a community-building tool through the shared eating of a certain kind of food, but is also a political manifestation expressed through eating this certain kind of food. In other words: the personal becomes political.

In the JP GAIA has found a powerful tool to launch its environmental and social concerns into the public realm. The synergy between the various, intentional elements that constitute the JP transform it into something larger: into a TVZ. Being in the TVZ lifts the eater, albeit temporarily, out of his or her everyday life and routines.

The TVZ is a place fertile with a charged and energetic potential for change.

Bruner defines Victor Turner's concept of the anthropology of experience as *lived* experience as follows:

> how individuals actually experience their culture, that is, how events are received by consciousness. By experience we mean not just sense data, cognition, or in Dilthey's phrase, 'diluted juice of reason', but also feelings and expectations. As Fernandes points out, experience comes to us not just verbally but also in images. (...) Lived experience, then, as thought and desire, as word and image, is the primary reality. (Turner and Bruner, 1986: 4–5)

And what if the eaters are considered participating actors in staging a public play, the play being the JP? Then, perhaps the JP can be seen as a manifestation of "communitas"[4] as suggested by Victor Turner:

> The dominant genres of performance in societies at all levels of scale and complexity tend to be liminal phenomena. They are performed in privileged spaces and times, set off from the periods and areas reserved for work, food and sleep ... One may perhaps distinguish between secret and public liminality, between performative genres that are secluded from the gaze of the masses and those that involve their participation not only as audience but also as actors—taking place, moreover, in the squares of the city, the heart of the village, not away in a bush, hidden in a cave or secreted in a catacomb or cellar. (Turner, 1988: 25–6)

Turner also believes that "an increase in the level of social arousal, however produced, is capable of unlocking energy sources in individual participants" (1986: 43).

Coming back to Cele Otnes' entry on consumption rituals in *The Blackwell Encyclopedia of Sociology*, she writes: "Functionally, consumption rituals can provide us with what Tom Driver (1991) describes as the 'three social gifts' of ritual—order, transformation and 'communitas'" (2007: 754).

Applying the notion of the three social gifts (Driver, 1991: 119ff.) to the JP as a consumption ritual, the JP as a weekly event provides structure to life and actions (order); transforms participants in either a slight or a significant manner because "eating in common" becomes 'activism through commensality' (transformation) and strengthens the social bonds with the other participants in the TVZ (communitas).

The observations made about the JP by people involved in its creation strengthened my idea that the nature of the JP is that of a public event staged to create a vegan TAZ in which people can simultaneously experience *and* expose themselves to new ideas through active participation.

Eating in the TVZ, offers an opportunity to think and exchange ideas with other people through every bite that is taken, making eating an affirmation of life. During the JP, the eater is temporarily free to experience an alternative food reality. At the same time, the space where the JP is happening, becomes a place.

Conclusion

Throughout this chapter the focus has been on the JP as a direct action by volunteers involved with GAIA, an environmental activist group in Lisbon, firmly inserted in a global network of environmental social movements.

As such, GAIA is part of a vast counterculture movement spanning the globe and has its roots in, for example, the dietary reform movements in Europe during the second half of the nineteenth century. Those movements were opposed to the "modern industrial urban diet" of animal proteins, sugar, and alcohol (Carton, 1912) replacing the traditional diet of grains and starches. Those groups established a link between dietary reform and reforming the way of life and society. Not only vegetarian and naturist groups embraced this mission, but it was also adopted by political movements such as the anarchists and intellectuals like Henry David Thoreau. His book *Walden* (2008 [1854]) would inspire the counterculture of the 1960s, which in its turn inspired contemporary global counterculture groups like GAIA.

GAIA's intention is to bring about individual and social change through direct actions such as the JP. The JP proposes the alternative of a vegan diet as a political strategy to counter the dietary pressures provoked by the global corporate food system.

In the JP, GAIA has found the perfect tool for political activism through commensality. When people eat together in a group, they bond around the food. When the food that is eaten is connected to global economic, political and social trends, the meal turns into a consumption ritual that becomes a political act.

Once again food has proven to be an incredibly analytical tool to think with.

6

Cooking in the Fourth Millennium BCE: Investigating the Social via the Material[1]

Maria Bianca D'Anna and Carolin Jauss

Introduction

In recent years, studies concerning communal food consumption and social identity have burgeoned in the archaeological literature (see Twiss, Chapter 7). One of the reasons is the major impact of the concept of feast(s) as formulated in the now classic volume *Feasts. Archaeological and Ethnographic Experiences on Food, Politics, and Power* edited by Michael Dietler and Brian Hayden (2001a). More recently, everyday commensality and topics such as hunger have also begun to be considered in archaeological research (Pollock, 2012b, 2012c). This interest in everyday commensality mirrors the use of the feast as a key concept to read social dynamics in relation to food, and it stresses that extraordinary and ordinary practices should be considered alike.

In this chapter we will also focus on the everyday; however, we will discuss another fundamental part of the broad realm of culinary activity, i.e. the preparation of food. Liquid and solid ingredients can be combined and manipulated in many different ways. Among this spectrum of techniques we chose to analyze cooking in vessels. Cooking on open hearths was the most common method in ancient times and is still very widespread in poor countries nowadays. World Health Organization (WHO) studies (WHO, 2011c) reveal that almost 3 billion people still rely on open fires or hearths for cooking and heating as well as drying or flavoring food, drying fuel or housing material, and controlling insects (Figure 6.1). An aspect that will not be discussed further here, but that nevertheless should not be forgotten, is the indoor air pollution that open hearths generate, which has tremendously negative effects, mainly on women's and children's health.[2]

Cooking not only requires specific skills to properly coordinate the heating source, pots, and ingredients in order to obtain the desired dish and taste, it also takes a considerable amount of time and is usually assigned to certain persons who develop special skills in this activity. In many societies cooking was and is a gendered

Figure 6.1 Woman with baby cooking on a three-stone fire, San Marcos area, western Guatemalan highlands (photo: Nigel Bruce)

practice carried out predominantly by women, at least in domestic contexts (Bray, 2003b; Bruce et al., 2002: 30; Hastorf, 1991; Murdoch and Provost, 1973; WHO, 2011a). Within the broader realm of foodways, cooking builds a link between food production and consumption, the actual commensal act. Cooking, like consuming food, can take place in various social contexts, and how, where, when, and by whom food is cooked plays a crucial role in commensal practices and may reveal social relations that shape the background of the act of eating and drinking together.

Our starting point is cooking as a social practice. From a practice-oriented perspective, social organization is grounded in practices and is therefore intrinsically "done" by acting (Reckwitz, 2003: 291).[3] Practices are generally characterized as organized, regular, and repeated actions consisting of an interplay between bodies, know-how, nonhuman organisms, artifacts, and things. Although distinct approaches take differing stances toward practice, bodily acts and gestures performed in interaction among these entities form the basis of the social (Hofmann and Schreiber, 2011; Hörning and Reuter, 2004: 13; Reckwitz, 2002b, 2003: 289, 291; Schatzki, 2006: 2, 2002: 38, 70–88). Concerning this interaction, artifacts are ascribed different levels of importance (Reckwitz, 2002c). At one extreme stands Bruno Latour's actor network theory based on the *principle of generalized symmetry*, which assumes that things and humans are equally active participants in networks

(Callon and Latour, 1992). Although this approach is viewed positively in some recent archaeological essays (e.g. Hodder, 2011), we adopt the standpoint of other scholars, such as Karl H. Hörning or Andreas Reckwitz, who focus on the materiality of practices but consider people as active actors at the center of practices and perceive the role of things in initiating, enabling, and restricting certain possibilities for behavior (Hörning, 2001; Reckwitz, 2002c). It is specifically this materiality of practices, their being grounded in material culture and bodily acts, that forms the starting point for our research. As archaeologists our main source of information for studying ancient practices is material culture—as Rosemary A. Joyce puts it: "[…] material that we interpret as signs of action" (2008: 27). Therefore tracing actions in archaeology means looking at the interplay between material culture and people. From material culture we infer actions that took place and people who acted, and finally practices and their place within wider society. Consequently we approach the social via the material.

In this chapter, we present a study of cooking pots from two Uruk period sites (second half of the fourth millennium BCE), i.e. Chogha Mish in southwestern Iran and Arslantepe in southeastern Turkey (Figure 6.2). We show how a close look at everyday practices helps us better understand the complex role that food and commensal politics played during the later Uruk period.

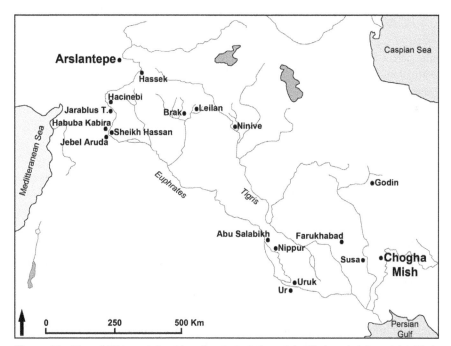

Figure 6.2 Map of Western Asia with archaeological sites of the Uruk period (copyright: Maria Bianca D'Anna and Carolin Jauss)

The Uruk period is described as the time when urban life and states first emerged in southern Mesopotamia. The economic base of this process was a high agricultural productivity. The production of food surplus allowed the maintenance of both an elite that centralized primary goods and artisans or "specialists" not involved in food production. In southern Mesopotamia, the Uruk period covers the fourth millennium and derives its name from the site located in southern Iraq. In addition to southern Mesopotamia, the Susiana plain in Iranian Khuzestan has been identified as another important area for tracing fourth millennium cultural developments. In the 1960s–1970s excavations were carried out at the site of Chogha Mish (Delougaz et al., 1996; Alizadeh, 2008), the first case study of this chapter. Surveys and excavations also revealed Uruk sites in northwestern Syria and in the Syrian and Turkish Euphrates river valley, among them Arslantepe (Frangipane and Palmieri, 1983; Frangipane, 2010), the site from which we draw our second case study.

Concerning the social, a key concept discussed in historiographies on the Uruk period is hierarchy. A leader figure is depicted in various images, and officials responsible for certain administrative tasks and crafts are listed in the "Standard Professions List" and a list of officials from Uruk. Both texts and pictorial evidence show people in groups distinguished mainly on the basis of their work. The elite who held administrative control in this early urban society appears strictly structured through a complex hierarchy (Damerow, 1998; Vogel, 2009; Wagensonner, 2010). Central authorities controlled people's lives in many ways. Through centralization and redistribution of foodstuffs, elites regulated a large sector of the economic and social life. Thus, during the Uruk period, food was not only the economic base of elite power but also a powerful instrument for controlling people (Pollock, 2003). Meticulous administrative documentation reflects the important role that state control over food played in Uruk society and the high degree to which access to food was connected to social status (Damerow, 1998). Dependent laborers can mainly be identified in archaic texts through the rations they received. The "Standard Professions List" mentions male cooks, but texts neither provide information on where cooks worked nor on the kind of food they prepared (Nissen et al., 1990: 156). However, Uruk culinary reality was certainly much more heterogeneous than what we learn from administrative sources. If we want to understand Uruk foodways better, aside from the elite perspective, we have to look more closely at what people actually did.

Already in 2002, Reinhard Bernbeck and Susan Pollock criticized narratives concerning Uruk Mesopotamia and suggested approaching this topic by identifying and analyzing different "spheres of life" through multiple narratives. Among their assumptions is the idea that "The '*Sitz im Leben*' of any past practice, institution or belief needs to be researched rather than assumed at the outset" (2002: 179). One sphere of life they suggest analyzing in more depth is that of routinized consumption of food rations. Some other recent studies have approached different aspects of commensality during the Uruk period (Helwing, 2003; Pollock, 2003; D'Anna,

2012). In this chapter we attempt to open two more windows on Uruk food practices by analyzing cooking pots at two sites at the edges of the "Uruk world." Research on pottery has so far mainly focused on formal aspects, such as the presence of genuine southern Mesopotamian ceramics (like bevelled-rim bowls and spouted vessels) or more or less Uruk-related assemblages. These have often been used as an indicator of the degree of "Urukness" of a specific site or region. However, we will not attempt to test our material according to this criterion (this analytical process would set Chogha Mish at the *degré zéro* and Arslantepe as Uruk-influenced), nor do we want to compare the two assemblages in terms of shapes and fabrics. Rather, we study cooking vessels from Chogha Mish and Arslantepe to infer how they were handled and used on the fire as well as in which ways and in which contexts food was cooked. As cooking is a practice that was executed in both public and domestic settings, it constitutes an interesting starting point to gain better insight into the diverse spheres of Uruk foodways and adds some heterogeneity to the picture of Uruk commensality.

It is through careful analyses of performance characteristics and use traces on artifacts that we are able to build a bridge between material culture, gestures, actions, and people, and to investigate the functional and social dimensions of cooking practices. For our case studies we choose to analyze vessels with traces of having been used in connection with fire.

Techno-morphological aspects relevant for functional restrictions and affordances of the cooking vessels analyzed here are volume, access factors such as the size of openings in relation to volume and shape of the vessels (restriction ratio), heat distribution and thermal shock resistance characteristics like paste and profile shape (Figure 6.3), and formal aspects relevant for handling vessels like handles (Smith, 1985). The study of use-wear traces on cooking vessels mainly focuses on

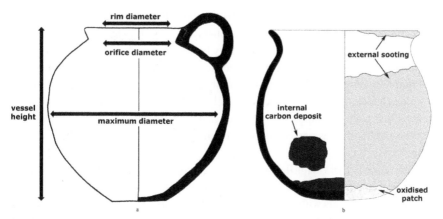

Figure 6.3 (a) Vessel measurements; and (b) cooking vessel's use wears (copyright (b) Maria Bianca D'Anna)

both internal carbon deposits and external sooting. The internal deposits are caused by the carbonization of food residues from repeated cooking, and they are affected primarily by three factors: the kind and density of ingredients, thus the degree of moisture present inside the vessel; heat intensity; and distance from the heating source (Skibo, 1992: 147–73; Kobayashi, 1994). The exposure to the fire may alter the external colors of the cooking pots. Variables affecting sooting formation and pattern as well as the presence of oxidized areas are: the distance from the heat source; the position in relation to the heating source; the presence of permeated moisture on the external surfaces; and the type of fuel (Kobayashi, 1994). Our analyses also take into account contextual data, such as the character of occupation at the two sites, and, if possible, vessel distribution to place our findings within the broader framework of food and the social.

Chogha Mish

Chogha Mish (Figure 6.2) in lowland Susiana, modern day Khuzistan, comprised about 17 ha during the later Uruk period and can be considered a regional center with public as well as residential buildings and evidence of accounting.

At Chogha Mish the main vessel types used for the preparation of food in connection with fire are strap handled jars and squat, round bottomed, wide mouthed jars with everted rims (Figure 6.4).[4] The vessels seem to have been made by a combination of techniques.[5] The wheel definitely played a role in their manufacture, as wheel traces, mainly on rims, testify, and scraping on the outer surface could be the result of reducing the wall thickness caused by throwing the lower part of the vessels. However, vessels show traces of handsmoothing, and the mineral temper sometimes is so coarse as to make it seemingly impossible to throw these pots with bare hands.

Strap handled jars can be divided into two groups: one with round and one with flat bases. Within these two groups the jars can be considered homogeneous concerning their functional performance characteristics, despite some differences in vessel form and decoration.[6] Generally they bear a short neck with a rounded lip and a rounded, sometimes carinated, body profile. Strap handled jars were certainly used for purposes other than cooking, such as short-term storage or transport of liquids. For this chapter, however, the focus is solely on their use as cooking vessels. Of the vessels that were examined for use wear (among which a considerable proportion of the vessel body was preserved), about half showed traces of having been used in a fire.

Strap handled jars with flat bases range in capacity from 100 ml to 4.5 liters.[7] There are concentrations of vessels with a volume of around 300–400 ml and around 1 liter. Vessels with rounded bases are generally bigger, their volume ranging between 4.4 and 9 liters (Figure 6.4(a)). Orifice diameters of strap handled jars do not exceed 12 cm, but are in most cases big enough for the vessels' contents to be

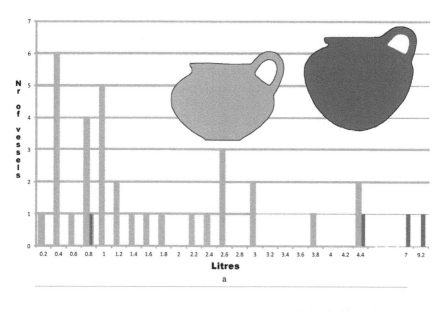

a

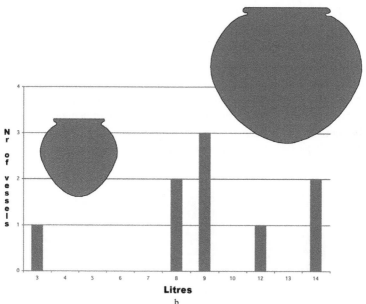

b

Figure 6.4   Chogha Mish: volumes of strap handled jars and everted rim jars (copyright Carolin Jauss)

accessed with an adult hand. The average height of the vessels is 16 cm and does not exceed 33 cm. Therefore, the accessibility of strap handled jars for manipulation of the contents and cleaning was moderate, and at the same time the restricted orifice would have prevented spilling of liquid contents during short distance transport as well as rapid evaporation during the cooking process. The handle would have made it difficult to place lids on these jars to completely prevent evaporation. Vessels with flat bases were suited to stand on a levelled surface and could be pulled across the floor. This might have been useful when a full vessel with hot contents had to be moved. On the contrary, vessels with round bases needed some kind of support to stand stably on a floor as well as in the fire, and to move them they had to be lifted.

Some larger vessels, most of them with round bases, would have had a weight of around 8 kg when filled with liquid content. A person would have needed both hands to handle such a vessel comfortably and it would have been a particularly difficult task when the vessel was hot. However, many of the larger vessels show semicircular widened lips on the side opposite the handle. This ledge handle might have helped considerably to grasp and move the vessels. Some of the vessels are incised on the upper strap handle as well as on the ledge handle, which could have served to give a better grip on the vessel, e.g. when greasy contents made the vessel slippery (Figure 6.5).

Sooting on strap handled jars with flat bases is mostly concentrated on the front part of the vessel, on the side opposite the handle. Often it forms an oval around the height of the maximum diameter of the vessel, and in some cases soot stretches to the upper part of the vessel over the lip on the interior of the rim or reaches down to the base and sometimes covers the whole base (Figure 6.6(a)–(b)). These vessels were placed at the side of the fire with only the front part being exposed to the heat and the hottest spot concentrated in an oval at about the height of the maximum expansion of the vessel. This is confirmed by carbon deposits of burned contents,

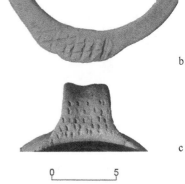

Figure 6.5 Chogha Mish: (a) widened lip on strap handled jar; and (b, c) incisions on strap handle and ledge handle (copyright: Carolin Jauss)

a   b   c

Figure 6.6 Chogha Mish strap handled jar: (a, b) external sooting; (c) internal carbon deposit (copyright: Carolin Jauss)

which are located on the front interior wall corresponding to the external sooting (Figure 6.6(c)). The round profile of vessel bodies is well suited to cope with thermal shock effects and distribute heat efficiently (Smith, 1985). In addition, a position next to the fire ensures easy handling of the vessel, because the handle stays away from the fire and remains cool if the vessel is not heated for too long. Other strap handled jars show sooting all around the vessel, mostly around the widest diameter. If deposits of charred food are preserved in these vessels, they stretch over the interior base. These vessels were placed in or slightly above the heating source, although their actual position cannot be determined because no complete bases are preserved.[8]

Apart from strap handled jars, squat, round-bottomed, wide-mouthed jars with everted rims were used for cooking (Figures 6.4(b), 6.7(a),(b)). Compared to strap handled jars with round bases, they are generally more globular in shape with a lower center of gravity and bear a shorter neck with a folded rim. Their mostly mineral paste is coarse and the outer surface rough, which can improve heating performance in the fire. According to the excavators, this type of vessel is omnipresent on the site, although unfortunately only ten specimens were accessible for this analysis.[9]

The jars range from 8 to 14 liters in capacity and they could be as heavy as 17 kg when filled with a liquid content (Figure 6.4(b)). Orifice sizes range from 10 to 13 cm in diameter, thus, on average, they are slightly bigger in comparison to strap handled jars, but they still fall in a medium accessibility range. Lids could be easily placed on the jars to accelerate the heating process.

Soot is preserved on these pots around the maximum vessel diameter; sometimes it reaches the base and is occasionally also visible on the rim (Figure. 6.7(a)). If preserved, carbon deposits were found only on the interior base (Figure 6.7(b)). The traces let us infer that the cooking vessels were placed in a moderate fire with the lower vessel wall in the hottest spot. None of the vessels shows carbon deposits on the interior wall above the base, which indicates that the content heated in these vessels was most probably watery. From semi-solid or solid contents one would expect particles to adhere to the interior wall at the uppermost line of the content, burn there, and form a ring of interior carbon deposit (Skibo, 1992: 151).

Performance characteristics of strap handled jars point to liquid or semi-liquid contents, which could have been poured from the vessels even when hot. These vessels were most probably used for quickly heating liquids next to the fire rather than simmering them for a long time. The bigger strap handled jars could additionally have been used as cooking pots to prepare larger quantities of liquid food. All strap handled jars were well suited for short distance transport and handling by one person. By contrast, the larger cooking pots without handles and rounded bases were considerably more difficult to move. It would have been rather difficult to transport a full vessel with hot content and most probably two persons would have been necessary to lift it. Devices to stabilize the vessels were needed to place them on the floor or in the fire. They were by far less flexible in handling than strap handled jars. Judging from their size, they fit within the medium range of family cooking pots reported from ethnographic contexts by Elizabeth F. Henrickson and Mary M. A. McDonald (1983: 631)[10] and their volume is comparable with cooking pots from domestic contexts at Arslantepe (see below; D'Anna and Piccione, 2010: 236).

Both vessel types were presumably used for liquid rather than for semi-liquid or solid contents, and boiling or simmering were the most common cooking techniques that were practiced with these vessels.

Figure 6.7 Chogha Mish everted rim jar: (a) external sooting; (b) internal carbon deposit (copyright: Carolin Jauss)

Information on the contexts in which the vessels have been found is limited, although most of the above presented material stems from the East Area (Alizadeh, 2008: 26, 243, Figure 17).[11] This area is characterized by several separate architectural units which are considered to be houses. There is evidence for pottery production and artifacts connected with accounting—such as sealings, clay tablets, and *bullae*—point to considerable administrative practice. The excavators interpreted this area as residential with workshop activities (Alizadeh, 2008: 26, 44–6; Delougaz et al., 1996: 30–1, 35). The excavated architectural units can be considered as belonging to households. A hypothesis is that the households consisted of extended families; however, it is unclear how many persons actually lived there.[12] Furthermore, lack of information concerning the number of vessels related to each architectural unit prevents precise statements on the purpose(s) or for whom cooked foodstuffs were prepared in this area. However, there are a few probable scenarios.

Arguing from the above described characteristics of vessels, simple fireplaces or open hearths, possibly equipped with stones to support vessels with round bases, would have been sufficient for cooking. This fits with the information we have on fireplaces at Chogha Mish. Hearths are reported in rooms and range in size from a few centimeters to 1 m in diameter.[13] Fireplaces are also reported from open spaces which were most probably used by several architectural units (Alizadeh, 2008: 26).[14] It seems likely that cooking was practiced either within the houses or in their close vicinity in open spaces. If cooking took place in open spaces between houses, it was an openly visible practice. The people who cooked would have formed a loose community of practice exchanging skills and recipes (Wenger, 1999). Also, people not practicing cooking themselves would have been involved by observing the activities going on and smelling the food. Indoor cooking would have been a more restricted activity; most rooms for which fireplaces are reported are small, and vessels were all suited for handling by one or two persons, which is an argument for cooking being a practice executed by few people in each household.

The capacity of most of the strap handled jars with flat bases is below a size suitable for preparing meals for several people. This suggests that these vessels could have been involved in the production of secondary foodstuffs (Jauss, 2013). Caprine and cattle husbandry is depicted on seal imagery from Chogha Mish (Delougaz et al., 1998: Plates 143, 145) and a suggestion would be that strap handled jars were used for the manipulation of milk from these animals, to produce, for example, yoghurt or clarified butter. Heating butter to separate fat from water is a common procedure to make milk fat storable (Palmer, 2002) and there is evidence for dairy fats being an important secondary foodstuff in texts from around 3000 BCE. In proto-cuneiform texts from Uruk, dealing with cattle and dairy products, some signs representing dairy fats bear the form of a handled vessel (Green, 1980: Figure 3; Englund, 1995: Figure 19) and in his analysis of texts from Susa, a site neighboring Chogha Mish, Jacob Dahl suggests that clarified butter from sheep and goat milk played an important role in the dairy economy (2005: 113–15).[15]

These texts are administrative records that list, among other data, the amount of secondary milk products that had to be delivered from animal herders to the owners of these animals (Englund, 1995: 38; Dahl, 2005: 113–15, 119). Herding and preparation of secondary products seem to have been connected tasks executed by people other than those who owned the animals, and who later on administered the products within a central settlement. That milk was actually processed in strap handled jars is a hypothesis which remains to be tested;[16] however, if secondary milk products— from cattle, sheep, or goats—were prepared in the East Area this means that the labor put into processing them was invested by persons connected to households within the regional center itself rather than in the surrounding countryside.[17] Whether the products were intended for intra-household storage or for extra-household purposes, or both, we do not know.

Everted rim jars could additionally have been involved in the production of secondary foodstuffs but, as they fit in the range of domestic cooking pots, it is also likely that they were used for preparing meals. The size of vessels as well as the size and location of hearths in mainly small rooms limit the amount of food that could be cooked indoors for meals to a volume suitable for a group of people somehow related to a household, rather than for a larger contingent of people—at least if the food were to be consumed right after cooking and not to be stored. Bevelled rim bowls, a type of container commonly interpreted as a dish for the distribution of food as rations, are as abundant at Chogha Mish as at other contemporaneous sites. To what degree cooked food was involved in rationing is a question for further research. This analysis points to the fact that cooked food, or more specifically food heated, stewed, or boiled in vessels, was only one of many facets of the diet, and probably only a small part. Other techniques such as drying, fermenting, or roasting, as well as baking in ovens, might have played a major role in food preparation (Pollock, 2012c). More research on other types of vessels as well as archaeobotanical and faunal remains will hopefully lead to a more precise picture of cooking as well as eating and drinking practices at Chogha Mish.

Arslantepe

Arslantepe is located in the Malatya plain (see Figure 6.2). The mound is about 4 ha, but Late Chalcolithic 5 remains (corresponding to the Late Uruk period in Southern Mesopotamia and Susiana) have been exposed only in the southeastern part of the mound. They comprise one architectural phase uncovered in two distinct areas, revealing a large public complex with edifices intended for different activities and some residential buildings (Figure 6.8).[18] During this period, which is called VI A in the site sequence, goods—mainly large quantities of different foodstuffs—were stored both in storerooms and temples, and then either redistributed in the form of meal-rations or consumed during ritualized feasts. The role of staple finance, meal redistribution, and ritual commensality has been recently discussed (D'Anna, 2012; see also D'Anna, 2010 and Frangipane, 2010)[19] but some questions still remain open. How and where was food cooked? Did cooking and cooked food play a role in different commensal spheres distinguished by location and people involved?

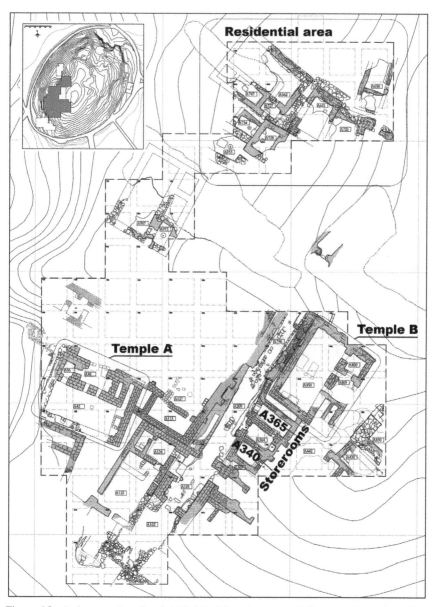

Figure 6.8 Arslantepe: plan of period VI A buildings (courtesy of Missone Archaelogica Italiana nell'Anatolia Orientale)

First of all we will have a closer look at cooking pots, which, in the period VI A, were always handmade, with a medium to coarse fabric with both vegetal and mineral temper. The exterior of the vessels is either smoothed or slightly burnished, while the interior is often left unfinished after being regularized with a hard tool. From a functional point of view, different profiles can be grouped together. The

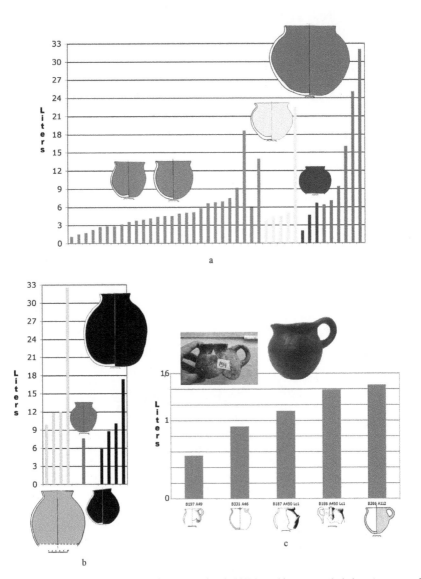

Figure 6.9 Arslantepe: distribution of volumes of period VI A cooking pots and pitchers (courtesy of Missone Archaeologica Italiana nell'Anatolia and Maria Bianca D'Anna)

majority of Arslantepe cooking pots present a globular, ovoid, or biconical body and a short outflaring collar (Figure 6.9(a)). The lip is simply rounded or slightly flattened. In most cases, cooking pots have a flat or gently flattened base, which of course grants better stability. Rarely is the base rounded. At any rate, the vessels' base and body never create any sharp angle, and this improves resistance to thermal shock. The majority of this first group of pots ranges between 1 and 7 liters in capacity, but six exceptions are worthy of note. Their capacity ranges between 14 and 32 liters. Typically, half to two-thirds of the vessels' walls fall under the point of maximum expansion, thus the percentage of vessel wall exposed to the heat is fairly high, allowing foodstuffs to be heated quickly and easily. The inner diameter of the orifice ranges between 8 and 28 cm, meaning the content was easily accessible but the evaporation rate was moderately high.

In the Arslantepe assemblage, traces of charred food in the interior of these pots are often visible. A black and thick carbonized area covers the base but often it does not reach the surface of the inner walls of the pot. In a few cases, one or more dark areas of carbonized deposit are present on the internal walls, in general along the point of maximum expansion and in correspondence to sooted zones or oxidized patches on the outside (Figure 6.10(c), (d), (e), (g)). The presence of this use wear on the pots may testify that sometimes food was simmered next to the hearth. In most of the cases, an oxidized patch is located on the external base and the very lower side of the vessels (Figure 6.10(b), (f)). The lower part of the body under the shoulder or the point of maximum expansion is markedly sooted, and, in some cases, the lip is also black or dark brown in color, while the shoulder is almost never affected by traces of sooting (Figure 10(a), (f), (g)). This pattern of internal carbon deposit and external sooting suggests that at Arslantepe VI A cooking pots were often located very close to, or even directly placed in, the heating source, which probably was not a high flame fire. The absence of dark sooting on the base proves that vessels were not suspended over the fire and, actually, no portable elements to sustain pots have ever been found.

A second group of cooking pots shows smaller openings and more or less elongated profiles (Figure 6.9(b)). At any rate, their constriction is more marked than those of the first group. They are almost all rather large pots (their volumes range from c. 6 to 32 liters, with the majority bearing more than 9 liters in capacity). In these vessels, the internal carbon deposit is almost always lacking. Both the narrowness of the orifices and the absence of thick internal carbon deposits suggest that these pots were used to process rather liquid ingredients, for which preventing evaporation was quite important. However, the outer sooting is consistent with that of the more open shaped pots (Figure 6.10(h)), meaning it is likely these vessels might have been placed in the same way directly in the heating source.

Five small pitchers show external sooting, suggesting they were used on the fire (Figure 6.9(c)). In two cases, the side opposite to the handle is sooted with a similar pattern to that seen on some strap handled jars from Chogha Mish. Therefore, it

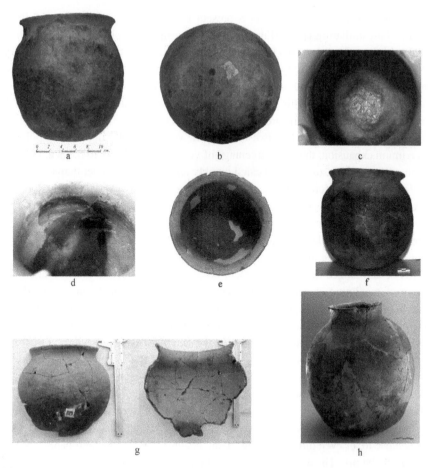

Figure 6.10 Arslantepe cooking pots: (a, f, g) external sooting; (b, f) oxidized patches; and (c, d, e, g) internal carbon deposit (copyright Maria Bianca D'Anna)

might be possible that these handled pots were used with the front part next to the fire. No pitchers have internal carbon deposits, which—along with the presence of the handle—confirms that they were used to process fluid ingredients, even though some liquids, like milk for instance, burn easily. These pitchers' volumes range from half a liter to 1.5 liters and their heights do not exceed 15 cm. Thus they were easily movable with one hand; the content had to be poured out of them while direct access was possible but rather uncomfortable because the inner diameter of the orifices is never larger than 10 cm.

Food processing was a crucial activity not only in the daily meal preparation, but also in relationship to the formal commensal contexts of meal redistributions and feasts. In period VI A buildings and open areas, no ovens have been found, but fireplaces are common inside rooms. As shown, the cooking pots are more or less all close-shaped vessels and neither trays nor bowls were ever used (Henrickson and McDonald 1983: 631–2). Boiling and stewing appear to have been the most common cooking techniques. Along with a large number of other kinds of containers, vessels

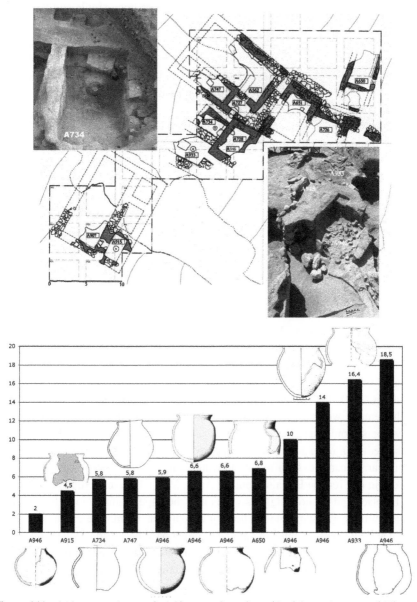

Figure 6.11 Arslantepe: volumes of cooking pots from the residential area (courtesy of Missone Archaeologica Italiana nell'Anatolia and Maria Bianca D'Anna)

with fire clouding are also found in spaces with no fireplaces. These areas are interpreted as storerooms.[20] Cooking is a way to preserve food for longer periods of time, and ceramics absorb the smell and taste of foodstuffs. It makes perfect sense that cooking pots were "also" storage vessels. Another hypothesis is that cooking pots were stored in those areas when not in use.

Both groups of cooking pots, the first with a more open profile and the second more closed, and similar use wear are found in the residences, the two temples, and the storerooms, but larger cooking pots only characterize the assemblages in both Temple B and the stocking area A365 within the storerooms sector. However, it is the ratio of cooking pots to vessels interpreted as storage jars and *pithoi* which defines differences between diverse areas (public and residential areas as well as within the public sector: see also D'Anna, 2010).

In the residential buildings, where no evidence of any administrative activities is documented, one very small and four large pots (10 to 18 liters in capacity) have been found, but the more common group is that of 5 to 7 liter capacity pots (Figure 6.11). This pattern resembles that of the cooking pots found in the houses of the Early Bronze Age I village (period VI B2, dated to the first centuries of the third millennium BCE): although the total number of cooking pots is much higher in the EBA houses, the characteristics of both collections are very similar in mean capacity and standard deviation (D'Anna and Piccione, 2010: 236).

Within the complex of public buildings, food processing, cooking, and consumption of meals certainly took place in both temples A and B, where—although scattered in different areas of the two buildings—large storage vessels for dry and semi-liquid contents, bottles, cooking pots, animal bones, and stone tools used in processing both animal and vegetal products have been found in abundance.[21] In Temple B, cooking pots were few in number (five) and large in capacity (altogether their total volume is 70 liters). Moreover a 70 liter *pithos* shows external sooting near the base, suggesting it might have also been used on the fire (D'Anna, 2010: 181, 2012: Table 1). All the vessels were placed in the main room of the temple, where a large hearth was also located, and it is unlikely that these heavy pots would have been moved around, especially when full. Before being consumed by a restricted number of people who actively took part in the feasting events, large quantities of different foods and drinks were stored, processed, and also cooked in the Temple B main room (D'Anna, 2012). One interesting aspect is that the fireplace and the cooking pots were all in the larger main room of the building, while a mortar was sunk into the floor of a small side room, where a millstone was found as well. Thus cooking, in particular, might have been part of the events taking place in the main room, contrary to other methods of food preparation. The size of the vessels suggests that cooking involved several persons, and it must have been rather time and energy consuming. Moreover, as hypothesized for the rituals and/or "feasting" happening in the main room, cooking was at least partly visible from the outside through the two windows connecting the entrance and the main rooms. The sensorial involvements of people standing in the entrance room could have played an important role in maintaining their degree of inclusion in all moments of these events (*ibid.*).

Concentrations of clay sealings, standardized mass-produced bowls associated with different kinds of storage containers and cooking pots testify to an intense practice of disbursement of rations in exchange for labor (Frangipane and Palmieri, 1986; Frangipane, 2010). The use of bowls as containers for redistribution points to the understanding of these rations as meals and not unprepared foodstuffs. This practice, which has also been defined as "asymmetrical provisioning" (Pollock, 2012b), served to construct contexts for everyday formal commensality (Pollock, 2003: 27–32; D'Anna, 2012). At Arslantepe VI A it seems that cooked food entered only marginally this circuit. In the main redistribution area (A340), for instance, cooking pots are small, with the exception of a large fragment of a 25 liter capacity pot found on the floor of the room. In A340 there were no fire installations, so it seems impossible that cooking took place in here, too. Cooked food was redistributed, but from a quantitative point of view it was not the most significant part of the redistributed goods and possibly other kinds of processed foodstuffs were employed more frequently. In fact, middle- and large-sized containers were also present in the room and they had either large openings or constricted cylindrical necks, which seem suitable to preserve respectively dry goods (such as flours or crushed grains)[22] and liquids or semi-liquids (such as beer, porridges, dairy products, and the like: D'Anna, 2010: 171–4). However, these products must also have been processed elsewhere within or outside the public compound. It might be that the entire cycle of food production for the redistribution was not visible in the public sphere.

Cooking transforms the taste of ingredients, and cooking habits shape taste and culinary tradition. Different kinds of food preparations took place at the site, and various processed foodstuffs circulated in the public sector and characterized different commensal events. Also the distribution of animal bones in the period VI A buildings shows that meats consumed in the commensal, ritual events taking place in the Temple B were different from those redistributed in the meal-ration system in terms of both kind of animals and cut quality, and therefore also flavor (see also Palumbi, 2010: 154). Although the cooking pot assemblage does not appear to be extremely varied, it seems that distinctive tastes and culinary traditions might have characterized different moments of people's social life. In particular, commensal events in formal contexts were not only differentiated in terms of location and degree of inclusiveness, but also by kinds of food and ways in which food was prepared. On the one hand, mutual social identities were defined and reinforced through these commensal—and therefore also culinary—spheres; and, on the other hand, the role of people cooking and preparing food to be consumed in the different spheres was differentiated in terms of physical and social contexts in which the practice of cooking took place.

Conclusion

In the two case studies we analyzed material components of cooking practices preserved in the archaeological record. Through the analysis of cooking vessels, architectural features, and the location of fireplaces, we reflected on how food was cooked and where food preparation could be situated both spatially and socially within the two communities. The case studies illustrate several overlapping and differing facets of cooking within Arslantepe and Chogha Mish, as well as between the two geographically remote sites.

At Arslantepe, the majority of cooking vessels were handmade and exclusively produced for cooking, whereas at Chogha Mish strap handled jars and everted rim jars were used for cooking only as one among several possible functions, as it is indicated by many specimens that do not bear sooting. Moreover they were rather standardized concerning their proportions and presumably made in workshops producing all kinds of pottery.

Concerning time and space, cooking could be connected very closely to commensal activities, especially if these included hot meals. At Arslantepe Temple B, it is possible that cooking was temporally and spatially connected to the commensal events taking place there. Yet cooking could also be distant from other commensal activities, as in the case of the preparation of secondary foodstuffs. Clarified butter, which was possibly prepared at Chogha Mish, or the different foodstuffs produced for the central storerooms at Arslantepe, could be stored and consumed later in time and away from the place of production. Spatial and temporal proximity or distance of cooking to other activities also determined whether the sensual aspects of smelling and watching food being cooked would have mattered only to the people directly involved in cooking or embraced a broader group of persons. At Arslantepe circles of exclusiveness and inclusiveness to certain events could have been determined by these aspects as well.

Spatial aspects of cooking also let us infer the social affiliations of the persons who cooked. At Arslantepe people cooking within or for the public complex would have been connected to this institution, and cooking in Temple B was an activity spatially restricted and conducted by special equipment, such as very large pots. It most probably involved more than one person and the people who cooked took an active part in the institutionalized feasts or rituals. Cooking in Arslantepe residential contexts was possibly carried out by a smaller number of people. This is in accordance with the results from Chogha Mish, where the social setting in the East Area was domestic and workshop-like, and the easy-to-handle vessels as well as the size and location of fireplaces within the houses seem to imply few people cooking. However, if secondary products were prepared in this part of the settlement, the products as well as the labor invested in their preparation could have served other social realms, such as a central authority.[23] This scenario is comparable to that hypothesized for the redistribution area at Arslantepe, where the food was surely not entirely processed on the spot.

Our examples illustrate that cooking is a practice that transects social spheres and can separate as well as link them. Cooking is a specific moment within the broader network of social relations connected to foodways, food politics, and commensality, and touched multiple spheres of life of Uruk communities. Looking at vessels and how and where cooking was practiced, we traced the interplay between material culture and people as well as the different roles of cooking practices at Chogha Mish and Arslantepe. Differences in skills and gestures, in the number of people involved in cooking and their social affiliation, as well as in the role of cooked and uncooked food within food politics, show some of the many facets of cooking and labor organization connected with cooking in later Uruk times.

Part II
Special Commensality

Part II
Special Communication

7

Methodological and Definitional Issues in the Archaeology of Food

Katheryn C. Twiss

The methodological challenge of food archaeology

All archaeologists recognize that methodological factors determine the validity of archaeological interpretations of ancient foodways. If an excavator has not practiced soil flotation, then interpretations of the ancient plant diet at her site are chancy at best; if an analyst ignores the fact that one assemblage was created over a day and another over a year, then his awe at the culinary diversity represented in the longer-term one is invalid. All researchers interested in ancient foodways need to be informed about the methods that have produced the data that we want to interpret, or which produced the interpretation that we are reading. My goal in this section is to alert nonarchaeologists to issues with which they may be unaware, and to begin a longer-run conversation across disciplines and subdisciplines as to what each of us would like nonspecialists in our areas to understand as they (we) read (and write) about food.

Food is an excitingly multifaceted phenomenon. The body of literature published only recently on the archaeology of food comprises a tremendous diversity of studies. Some papers address social stratification (Curet and Pestle, 2010; Dawson, 2008; Hastorf and Weismantel, 2007: 313; Thomas, 2007; van der Veen, 2007: 124), some focus more tightly on its political concomitants (Lewis, 2007; Margomenou, 2008; Sykes, 2006). Some examine food's economic implications (Dietler, 2003; Fox and Harrell, 2008; Kieburg, 2008), while others study its role in the expression and/or negotiation of ethnic identities (Amundsen, 2008; Pierce, 2008; Sunseri, 2009; Sykes, 2005), and still others the social impact of gendered food behavior (Gray, 2009; Joyce, 2010; White, 2005). Some investigate how religious proscriptions structured human diets (Daróczi-Szabó, 2004; London, 2008), others consider food's part in human interactions with the supernatural (e.g. Hamilakis and Konsolaki, 2004; Stross, 2010). Furthermore, such studies employ a tremendous range of data sets: ceramics (Howie et al., 2010; Junker and Niziolek, 2010; Mills,

2007; Tomkins, 2007; Urem-Kotsou and Kotsakis, 2007), architectural features (Haaland, 2007; Papaefthymiou et al., 2007), spatial arrangements (Buxó and Principal, 2011; Kieburg, 2008; LeCount, 2010), faunal remains (Aranda Jiménez and Monton-Subias, 2011; Halstead, 2007; Marom et al., 2009; Spielmann et al., 2009), botanical remains (Jamieson and Sayre, 2010; Mrozowski et al., 2008), art and texts (Delgado and Ferrer, 2011; Mylona, 2008; Wright, 2004), and more.

It is clear that food is physically ubiquitous: direct and indirect traces of foodways are perceptible in virtually all aspects of material culture. It is also socially ubiquitous, knotted into any society's economic strategies, political structure, cultural identity, gender organization, and religious beliefs. I would argue that much of the excitement we feel when studying ancient foodways lies in this very omnipresence, in food's ability to testify to so very many different aspects of life. Yet the fact that foodways are constructed out of many social *and* physical components makes them challenging to study. Since no single data set can reflect a people's entire diet or entire food technology, researchers must integrate multiple data sets in order to build an interpretation of how people ate. However, different types of data have different interpretive implications. To integrate them into one cohesive interpretation, one needs some understanding of their distinct characteristics.

What knowledge, then, is necessary to understand (or practice) food archaeology? A detailed discussion of this topic, addressing such issues as discipline-specific quantification methods, or the interpretive implications of differential breakage patterns, is beyond the scope of this chapter. On a broad level, however, three very general issues are broadly relevant.

Issue 1: Different data sets have distinct relationships to human society

Different foods often play distinctly different social roles, with, for example, cereals being everyday foods, but meats being too costly for quotidian consumption and thus being served primarily at "special" occasions. Different data sets may also represent different segments of society: ceramic dishes being reserved for elites, for instance, and wooden ones used primarily by plebeians.

Different data sets may represent different stages of food's interaction with humans as well, and thus reflect separate aspects of social diversity. Such is the case with plant and animal remains. Animal remains include bones from animal parts that people may not have eaten, such as heads and feet; they also include bones that are essentially leftovers, the past equivalent of chicken drumsticks, barbecue ribs or steak T-bones. In contrast, most plant parts that humans would have brought onsite for eating—seeds, tubers, etc.—would presumably have been consumed and thereby destroyed. As a result, assemblages rich in edible plants and plant parts were probably produced accidentally. It is assemblages of inedible plant parts, many of which are the byproducts of preparing staples such as cereals, that could easily reflect habitual behaviors such as waste disposal or use of plant debris as fuel or temper. Since accidents are inherently less common than are normal activities, inedible plant remains such as weeds and chaff constitute the bulk of the macro-botanical record, and represent only *indirect* evidence of plant foods. In sum, the paleoethnobotanical record largely reflects processing prior to consumption, while the zooarchaeological record commonly contains both preparation debris and the leftovers from consumption.

Different data sets may even diverge with respect to the degree that they reflect human food activity at all. Ceramic, metal, and glass artifacts were, of course, intentionally produced; remains from mid-size and larger animals usually indicate a human desire for their presence onsite as well. However, for plant food remains it can be a significant challenge to separate those consumed by humans from those consumed by animals, especially in areas such as southwest Asia where dung has long been a key fuel source. Burning animal dung as fuel is very likely to introduce huge amounts of charred-plant remains onto a site. Of course, many animal foods can also easily become human foods when hunger strikes (e.g. Halstead, in press), so determining the extent to which floral remains reflect human foodways can be extraordinarily complicated.

Issue 2: Context and sample character are key

This is an issue that would benefit from considerably more attention in the archaeo-logical literature. A statement in a paper that food remains were found "in an oven," for example, does not reveal whether those remains were on the floor of the oven and so were left there at the time the oven went out of service, or whether they were higher up inside the oven and could simply have been part of the room fill that happened to end up there. In general, only when remains are found *on a surface* are we entitled to argue that they reflect food activities in that location.

We also need to consider the samples' size and duration of deposition, especially when making comparisons. A larger sample, or one deposited over a longer time, is inherently more likely than a smaller or shorter-term one to contain a variety of food remains.

Issue 3: Truly integrating multiple data sets remains a challenge

The practice today, when ostensibly integrating data sets, is generally to simply consider the results of separate analyses in the interpretation. Thus we see numerous papers presenting, for example, both faunal and botanical results (Kansa et al., 2009; Spielmann et al., 2009; Troubleyn et al., 2009), but relatively few constructing analyses that involve both kinds of data from the start. In wrangling with this challenge, the approach that my collaborators and I have used in the past is to calculate the density (grams per liter soil) of both plant and animal remains, to study the spatial distribution of each kind of food (Twiss et al., 2009). While we have found this very rewarding for investigations of domestic organization and public/private boundaries, it is not a strategy applicable to numerous other research questions. Similarly, correspondence analyses combining archaeobotanical and zooarchaeological data can provide insight into regional economic and landscape exploitation strategies (Smith and Munro, 2009), but are difficult to apply in other contexts.

Given that different types of data have separate cultural roles, taphonomic histories and quantitative issues, additive strategies may be the best we can do in many cases. However, given the potential interpretive value of full integration, I suggest that this is a realm worth exploring further. Cross-disciplinary collaboration is key to full understanding of past foodways; the more closely we can integrate different specialties throughout the analytic and interpretive process, the stronger our interpretations of the past should be.

Definitional issues in the archaeology of food

Like all archaeologists, those of us who study the archaeology of food rely— necessarily—on various assumptions as we conduct our studies. Among those assumptions, some common ones relate to the most basic definitions of what we are doing and what we are studying. Two of those are what food is, and what feasting is.

Food

As defined in the *Oxford English Dictionary*, food is 'Any nutritious substance that people or animals eat or drink in order to maintain life and growth' (www.OED. com, accessed January 24, 2012). It is generally acknowledged, however, that we do not eat everything that could give us nutrients—no more than do people in other cultures. In reality, we humans eat what we perceive as food, rather than what can technically nourish us.

We thus tend, in my opinion, to conceptualize "food" in an archaeological context, in one of two ways.

In the first, we define food as a subset of all theoretically available nutrients: a Venn diagram, as it were, wherein "food" is a smaller circle within a larger one of "available nutrients." Yet this is a problematic view of food, at least for those of us who view food primarily as a tool for investigating ancient social life, rather than as an element in behavioral ecological reconstructions of past human adaptations. This is because consumable substances are culturally categorized into multiple types, each of which may or may not play a distinctly different, and important, social role. If we conceptualize a culture's food simply as a subset of the nutrients available to it, we silently ignore cultural distinctions between, for example, solid foods and beverages, or foods and medicines, or foods eaten for their nutritional contents and those that do provide nutrients but that are consumed instead for their psychoactive properties (e.g. "magic mushrooms").

Alternatively, we archaeologists conceptualize food (implicitly: this is rarely stated) as solid consumables: ones that we put in our mouths, usually chew, and swallow. This is also a problematic conceptualization in that it makes consideration of the complex links and relationships that exist between solid foods, beverages, inhalables, and swallowables such as "medicines" more difficult. To include beer, vodka, or psychoactive fungi in our interpretation of past food production strategies, in other words, we have to mentally re-add them to the study; they are not already there.

This is potentially problematic if a person is interested in any one of a wide range of topics: If one wants to study agricultural production, for example in many societies how much grain a group chose to grow would have taken into account both subsistence and alcoholic needs. If one wishes to examine grain processing, wheat or barley bread may be made as an intermediate step to brewing beer, not as an end in and of itself (Jennings et al., 2005: 280–1; Samuel, 2000). If one desires insight into ancient nutrition, beer contributed significantly to ancient Near Eastern sustenance (Homan, 2004). If one is interested in mealtime rituals, there is a common temporal association between eating and drinking—and, in some groups, smoking as well. How would one discuss the rituals of an elegant French meal without touching on wine tasting, pouring, and sipping? (The converse of these points is of course also true: drink is commonly temporally and culturally linked to solid food.)

We are thus left with a definitional challenge: if we adopt a generalized definition of food, we fail to recognize the existence of socially important subcategories within that broad definition. If we conceptualize food as essentially solid chewables, then we make it more difficult for ourselves to keep in mind that the boundaries between solid foods, beverages, and other consumables are porous and shifting; that, as Dietler (2007: 219) has said, beer is really just "special forms of food with psychoactive properties."

Ergo, it is not merely that what people consider eating varies contextually; I argue that the appropriate definition of food itself does as well. We need to let our research questions guide the boundaries we draw around our conceptions of food, shrinking or expanding to encompass various consumables as we consider potential relationships between them.

Feasting

Feasting pervades the archaeological literature on food (Aranda Jiménez et al., 2011; Bray, 2003a; Dietler and Hayden, 2001b; Klarich, 2010; Mills, 2004). The issue that underlies all of this literature is, of course, what is feasting? What precisely is the social phenomenon under investigation? This is a question with which Dietler and Hayden (2001b) opened their edited volume *Feasts: Archaeological and Ethnographic Perspectives on Food, Politics, and Power*.

Dietler and Hayden (2001b: 3) state that while definitions of feasting vary in their details (e.g. how many participants must be present, or how big the gathering must be), in general the authors in their volume agree that "feasts are events essentially constituted by the communal consumption of food and/or drink. Most authors are also explicit in differentiating such food-consumption events from both everyday domestic meals and from the simple exchange of food without communal consumption." Separately, Hayden (2001: 28) defines a feast as "any sharing between two or more people of special foods (i.e. foods not generally served at daily meals) in a meal for a special purpose or occasion," whereas Dietler (2001: 65) insists that a feast is "an analytical rubric used to describe forms of ritual activity that involve the communal consumption of food and drink."

These are obviously very broad definitions. Such generality is necessary because, in the ethnographic literature, tremendous cross-cultural variations exist in the scale, meaning, and practice of feasting. Even in a single society there can be tremendous diversity in feasts. Among, the Akha of northern Thailand, for example, "some feasts ... involve only a few people and the ritualized consumption of a very small amount of food, whereas other feasts are enormous, involving many hundreds of people and the consumption of several water buffalos, pigs, and chickens over a period of weeks" (Clarke, 2001: 151). Therefore, as Hayden (2001: 38) notes, feasts "vary enormously in size from a minimum of a two person (dyadic) solicitation or friendship (solidarity) dinner to an inter-community event involving hundreds or thousands of people."

Despite our recognition of the varied scale and meaning of feasts, in the archaeological literature feasting tends to be presented as a communal activity that involves food preparation and consumption on a larger scale than is habitually the case. This conceptualization allows us to identify it on the basis of large-scale cooking or serving equipment, or large collections of food remains. Feasting is also commonly presented as involving the use of prestige goods such as exotic ceramics (e.g. Junker and Niziolek, 2010) or valuable materials such as shells or colored stones (e.g. Turkon, 2004: 234). This conceptualization of feasting as a large-scale, materially elaborate activity has two clear effects. First, it simply means that archaeologically we almost inevitably overlook small feasts, involving relatively few people. Second, we may also overlook feasts that don't involve special or prestige items.

I am not challenging this habitual focus on large-scale, elaborated feasts rather than small, materially simple ones (see also Hayden, 2001: 38). I perceive this as a matter of general necessity—of focusing on events that leave noticeable traces in the archaeological record, rather than those that have minimal perceptible impact. If someone can develop a good way to regularly identify the remains of the ancient equivalent of a family birthday party, or a couple's anniversary dinner, I will be as thrilled as anyone. In the meantime, I am comfortable with the fact that, in most archaeological contexts, we can only discern feasts that are pronouncedly distinct from daily eating habits—those toward the far end of the feasting-daily meal continuum of scale and elaboration.

However, given that in reality we are virtually always talking about large-scale and elaborated events, my question is whether or not we should continue to refer to these practices simply as "feasts," which, as we have established, in ethnographic contexts can include a far wider variety of events. We certainly can continue to do so: indeed, we can point at the dictionary definition of feasting to support our decision. According to the *Oxford English Dictionary* (www.OED.com, accessed September 19, 2011), a feast is definable as:

[…]
2. A gathering for pleasure or sports; a fête.
3. A sumptuous meal or entertainment, given to a number of guests; a banquet, esp. of a more or less public nature. […]
4. An unusually abundant and delicious meal; something delicious to feed upon; fig. an exquisite gratification, a rich treat. to make a feast: to enjoy a good meal, eat luxuriously (of, upon).

We can simply note that abundance and elaboration figure prominently in two of these definitions, and declare those definitions as the ones that we archaeologists choose to utilize. If we do this, then we essentially reject the model of feasting embraced by ethnographers who include smaller and simpler gatherings; we shift the problem of defining the scale of feasting into another discipline. This may complicate our intellectual relationship with sociocultural anthropologists in that they and we would be using different definitions of a common term. Arguably, however, it need not complicate our selection of ethnographic analogies for interpreting archaeological data. If we are interested in the social implications of an archaeological assemblage that reflects a large communal gathering, then we shouldn't be looking at small-scale ethnographic analogues anyway: we should be looking for practices that appear materially comparable to those we think we are seeing archaeologically.

Furthermore, sociocultural anthropologists' application of the term "feasting" to a broader range of consumption events than we would use could actually be a useful reminder to us that feasts, whatever their definition, do not stand alone in a culture's dining repertoire. If we see a relatively small-scale meal or ceremony referred to as a "feast" in the ethnographic literature, it might remind us that in any culture, small- and large-scale meals are related phenomena. As Mary Douglas (1975) pointed out, there is commonly a metonymic relationship between even daily meals and feasts, and this important relationship intensifies and extends the messages communicated in each meal.

The second issue raised by our tendency to identify feasts as essentially "the large-scale, special other" is the extent to which we agglomerate very distinct social practices into one large "special" category, and thus miss important distinctions of cultural meaning. Consider the *sihk puhn*, a Cantonese banquet (Watson, 1987). At a *sihk puhn* banquet, attendees squat around communal basins in which various foods are mixed all together into a largely unidentifiable mass: a style of preparation usually associated with schools, armies, or work gangs (Watson, 1987: 392). Feastgoers eat without talking, first come first served, without ceremony, without speeches, without toasts, without observing any complicated etiquette; diners are not ranked, no one acts as a host, and there is no head table for prominent guests. These banquets, which are required to legitimate marriages, male offspring (whether born or adopted), and village guardsmen, bring the entire community together. Every household must send a representative, so that the host symbolically feeds the entire village, while the village in return signals its acceptance of the marriage, son, or village appointee. In other words, these feasts act as important mechanisms of social cohesion.

Archaeologically, *sihk puhn* banquets should be easily identifiable as feasts. The foods are prepared in giant woks, so they possess the classic archaeological feasting criterion of unusually large cooking vessels. The foods also are varied: nine distinct items go into the basins (Watson, 1987: 394), so we have the criterion of a diversity of foods. Furthermore, the proportions of those foods are dramatically altered from normal daily consumption: instead of the daily norm of mostly rice with a small amount of meat or vegetables, at the banquets fish and meat are abundant, and rice is "almost an afterthought" (Watson, 1987: 393).

Sihk puhn banquets are not the only form of feast recognized by Cantonese villagers. Indeed, older villagers "draw a clear and unambiguous distinction" between *sihk puhn* banquets and *sihk piu* celebrations, which are held in restaurants in nearby market towns. As the most prestigious form of dining available, *sihk piu* banquets promote the status of host families. At these celebrations the food (usually nine dishes, nicely paralleling the nine distinct foods added to a *sihk puhn* bowl) is served in a sequence of courses on separate plates. These cost five to six times more per attendee than do *sihk puhn* feasts, and personal invitations are required to attend. Even elders must be individually invited, and many are left out. Guests must bring money for the host, and a public record is kept of all gifts. Etiquette requirements are complex and rigorously observed, and the whole experience is characterized by tremendous formality (Watson, 1987: 397). These feasts act as important mechanisms of social distinction.

Archaeologically, there would be clear material distinctions between these two types of feasts in terms of setting (village hall as opposed to restaurant) and associated material culture (large communal vessels as opposed to separate dishes). Such differences would, I hope, spur us to contemplate the likelihood that these two forms of feasts had different social implications.

Given that the two forms of banquets occur in separate locations, however, we cannot necessarily expect that archaeological excavations would uncover both sets of remains: we commonly only have the time, the funding, or the opportunity to dig at a single site rather than two or more. It is also possible that since the *sihk piu* banquets take place at restaurants, we might not be able to archaeologically identify "feasting" there, as opposed to what we might consider non-feast consumption in a communal setting. We thus might well be left with only *sihk puhn* banquets as our feasting evidence for Cantonese village society. In addition, we would not have a helpful material prompt that a variety of practices were socially important. Then, if "feasts" are simply "the large-scale, special other," what we could end up with is a generalized view of village communal consumption, with perhaps a single inter-pretation: they were competitive, they were integrative, they were both at the same time. In other words, in the absence of a material prompt such as remains found in both restaurants and town halls to remind us of diversity in communal dining, simple use of the term "feasting" does not provide such a prompt either. Instead, it both allows us and assists us to mask our collapse of a variety of practices into a less-than-meaningful "special dining" category.

Obviously, several people have ethnographically and ethnoarchaeologically distinguished between types of feasts: competitive feasts, diacritical feasts, work party feasts, solidarity feasts, patron-role feasts, and so forth (e.g. Hayden, 2001). I have seen relatively few of the many offered categories actually identified in the archaeological literature. Competitive feasts and solidarity feasts appear regularly, but punishment feasts or maturation feasts rarely if ever. Part of this is because, as is widely recognized, few if any feasts are completely pure in intention (e.g. Hayden, 2001: 36; Dietler, 2001), and part is because establishing archaeological criteria for specific feast types is extremely challenging.

Therefore, we archaeologists recognize the existence of a wide variety of social phenomena involving communal consumption, which we subsume under the general rubric of "feasts." The extent to which these should all be thus subsumed is what I consider debatable. On the one hand, using a single term to refer to all of these hugely diverse practices abets our hybridizing them all into a less-than-meaningful "special consumption" category. Adding modifiers to that basic term breaks up this hybrid into separate social phenomena—but they are modifiers, which are easy to leave off, and which do not all necessarily come under consideration when a researcher is deciding what to label the thing he or she has found in the archaeological record.

On the other hand, we archaeologists do have real trouble separating the different categories of feasts, not only because it is difficult to come up with sufficient archaeological criteria, but also because single feasts serve multiple social functions. If we segregate different types of feasts into separate categories, we verbally efface the multifaceted nature of many events. We would, in all likelihood, end up in a situation arguably even more problematic than that imposed by our use of "meals" vs. "feasts."

At present, I have no solution to this dilemma. I do find generic reference to "feasting" in the archaeological record is problematic, due to the immensely varied character of ethnographic feasting. I also believe that "feasting" does generally have definitional implications when used in an archaeological context that it does not necessarily have in an ethnographic one, with regard to the scale and often the material elaboration of the gathering. In regard to this issue of size and elaboration, I argue that we archaeologists need to be open with the broader food community about what kinds of events are and are not including when we refer to feasts. My tendency would be for us to simply say that we are using the word feast as I think the general populace does, to imply meals that are unusually large as well as elaborate in one fashion or another.

As for "feasting's" lack of specific social meaning, that can be largely solved by following up the use of the term with a discussion of its social implications in one's particular cultural context. I suspect that is what is best, as it avoids any need to slot archaeological data into single or ill-fitting categories, and allows inclusion of multiple social motives at the event or events in question. It runs significant dangers in that evaluation of social motives is not built into the label itself, but for informed and careful researchers I believe that at present it is the most straightforward solution.

Conclusion

Archaeologists investigating commensality and other aspects of food behavior in the past face significant methodological and interpretive challenges. I have attempted here to list a few broad methodological issues of which I think interested people should be made aware. I look forward to other voices in the discussion.

8

Medieval and Modern Banquets: Commensality and Social Categorization

Paul Freedman

Introduction

I propose to discuss banquets across different time periods in European and American history, looking at them as more complicated forms of commensality than mere catered celebrations, focusing especially on excess and hierarchy. Excess: for most of European and American history a banquet, in the sense of a major feast, was an occasion where normal boundaries of food supply, appetite, and appropriate consumption were not merely surpassed but rejected. For the peasant, whose usual diet was sparse, fairly monotonous and often inadequate, major church festivals or harvest celebrations represented relief from a penurious routine, so the appeal of large quantities of food, and the opportunity to eat not only one's fill but more, are easily comprehended.

The excess practiced by the aristocracy goes beyond this temporary change from privation to plenty. The nobles' banquets of the Middle Ages and the *ancien regime* were ceremonies of competition (how elaborate one could make the offerings), magnificence (many more dishes than any single person could taste), and largesse. Anthropological approaches to gift-giving and such competitive generosity as is enshrined by the Pacific Coast Indians' "potlatch" are useful in understanding implications of excess among European aristocrats, but not really as pertaining to the role of food which, unlike the potlatch presents, is an ephemeral offering. Food is a common but nevertheless peculiar kind of gift.

In addition to excess, I would also like to consider hierarchy. Pre-modern banquets demonstrated hierarchical divisions that counter the norms of commensality which we think of as tending to break down social distinctions. Who sat where, who was served what and the interaction of ceremonial and informal elements complicate, in creative ways, how we think about dining together.

This chapter concerns formal occasions of feasts usually marking particular events such as religious holidays, treaties, weddings, or diplomatic visits. Nevertheless, far from being exceptions to the social rules in the way that village feasts might be holidays from a normal regime of austerity, banquets have tended to reify social differences and so subvert their own apparent commensal purpose. They are, for their participants, mundane, or at least repeated and confirmatory. It's not just that people of wealth or political power can show their distinction by being invited to or hosting such functions, but that distinctions are made among those attending the banquet. Especially in the setting of a princely court, be it the Versailles of Louis XIV or Stalin's Kremlin (both rulers profligate, if sinister hosts), the instability of rank and the capriciousness of favor provide strong counter-narratives against the surface celebratory coming together.

Commensality and its discontents

Commensality has many forms as the chapters in this volume demonstrate. The English word is quite venerable, so, although it might seem to be a typical piece of modern social-science terminology, the use of "commensality" is attested since the seventeenth century. The peerless eighteenth-century English lexicographer Samuel Johnson defined commensality as "Fellowship of the table; the custom of eating together." In 1826, writing about members of the House of Commons being invited to meals with the Speaker, an observer imagined that Dr. Johnson might have remarked *à propos* "eating together promotes good will, Sir, commensality is benevolent" (Anonymous, 1826). Indeed, eating together is so common that it has tended to pass unnoticed, much as the subject of food itself has failed until recently to interest historians, in part because of its ubiquity. One might say we have been practicing commensality without being aware of it.

Commensality has been discussed by social scientists, however, in terms of the socially healthful effects of dining together versus the isolated individualism of contemporary customs (Fischler, 2001). Sociability at the table in the developed world has waned in recent times as meals have tended to become brief, solitary opportunities to grab utilitarian sustenance. Academic and popular discourse laments the decline of taking meals with others, part of a supposed crisis of community and the public sphere. In the U.S., Starbucks and other coffee shops are wrestling with the problem of computers and digital devices which not only keep customers occupying space at the expense of potential sales but also create an atmosphere of self-absorbed solitude in what is intended as a communal space with opportunities for exchange and discussion. Some independent coffee shops now ban these devices.

A similar and more generalized loneliness results from the near-disappearance of family meals. I participated in an advertising agency meeting in the summer of 2011 in which experts on housewives were asked about the tensions American mothers felt in trying to get family members to sit down to the same meal. The schedule conflicts, the moms' own activities, the volatile likes and dislikes of older children, and the tendency even when at the table to tune into other media have so subverted the 1950's ideal of the family dinner that one of these experts hoped that one 15-minute segment of such idealized family time *per week* might be preserved, a forlorn habitat for an endangered species. Probably the reality is not quite that dramatic, although in Robert Putnam's *Bowling Alone: The Rise and Collapse of American Community* we learn that this form of commensality, family dinners, declined in the U.S. by 43 percent in the last quarter of the twentieth century (2000: 100–2).

Of course not all examples of commensality, the imagined Dr. Johnson notwithstanding, are occasions for benevolence. Studies of commensality tend to emphasize its positive effect of breaking down selfish individualism (Hirschman, 1996; Simmel, 1997: 130). However, the pull towards sharing and festivity can be resisted, often dramatically. Fights at festive family meals are a staple of novels and dramas—the terrible altercation over Irish politics at a Christmas dinner in James Joyce's *Portrait of the Artist as a Young Man* (1993: 25–39), for example. And during mundane, non-celebratory meals as well—Jonathan Franzen's *The Corrections* (2001: 25–39) includes a harrowing description of a boy refusing to eat liver, beet greens and rutabagas and being kept at the table for hours by his parents for this defiance.

Business meals form an entire category of charged and often negative commensality. In the movie *Pretty Woman* (1990) the corporate raider played by Richard Gere demonstrates his domination of one such dinner by his flawless, confident gourmet expertise. By means of hurried special coaching, the Julia Roberts character learns something of the necessary table etiquette, although not quite mastering an awkward encounter with snails. The uplifting Pygmalion theme, however, is displaced by the breakdown of commensality. The meal ends in abrupt discord, a confrontation over the predatory machinations of the raider. His "guests," whose company he is taking over, walk out. Not only is this a failure of commensality, but, once having humiliated his opponents, the business tycoon loses all interest in the meal itself. It has been merely a vehicle for insulting behavior, with the pseudo-fellowship of the table heightening the insult (Parasecoli, 1999: 175–6, 188, 340). In all these examples, the official agenda is sharing, but there are other currents and conflicting circumstances.

Banquets are a particular kind of commensality because of their scale and effort at delight or intimidation. They are celebrations of events such as alliances, dynastic weddings or victories in battle, but their public festive nature and apparent commensality fail to cut across the divisions of society. I turn to the more complicated exclusivity of the elite banqueters.

Excess

For the wealthy, banquets perform a commensality of excess, but a certain type of excess. The food has to be copious, of course, but also difficult, rare, and expensive as well. Mere quantity is not sufficient—rural villages have excessive quantities of food as depicted in the peasant weddings painted by Dutch artists or before them in German woodcuts in which rustics feast on beer and sausages while fighting, dancing, vomiting, and enjoying a diversion from normal life (Vandenbroeck, 1984; Moxey, 1989). This is excess, but not, however, a form of culinary distinction.

The banquets of the medieval elite do tend to involve ridiculous and inconsumable amounts of food, but what is offered is appropriate to the upper classes—meat, especially game, or large saltwater fish (during fast days) (*Banquets et manières*, 1996; Aurell et al., 1992; Altenberg et al., 1991; Albala, 2007). The dishes are fragrant with ingredients that must come from far away at great expense, not only the relatively well-known pepper or cinnamon but rarer spices such as galangal and nutmeg, or even perfumes such as musk.

At the enthronement of the Bishop of Salisbury in 1414, the meal began with boiled meats including capon, swan, peacock, pheasant, meatballs in aspic, wheat porridge with scrambled eggs and venison, and "mawmeny" (wine with sugar and spices thickened and mixed with ground pork and chicken). The second service of roasted meat featured piglets, crane, venison, heron, stuffed poussins, and partridges. Fried meats, small birds and, delicacies comprised the third course: meat (bittern, curlew, pigeon, rabbit), birds (plover, quail, larks), and delicacies (fritters, and puff pastries) (Woolgar, 1999: 159–60).

Master Chiquart, chef for the Duke of Savoy in the 1430s, envisaged a banquet for probably about 500 guests lasting two days. It would require six weeks to two months of preparation, mostly involving the collection of an extraordinary amount of game. Purveyors with 40 horses set out to acquire all manner of birds and mammals. Several hundred pounds of spices were needed as well as no less than 12,000 eggs. Twelve pounds of gold leaf was needed for decoration of the dishes to be presented at the meals. Some of the dishes included in Chiquart's cookbook give an idea of the final product—an edible castle with four towers and a courtyard with a fountain. Atop each castle was a different virtuoso dish typical of medieval culinary display: a pike cooked in three different ways, each way a different color, without being cut into pieces before serving (tricky); a skinned and redressed swan (i.e. cooked, but sewn back into its original skin and feathers); a glazed piglet, and a glazed boar's head adorn the fortifications. Each animal is breathing fire by means of a camphor-soaked wick in its mouth (Chiquart, 1986: 9, 22–4; Scully and Scully, 2002: 41–2).

Hierarchy

This must have been fun, but a key aspect of pre-modern celebrations is that not everybody got to eat the same delicacies. If the banqueters were sharply distinguished from the mere mob of envious observers, once they entered the site of the banquet it was the internal distinctions that mattered. The ruler often had his meal at a table apart from the others, eating food reserved for him and usually prepared in a completely separate kitchen. Such extravagant solitude was for reasons of security, to guard against poisoning, but served also to distinguish the ruler while depriving him of convivial company. This is especially noticeable in the ceremonial of Versailles. The king took most meals seated alone but surrounded by standing courtiers, either in a large company (*au grand couvert*) or in a more intimate setting (*au petit couvert*). The others did not dine—a break with a tradition of the king being first among nobles rather than completely set apart (Pinkard, 2009: 129–30). The dinner was a public event, but one without any literal commensality.

Grand dining in the Middle Ages was a bit more hospitable, but nevertheless hierarchical. There were 2,500 guests at celebrations following the enthronement of George Neville as archbishop of York in 1465 and they were seated at tables that spread out over several rooms of the castle of Cawood. A high table set at one end of the principal hall was occupied by bishops, dukes, and earls. Six other tables accommodated high monastic officials and noble lords, and then, at increasing distance from the high table but still in the hall, members of the York cathedral chapter, officials of the city of York, men of law and other lay functionaries, and young esquires of the royal court. Beyond the hall were further rooms seating ladies of prominence, lesser gentlemen and their wives, and finally a gallery where servants of the various guests ate. Each table got a different set of courses, essentially more variety at the higher-rated ones (Benson, 1919: 88–90).

At a series of wedding banquets in Florence in June of 1469, the guests celebrating the marriage of Piero de'Medici and Clarice degl'Orsini were arranged not by status but according to a more complicated demography. The bride and 50 of her girlfriends dined in the garden of the Medici Palace. Invited citizens of Florence sat in the courtyard; young men were served in the ground floor *sala*, and the older women were upstairs on a balcony. The girls were visible to all, but protected by their separate space, intermittently available to talk to when, for example, they went out into the street to dance (Agresta, 2011). Here hierarchy interacted with staging as the young women were favored because of their beauty rather than rank.

Sometimes the carefully performed celebration broke down and disorder and gate-crashing replaced the calibrated hierarchical arrangements. Here excess and hierarchy comically interact. The scale and complexity of pulling off both a public fête and more *soigné* private meal create all sorts of logistical problems. The boy King Henry VI of England was crowned twice, once at Westminster in 1429 at the age of seven, and then two years later in Paris as the English were starting to lose the 100 Years War to the French. The Parisian event was disastrous at least as a catering spectacle. The populace forced their way into the hall where the feast was supposed to take place, eating what had been already set out, stealing salt cellars and other portable table-service items, and resisting all attempts to move them to make way for the invited members of Parliament, university faculty, merchant officials and other urban dignitaries who very reluctantly shared the disorganized revels with their social inferiors (Huizinga, 1949: 50).

Similar problems occurred in the modern era: for example, the coronation banquet for King George IV of Britain on July 19, 1821 was ludicrously extravagant and the banquet involved almost 4,000 dishes, but the confectionery sculptures melted and, in the near stampede to get something to eat, the guests more-or-less trampled the food (Kelly, 2003: 196–8). Arrangements miscarried similarly at the less ostentatious inaugural celebration for the American president Abraham Lincoln's second term on March 6, 1865. A large table was set up in the corridor of the West Wing of the White House. The menu was quite extensive, although the dishes were fairly plain (roasts, smoked meats). There were 53 items served of which more than half were what we would consider desserts: cakes, tarts, creams, ice creams and fruit ices. Three hundred people were invited to attend the event standing (only the most select of the company actually sitting down to dine), but 5,000 crowded into the building. According to the *New York Times* newspaper, "The crush which followed can better be imagined than depicted … in less than an hour the table was a wreck … a demolition in a twinkling of an eye of all the confectioner's handiwork … as much was wasted as was eaten, and however much there may have been provided, more than half the guests went supperless" (Clarkson, 2009, vol. 1: 163).

President Obama's inauguration in 2009 also had various levels of access and even those who simply were able to get a glimpse of it were considered privileged. Above them were those who were at the White House. A portion of these dined somewhere in the executive mansion, and the elite actually dined with the President.

Thus even when arrangements went according to plan, there was a distinction among the guests that puts this form of commensality into a particular perspective. The interaction of excess and hierarchy made it more likely that the occasion would be difficult to accomplish and that the lower order of guests would not obtain the full satisfaction of the banquet as a meal: but that was part of the unfolding of the event, a combination of order and chaos.

Modern banquets

Certain key aspects of banqueting changed in modern times. Although we are inclined to think of modernity as less splendid, more severe, and altogether less ostentatious than the pre-modern period, in fact this is not at all true. Excess in nineteenth-century banquets was as frequent and extensive as during Middle Ages. What had changed is the diminution of hierarchical distinction among banqueters. To be sure at a royal or state occasion to this day there will be a head table, but banquets are now private affairs, not public spectacles, and even in France or China, home to extraordinary gastronomic and ceremonial traditions, the food served at official meals will be reasonable in quantity, unexceptional in quality, and served equally.

The nineteenth century witnessed some of the most extraordinarily elaborate banquets ever served. In his brief service for the British Prince Regent, the future George IV, the great chef Antonin Carême in 1817 put together a meal in honor of Grand Duke Nicholas of Russia that included 117 different dishes in nine courses, and these were elaborate preparations such as *Faisans truffées au Perigord* and *Filets de poulardes glacés aux concombres* (Kelly, 2003: 134–40).

To take some examples of modern excess from the United States the so-called "Gilded Age" after the Civil War was a notorious time of gastronomic ostentation. A spectacular meal was offered in 1865, just after the end of the War, by the English railway magnate Sir Martin Peto for 250 guests at Delmonico's in New York, generally acknowledged as the finest restaurant in the country. The cost of this meal was $200 per person, an astronomical amount at a time when the average weekly wage was $5 (Clarkson, 2009, vol. 2: 675–8). There were ten courses with 38 separate dishes. These included such difficult creations as *cassolettes de foie-gras, chaudfroid de rouge-gorges à la Bohèmienne,* and *Buisson de ris d'agneau Pascaline.* Within two years Sir Martin's speculations had failed and he was bankrupt. There was a kind of spectacular commensality to this event, but in fact it was like a publicity party in which the guests were not really that well-known either to their host or to each other.

A less well-known but quite interesting and friendlier dinner served in 1851 was part of a competition between a group of wealthy gourmands from New York and their fellows from Philadelphia. The New Yorkers of course chose Delmonico's for their banquet, but unfortunately we don't know what was served. The Philadelphia menu, which won against expectations, does survive and it is rather amazing: 17 courses, over 70 dishes and a service of 20 wines. The fish were difficult to obtain fresh—special messengers carried salmon from the Kennebec River in Maine to Philadelphia. The April 19 date was challenging as it is neither full spring nor anywhere near normal harvest time or game season. The meal was splendid but also innovative—roast turkey served with oyster sauce (more commonly seen with boiled fowl); a so-called "coup de milieu," usually Roman Punch, here was a sorbet made from old Tokay (Parkinson, 1874: 28–31; Hines et al., 1987: 29).

Still these American meals did not surpass what the French authority Grimod de la Reynière called for as a general standard in 1805. He actually criticizes pre-revolutionary dinners for 60 guests where the first course alone might contain as many as 128 dishes, proposing a more modest total of 108 dishes in three courses, again for 60 guests. The nineteenth century ended with the beginnings of a much reduced standard of excess. By the time of the monthly journal *La cuisine française et étrangère* (started in 1891), ten dishes were sufficient for 60 guests (Flandrin, 2007: 68–101).

In modern settings that replicate autocratic courts, such as the entourage of Stalin or Mao, there was a perpetuation of some aspects of traditional banqueting and commensality. Stalin practiced both an ostentatious simplicity and a peculiar kind of luxury and innovation. He would mix two soups and crumble bread into the result in rustic fashion, according to Anastas Mikoyan, but Stalin was also credited with inventing a dish called "Aragvi" (named after a river in Georgia) consisting of mutton, aubergines, tomatoes, potatoes, and black pepper in a spicy sauce. In addition to his many other talents, lauded so profusely by the cult of personality, Stalin was a gourmet. For many years the best-known restaurant in Moscow was the *Aragvi*. Stalin was both generous and intimidating, plying his guests with food, but also making them taste dishes first to make sure they weren't poisoned. He teased KGB chief Laverenti Beria about Polish communists ("where are they anyway?") who, as they both knew, had been killed by Stalin's orders while rejecting Beria's gift of 30 turbots alleging they were spoiled. Yet this erratic series of meals constituted the center of Soviet power, especially in the post-war era. Molotov states that the empire was "truly governed from the dining table" while the disillusioned Yugoslav observer Milovan Djilas noted that at these dinners "the destiny of the vast Russian land, of the newly acquired territories and ... the human race was decided" (Montefiore, 2003: 522–5).

How tame are the dining habits of the heads of state of major countries now by comparison! Perhaps some of the court culture has survived in the meals of dictatorial figures such as the former Libyan tyrant Mohammar Gadhafi. It's not that celebratory excess is gone—the new global plutocracy organizes spectacular parties, but the emphasis is on having stars entertain, as Rod Stewart did for an enormous fee for the private equity billionaire Stephen Schwartzman in 2007, or vulgar, non-gastronomic spectacle, as at the infamous birthday party on Sardinia thrown by the criminal business executive Dennis Koslovski at which, among other things, an ice sculpture modelled on Michelangelo's "David" spouted vodka from its penis. Country music singer Jimmy Buffett sang here at, presumably, great expense that surpassed that of whatever food was served (Anonymous, 2007; M. Jennings, 2009: 326).

By the late twentieth century, both excess and hierarchy in grand meals were diminished, but so too were banquets in general. It is not just a decline in community or retreat into private, familial life that is responsible for this, but new ways of combining business with pleasure, or, one might say, sociability with networking. In the Middle Ages entertaining was an important part of both friendship and business, from aristocratic open-handedness offered to followers, to court ceremony, to merchant guild occasions. In the nineteenth century as well, private dinners built, confirmed, and maintained social prominence. One is also struck by how many American menus survive from celebratory meals of private associations—the Shakespearean Society of Philadelphia, or the New York Sons of the California Gold Rush, for example. There has been a precipitous decline in such commensal events as well as in private entertainment. Academic dinner parties, a treacherous feature of my early teaching career, which began in 1979, are almost extinct. Business lunches are not what they were in an era that uses the phrase "three-martini lunch" as a term of opprobrium. And there is that crisis of familial dinners alluded to earlier as part of the general pattern of waning of commensality.

Magnificent meals are eclipsed, but not quite dead. In 2011, one of the farewell dinners at the celebrated restaurant El Bulli featured 44 dishes including classics such as Golden Egg, new items such as Peas 2011, and hard-to-decode offerings such as "Pond" or "Box." Nine wines were also served. Hundreds of thousands of people around the world attempted frantically to participate in this series of dinners marking the end of this restaurant at or near the pinnacle of its success.

It is worth comparing the publicity surrounding the demise of El Bulli with a famous (once-upon-a-time) 31-course meal served in November 1977 by the Parisian restaurant Chez Denis to the restaurant critic of the *New York Times* Craig Claiborne and his friend Pierre Franey. The garishly splendid occasion was the result of winning an American Express contest for a restaurant meal anywhere in the world, at any price. The bill came to $4,000 and the 11 wines were more expensive than the courses. These included a tart made with Mediterranean red mullet, a chartreuse of partridges, baked truffles with potatoes, ortolans, and chaud-froid of woodcock. This meal earned considerable notoriety and marks both the birth and death of culinary trends: the beginning of the restaurant critic as publicist, but also an important episode in the slow death of French culinary dominance (Davis, 2004).

Neither of these qualifies exactly as a banquet—the Claiborne-Franey *bouffe* was too intimate, the El Bulli fêtes too anonymous. But their differences illustrate the changing criteria of gastronomic prestige. At Chez Denis there was an agreed upon understanding of what constituted elegant dining. In the Paris of 1977, as in the Paris of 1877, or for that matter 1777, such things as ortolans and truffles were expected, even required at grand gastronomic occasions. The vocabulary changed little and there was always an effort to combine innovative delight with such dishes as were necessary to demonstrate that this was a serious event. Thus in Edith Wharton's novel *The Age of Innocence*, a depiction of upper-class New York in the 1870s, a successful dinner party must include terrapin (small turtles) and wild canvas-back duck, the two most prestigious dishes in America throughout the nineteenth century (Wharton, 1996: 18, 29). Five hundred years earlier, a medieval European banquet would have included a different roster of important dishes—glazed wild boar's head perhaps, or fish cooked three ways and in three different colors—but the expectations would be similarly clear. Still, today, many proper Chinese banquets have to feature birds'-nests soup and shark-fin soup.

The notion of a dossier of preparations considered *de rigueur* ended in late-twentieth-century Europe and America, to be replaced by an exaltation of creativity and originality, whether in the form of fusion, modernist cuisine, or even a stylized return to traditional or seasonal ingredients. Copenhagen today is the great gastronomic capital, of course, and very much a leader in creativity and unpredictability.

The eclipse of the banquet is related to this decline of the repertoire of expected and elegant dishes. However much of it is meant to dazzle or impress with its excess and choreography, a banquet has to be identified by certain gastronomic signs. Private, unceremonial commensality does not suffer from these limitations. Certain local traditions might be built up—the Golden Egg at El Bulli, for example—but they are site specific as opposed to the international demand for shark-fin soup or, in its time, foie gras.

The current gastronomic world offers more variety and opportunities, but fewer agreed-upon criteria of enviable gastronomic pleasures. We are certainly not witnessing anything approaching the end of festive dining, but we are seeing the fading of a certain kind of splendid commensality.

9

It is Ritual, isn't it? Mortuary and Feasting Practices at Domuztepe

Alexandra Fletcher and Stuart Campbell

Introduction

Archaeologists tend to categorize ritual and domestic activities as separate, discrete, even opposing spheres even though it is widely acknowledged that such a total separation is not found in all societies. In many cases it is exceptional commensality (see Grignon, 2001: 28), for the purposes of this chapter feasting, that is often the focus of archaeological research (Dietler and Hayden, 2001a). This is partly because the nature of exceptional commensal acts increases their visibility within the archaeological record compared with more mundane, everyday practices; even if everyday consumption cumulatively produces more ecofactual, such as animal and plant remains, and artefactual evidence (Grignon, 2001: 28). Equally, however, it is because archaeological practice tends to privilege the social impact of the exceptional over the repetition of the mundane. Although it has been long established that archaeological data are derived from a range of depositional activities whose relationships are often more complex than expected (Brück, 1999; Pollard, 2001: 318; Bradley, 2003: 11–12, 2005: 19–35; Hill, 1995: 106; Hodder, 1987), archaeologists tend to maintain a division between the material remains from highly structured "ritual" activities and other material. This treats the exceptional and unusual as something separate, and isolates these practices from other aspects of the archaeological record (Thomas, 1999: 62–88; Chapman, 2000b; Hill, 1995: 102–14; Martin et al., 2000).

The remains of feasting therefore tend to be treated as if they are highly structured, deliberate deposits that can be clearly defined. Hayden, for example, has attempted to categorize types of feasting and the variety of archaeological signatures that may be created therein (2001: 35–42). Other food-related artifacts and ecofacts tend to be considered separately in terms of discarded and unwanted waste, with little to no structure in their deposition (see Cameron 2006: 25–31). Nevertheless acts of enchainment and fragmentation can create links between ritual and mundane worlds (Chapman, 2000a) and thus feasting cannot be considered in isolation from other forms of eating. As always, the challenge facing archaeologists is investigating the relationship between material we excavate and the social processes that underlie its deposition (see Schiffer, 1987, 1995; Tani, 1995; Wilson, 1994; Papaconstantinou, 2006). The study of exceptional commensality arguably also offers insights regarding social change and the construction and maintenance of social relationships in prehistory, which perhaps can then be cautiously extended further into more mundane contexts (Dietler and Hayden, 2001b: 2–3, 16–18). This chapter will examine these issues through the evidence for commensal acts from Domuztepe; a late Neolithic (c. 6200–5400 cal. BC) settlement located in southeast Turkey.

Grignon (2001: 24) defines commensality as "a gathering aimed to accomplish in a collective way some material tasks and symbolic obligations linked to the satisfaction of a biological individual need." The identification and examination of commensality in the prehistoric archaeological record relies on the analysis of seemingly plentiful evidence. Primary evidence for consumption that survives well archaeologically consists of some food remains and cooking or serving vessels; mainly animal bone and ceramics in Near Eastern contexts. Such physical remains of commensal acts are merely a subset within a broader range of activities concerning the relationship between consumption and society (Grignon, 2001). Thus although artifacts and ecofacts give some insight into how "biological individual need" may

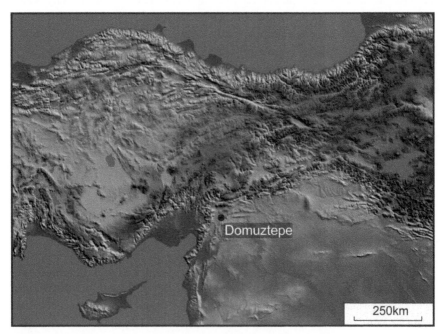

Figure 9.1 Location map for Domuztepe (map: Stuart Campbell)

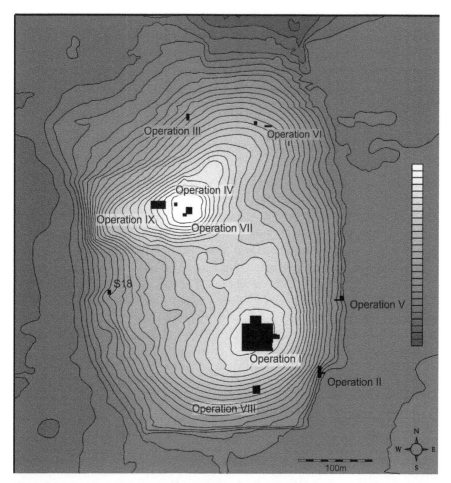

Figure 9.2 Site plan showing areas of excavation (map: Stuart Campbell)

have been met, it is more challenging to translate such evidence into the "symbolic obligations" that were also intimately linked to communal eating.

This chapter will focus on evidence from the site of Domuztepe (Figure 9.1). Located in southeastern Turkey between the Amanus and Taurus mountains and with an area of 20 ha, Domuztepe is the largest known example of a settlement from the Late Neolithic in the Middle East (Figure 9.2). Surface collections suggest that most of its 20 ha area was occupied in the mid-sixth millennium cal. BC (Campbell et al., 1999: 396–400). A largely continuous sequence of activity has been excavated from the late Ceramic Neolithic (c. 6250 cal. BC) to the Late Halaf period (c. 5400 cal. BC) (Campbell et al., 1999; Carter et al., 2003). This period of prehistory is particularly interesting as it is the first time that large-scale inter-regional communication can be identified suggesting widespread patterns of social change and interaction

(Campbell, 1999; Bernbeck 2008). Domuztepe appears to have been a part of the processes through which painted ceramics spread rapidly at the end of the seventh millennium cal. BC across a large geographical area covering southern Turkey to northern Iraq (Niewenhuyse, 2007). Large-scale open area excavation (c. 2000 m²) has encountered domestic, non-domestic, and mortuary deposits. Most of these have associations with the consumption of food and the disposal of food remains.

Mortuary deposits and exceptional commensality

The discussion will begin by examining an area of Domuztepe where evidence for food consumption and mortuary deposits were found in close association. The Death Pit was a multiple burial of at least 40 disarticulated individuals excavated between 1997 and 2003 (Carter et al., 2003; Kansa et al., 2009b). This large multiple inhumation was created toward the end of the Neolithic occupation at Domuztepe c. 5592 and 5562 cal. BC (Campbell, 2007) and was filled with layers of human and animal bones, mixed with other artifacts. The pit was situated in an open area that had possibly been deliberately cleared. Immediately to the north is a linear earthwork consisting of a raised bank, some 20 m wide, which is aligned east–west across the site (Carter et al., 2003: 118–19, Figure 6; Campbell, 2004: 4–5, 2005:

Figure 9.3 Photograph showing excavated Death Pit in foreground and Red Terrace in background (photo: Stuart Campbell)

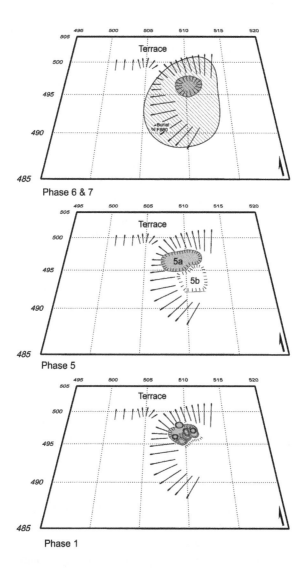

Phase 1: A scoop was made into the southern face of a terrace. Three or four shallow pits were dug into the base of resulting hollow and each filled with large quantities of articulating animal bones, stones and pot sherds (shaded).
Phase 2: More material was placed over the pits in the bottom of the larger hollow.
Phase 3: The hollow was then flooded and allowed to dry out, leaving a thick deposit of silt. This may have happened twice.
Phase 4: A small pit was probably cut into the silt lenses and filled with animal bones.
Phase 5a: In the northern part of the Death Pit, animal and human bones, especially the latter, were tightly compacted within a largely pisé-like matrix (shaded). The top of this hard packed deposit was modeled to create a shallow raised hollow.
Phase 5b: At the same time in the southern part of the Death Pit, more material was deposited, possibly to maintain a level with the hollow created by Phase 5a. This deposit contained abundant animal bones but few human remains.
Phase 6: Further bones, roughly equal proportions of humans and animals, were placed in the base of the raised hollow (shaded).
Phase 7: The entire area of the Death Pit was covered by a thick layer of ash, which probably lay over an area of 10-15m in diameter (hatched). Either at the same time as the ash was deposited (or very shortly before) the body of a child was placed on the southern edge of the Death Pit.

Figure 9.4   Sequence within the Death Pit (diagram: Stuart Campbell)

14) (Figure 9.3). This so-called Red Terrace was made from clean distinctive red clay, apparently a natural terra rossa, deliberately brought to the site from hills lying to the west (Gearey et al., 2011: 477–8). The soil was mounded up, then reinforced, and stabilized with lines of stones and areas of thin plaster wash. The distinctive character and color of the clay has allowed geoarchaeological survey to establish that the earthwork was at least 75 m in length and excavation suggests it was constructed and maintained over a considerable period of time (c. 500 years). The Red Terrace largely predates the Death Pit, which is dug into its southern edge. The two features appear to be closely linked and possibly derive greater significance and importance through their co-location (Campbell, 2007–8).

The burial within the Death Pit appears to have taken place over a short period of time; a few days, at most weeks, and had several phases (Figure 9.4). Initially three–four small pits were dug in the base of a shallow hollow and animal bones from different species placed within them. Significant quantities of cattle bones were placed above this, plausibly interpreted as the remains from feasting that included the slaughter of a small herd of cows. These come from a minimum of about eight prime-age female animals; sufficient to feed perhaps 2,000 people, which is potentially the whole population of the settlement (Kansa et al., 2009b, 2009a: 911–12). The exceptional nature of this commensal act is confirmed not only by the symbolic expense of the quantity of food made available but also the value of its source; prime-age females, would have required substantial resources to keep to maturity and would arguably have had a continuing long-term value as a source of milk and breeding stock (Kansa et al., 2009a: 911–12). Cattle were also afforded symbolic significance through their depiction as bukrania motifs painted on ceramics (Kansa and Campbell, 2002; Kansa et al., 2009a: 911). Therefore, although these bones appear to represent the disposal of food refuse, this discarding seems to have been done in a particular way, allowing us to suggest that these remains were closely linked to the creation of the Death Pit and a series of events associated with a specific social context; that is the "material tasks" and "symbolic obligations" inherent within commensal acts.

The cattle bones were flooded, creating a fine silty layer, which then dried out. Above this a dense mud layer was deposited with disarticulated and fragmented human remains concentrated in the northern part of the pit. A raised hollow was created above this by packing more animal and human bones with dense mud and more human remains were placed within this. This pit was then covered by a layer of ash that was about 10 m wide. The burial was later marked by two large posts and it was the location of subsequent burials of human remains ranging from small fragments of skull and jaw bones, the severed skull of a young woman, and a complete burial. Some were placed in shallow cuts, whereas others might have been placed on the surrounding surface. These examples cumulatively formed a structured placement of human remains in relationship with the Death Pit. The entire area was left devoid of domestic occupation for a period of perhaps 60–80 years.

The Death Pit therefore appears to have remained a focus for the community long after its initial creation.

The human remains deposited in the Death Pit are highly fragmented and processed (Kansa *et* al., 2009b). There are impact fractures, cut marks, chop marks, and thermal exposure consistent with the dismemberment and heating of bodies including the severing of skulls. The parallels with the treatment of the animal bones are striking (see Outram et al., 2005; Duncan, 2005; Whittle et al., 1999 for approaches to this). For the human bones, violent death and sacrifice can certainly not be ruled out and there is a strong possibility that cannibalism may have taken place (Kansa et al., 2009b). If cannibalism took place, the actual quantity of human flesh eaten might have been small but almost certainly it was highly symbolic and highly controlled within powerful social sanctions (Lindenbaum, 2004; Goldman, 1999; Sartore, 1994). The human remains may therefore have been regarded by the

Figure 9.5   Double oven on the Red Terrace (photo: Stuart Campbell)

participants in the commensal process as dangerous or powerful, and their burial might have been both associated with control and restriction. This might not, in fact, have been unique to human remains, although to our modern preconceptions it appears obvious. Other substances consumed on occasion might have had equally powerful or dangerous meanings, less obvious to archaeologists, which needed to be controlled through burial. At the end of the process, the physical location of the Death Pit had become a place with power and meaning that was intimately linked

Figure 9.6   Relative positions of the Red Terrace and Ditch (photo: Stuart Campbell)

with the living through acts of consumption and disposal (see McOmish, 1996: 75: Ullén, 1994; Thomas, 1999; Pollard, 2001).

To the north of the Death Pit, no domestic occupation was apparent on the surface of the Red Terrace but a number, five to date, of large ovens have been found, almost certainly used for cooking (Figure 9.5). This type of oven is rarely found in other contexts at Domuztepe. They are spatially disassociated with domestic architecture and, in at least one case, two adjacent ovens seem to have been in use at the same time, suggesting usage on a scale larger than necessary for a single household (see Hayden, 2001: 47–52, Figures 2.3–2.5). The specialized construction, maintenance of the structure including the cleaning and disposing of waste, and the nature of the features found upon the earthwork strongly suggest that the Red Terrace was a zone where special non-domestic activities took place, which perhaps were given a particular status or set of associations owing to their location. It certainly would have provided a good vantage point from which to view the creation of and activities associated with the Death Pit (Campbell and Healey, 2011: 328).

Figure 9.7   Thick burnished vessels with globular bodies and long restricted necks (photo: Stuart Campbell)

A series of segmented scoops and pits extended for c. 25 meters alongside the Red Terrace. For convenience these have been collectively termed the "Ditch" (Figure 9.6). The scoops might have been cut individually on a seasonal or annual basis. As many of the cuts themselves removed earlier cut lines, it is impossible to say how many times the process had been repeated. The fill of the Ditch was very distinctive. The soil was heavily gleyed, showing it has accumulated in a waterlogged environment that was rich in organic matter and, unlike the material that made up the Red Terrace, contained dense quantities of culture debris. Animal bones were plentiful. The gleying suggests the ditch was a wet environment that contained organic material, possibly derived from discarded meat but probably also including plant matter. It seems possible this debris represented the disposal of waste from activities held on the Terrace itself and the association between the presence of ovens and large quantities of animal bone strongly suggest feasting took place. It is interesting, however, that this feasting was not based primarily around the consumption of cattle, but animals that presented a smaller "package" of meat more-suited to sharing within smaller familial or kinship groups (Kansa et al., 2009a: 911). The Ditch also contained large quantities of pot sherds. Specific types of ceramics were found in large numbers, especially thick burnished wares and painted Halaf ware sherds with naturalistic decoration. Although the exact function of the thick burnished pottery eludes us, it is a remarkably consistent type of artefact (Irving, 2001: 229–32). Its shape with a round globular body and long neck, suggests uses associated with liquids (Figure 9.7). A different type of feasting from that reflected in the Death Pit is implied. Different food stuffs might have been consumed, with no indication of an association with human remains, and consumption of drink might have been a much more significant factor.

The painted sherds are characteristic of the earlier phases of the Halaf period at the site (c. 6000–5750 cal. BC). However, distinctive and unusual naturalistic designs dominate the painted motifs, suggesting it represents the breakage and disposal of a specific type of vessel. Since the vessels might have been associated with the serving and consumption of food or drink, this again emphasized the extent to which these deposits represent exceptional commensality. A frequently occurring motif shows a painted scene of a thatched two-floor building and its surroundings (Campbell and Fletcher, forthcoming) (Figure 9.8). The presence of storks on the roof suggests the scene depicted is during the late spring or early summer and anchors it within a particular time of year. It is possible that the building itself was only used seasonally, or that otherwise mundane, everyday structures were associated with special events at certain times of year (Bradley, 2005: 43–50). The recurrence of the exact image on pottery from other sites such as Sabi Abyad (Nieuwenhuyse, 2007: 10, Table 1.2.1, 20, Figure 2.2.4), Fistikli (Bernbeck and Pollock, 2003: Figure 22, g) and Arpachiyah (Hijara, 1978; Breniquet, 1992) however, implies such activities and associations were not limited to Domuztepe alone but might have been part of a much wider network of social behaviors. This might suggest that the events with

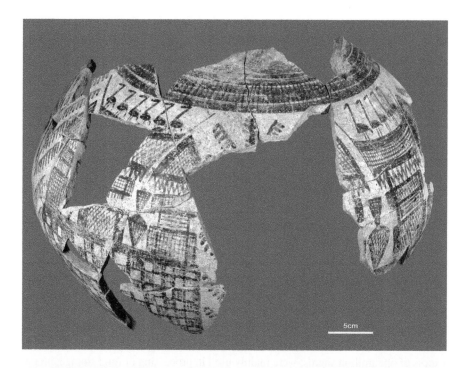

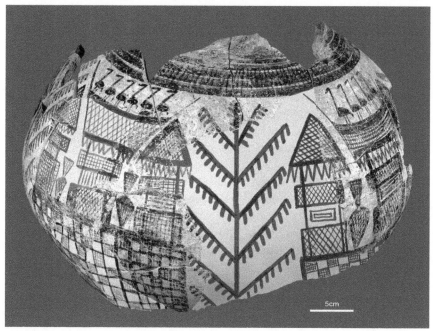

Figure 9.8 Painted vessel showing the building motif that is frequently found in the Ditch pottery assemblage (portions reconstructed) (photo: Stuart Campbell)

which the feasting was associated were themselves seasonal (Kansa et al., 2009a: 910–11) and perhaps further supports the suggestion that the cutting and re-cutting of the scoops that made up the ditch were also part of a recurring pattern of activities. In contrast to the spectacular consumption of cattle associated with the Death Pit, the feasting occurring on the Red Terrace might have been part of a regular seasonal cycle of events, perhaps within the category defined as Tribute Feasts by Hayden (2001: 58) with the result that meats of lower impact, value or prestige were consumed. We can therefore contrast the less spectacular but possibly seasonally recurrent feasts of the Red Terrace's 500-year history with the single short-lived spectacular event which accompanied the creation of the Death Pit.

Closing the gap between the extraordinary and the mundane

As well as these striking examples of consumption in particular contexts, the artefactual and ecofactual evidence from Domuztepe provides abundant evidence of repeated acts of much more mundane consumption. Animal bones are ubiquitous and most represent the by-products of food processing and consumption. Plant remains are equally widely preserved through charring and many represent food remains. Perhaps most obviously the huge quantities of broken pottery, now well in excess of one million sherds, were mainly used in processing of food storage, preparation, and consumption. Indeed the painted pottery most associated with the Halaf period might have been adopted as part of a process in which food consumption changed and became more symbolically loaded (Niewenhuyse, 2007). In general, it is impossible to unpick this general pattern of mundane consumption into individual episodes, although it undoubtedly had its own symbolism and small-scale rituals that shaped society through everyday practice. Nonetheless, it is possible to find evidence that links elements of extraordinary commensality to the mundane and the domestic.

In addition to the bone deposits, the Death Pit also contains large quantities of material that would be considered as straightforward refuse in a different context. No items in the Death Pit could be easily described as grave goods yet there is a large quantity of associated and largely fragmentary material culture including chipped stone, ground stone, stone bowls, bone tools, figurines, and jewellery in the form of beads or pendants. None of the objects are in positions that suggest deliberate placing (Campbell and Healey, 2011: 329). Owing to the method of excavation there has been an almost total recovery of everything deposited. It was therefore possible to assess the extent and nature of fragmentation among the ceramics and the spatial relationships between them though a joining study. Some 4,227 sherds were recorded weighing a total of 104.15 kg. Two hundred and thirty-eight sherds were joined and reconstructed into portions of a minimum number of 85 individual vessels and it was apparent that some sherds were from the same vessel even though they did not physically join (Irving and Heywood, 2004).

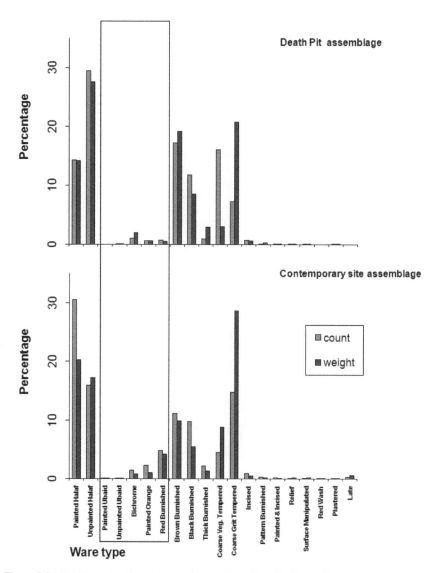

Figure 9.9 Relative proportions of ceramic ware types from the Death Pit and contemporaneous deposits. Fine and unusual wares are highlighted within the box (illustration: Alexandra Fletcher)

When the proportion of ceramic types present was compared with contemporaneous deposits elsewhere on the site, no significant differences could be perceived (Figure 9.9). A similar pattern was discerned for some of the lithic deposits (Campbell and Healey, 2011). This excluded the possibility that there were specific ritual vessels associated with the pit and could be consistent with the derivation of the fill from debris from the surrounding site that coincidentally contained pot

Figure 9.10 Sherd cut at the leather-hard stage of production (photo: Stuart Campbell)

fragments. Connections were identified between sherds found across different phases of deposition, however, which are more likely to represent deliberate distribution and incorporation of parts of broken vessels within the burial. It is notable that no complete vessels could be reconstructed from the sherds found. Even the most complete examples were still missing approximately a third of their total. It is therefore possible that the ceramics might have been subjected to deliberate fragmentation, with part of the broken vessel retained elsewhere, perhaps symbolizing an enchained relationship between the Death Pit and other arenas (Chapman, 2000a: 49–68). This idea was reinforced by the discovery of a sherd that had been cut through at the leather-hard stage of production before the vessel was fired (Figure 9.10). It was not broken after firing as it showed signs of dragging within the clay fabric. We can definitively state that the rest of the vessel from which the cut sherd came is not present in the Death Pit and therefore argue that its uniqueness makes it almost inconceivable that its deposition in the pit was accidental.

As the inter-phase connections identified between the pot sherds were not related to the deposition of unusual or luxury vessels, the pottery in the pit might have connected participants in the mortuary activities to a specific domestic sphere or location. The fragments retained outside the pit might have acted as a reminder of the activities surrounding the Death Pit's creation and expressed links to specific human agents that were involved, (see Chapman, 1996, 2000a, 2000b; Weiner, 1992; Wagner, 1991; Hill, 1995, 109; Garrow et al., 2005: 153–6; Beck and Hill, 2004; Bradley, 2005: 119, 2003: 16; Last, 2006: 127–35); specifically in the case of pottery vessels, the links might have been articulated in commensal acts. Unlike the animal-derived feasting debris, however, it is possible that the commensality represented by the potsherds was of a more mundane everyday nature as the range of pots encountered was so similar to the norm elsewhere within the settlement. The inclusion of pot sherds within the Death Pit might therefore have been related to forging connections between mundane and everyday aspects of life at Domuztepe and unusual, or extraordinary ritual events (see Weiner, 1992; Thomas, 1996: 150–77; Pollard, 2001: 327; Hodder, 2004: 50).

The disposal of mundane food-related material culture in the Death Pit leads us to re-examine other evidence for consumption at Domuztepe. As outlined at the beginning of this chapter, the most ubiquitous food-related artifacts and ecofacts tend to be treated archaeologically as discarded, unstructured, and unwanted waste. We have perhaps been misdirected by such preconceptions and so should establish if the disposal of food and its associated material remains anywhere else on the site show any similarities with the patterns of disposal seen in the Death Pit. In the northern part of the settlement, excavation revealed a dense concentration of animal bones deposited in association with an area of pebble surfaces (Campbell et al., 1999: 401). Over 90 percent of the bone fragments (52 of 57 bones) were those of cattle representing at least four individuals. The bones were not highly fragmented and came mainly from a single species. More than half the bones present were from meat-bearing parts of the carcass, providing striking parallels with the cattle bones found in the Death Pit and making it less likely that this was the remains of butchery. It seems likely therefore that these bones too, are primary refuse, deliberately deposited in the aftermath of feasting (see McOmish, 1996).

The Red Terrace, Ditch, and Death Pit therefore appear to be linked through the cooking, consumption, and disposal of large-scale feasts, acts of exceptional, some might say extreme, commensality at least some of which might have been associated with mortuary rites. There are striking parallels with the interpretation of Neolithic causewayed enclosures of the fourth millennium in Britain where episodes of feasting, mortuary ritual and deposition are evident, and where the ditches were subject to deliberate deposition, back fill and re-cutting (Pollard, 2001: 319; Fowler, 2003: 53; Richards and Thomas, 1984; Bradley, 2005: 15). At Domuztepe the recurring deposition of sherds showing buildings may suggest that specific vessels, decorated with significant images might have been used within these events and disposed of in special circumstances. As such, the Ditch may represent discard from a particular set of events, perhaps in an effort to control their associations, implications or powers. It is potentially significant that a potsherd painted with an image of headless bodies was also found within the Ditch. The cutting and re-cutting of the pits and scoops might also have served to renew people's connections to the activities that took place within the complex of associated structures. The feasting remains found in the north of the site also suggest these activities should not be viewed as isolated. We might therefore speculate that material created in unusual circumstances, such as feasts, was charged with power, perhaps of a dangerous nature, and that disposal in a specific way incorporated this power into a defined part of the site. The evidence relating to the disposal of potsherds in the Death Pit, however, points to a different set of associations and connections perhaps being created through the structured deposition of material culture intimately connected to mundane, domestic contexts. Ultimately all these activities can be regarded as part of the way in which meaning is ascribed to place and subsequently maintained.

Conclusion

At Domuztepe, and probably at a range of broadly contemporary sites, there are a range of socially loaded discard practices that are not best understood as an opposition between ritual activities and mundane refuse disposal. Commensality cannot easily be separated from actions of use and disposal, whether of human remains or of other categories of artefact and ecofact. Instead, it may be that food and its consumption should be placed in the wider context of the use of material and its structured discard. They are better regarded as a set of actions across a wide spectrum that can encompass mechanisms in which relationships can be defined and reinforced, dangerous, and powerful concepts contained and controlled, and the meaning of places defined and redefined within and beyond the settlement.

10

Drink and Commensality or How to Hold on to Your Drink in the Chalcolithic

Susanne Kerner

Introduction

The biological requirements of human beings concerning their nutritional needs are relatively well researched: the survival chances without breathing are minutes, the survival without eating can be weeks, while the survival without drinking is only days. Taking liquids is thus an essential necessity for humans, and today the lack of clean drinking water is one of the major problems in international health concerns.

But in drink, as in food, it has become clear that purely physiological considerations are falling short of actually explaining both the choices of food and drink as well as the social importance of drinking or the social meaning of imbibing.

Four different functions of drinking can be identified that are constituted by 1) drinking to quench thirst; 2) drinking to enjoy sensory aspects—closely connected to cultural questions of taste; 3) drinking for clearly commensal reasons, be they social or religious; and 4) drinking to obtain psychoactive effects (alcoholic effects). The physiological need of liquid intake can be fulfilled by any liquid and in extreme cases even by consuming vegetables or fruit cooked in liquids instead of actually drink.[1] Such nutritional questions will not be discussed in this chapter. While the sensory aspects of drink are noteworthy, touching upon aspects of taste as a social construct (Bourdieu, 1984) and taste as culturally learned habit,[2] it is one of the problems of archaeology that such aspects can only be studied under very particular and lucky circumstances. The only available evidence would be textual in the form of taste descriptions, and Near Eastern texts are not very enlightening on such introspective information,[3] as they tend to be more descriptive.

This chapter will instead concentrate on the third point, the social aspects of drink, which can include the psychoactive effects of alcoholic beverages. The diversity of ceremonies and rituals connected to drink is impressive, as Dietler quotes an informant in his ethnographic research in Africa that "if there's no beer, it's not a ritual" (Dietler, 2006: 232). Rituals extend from the so-called coma drinking of modern teenagers[4] to Kava drinking ceremonies in the Tongas (Bott, 2003), with their elaborate social make-up, to afternoon teas (Hazan, 2003). These examples clearly illustrate that each consumed liquid has its own culturally constructed aura and image depending on the cultural background and the practice connecting it to different people.[5] In the Western world, milk is a drink for children, with several researchers claiming ill effects on adults consuming milk. In the Cameroon girls are given milk to fatten them and to make them happy (Garine, 2001), while in Tanzania Massai warriors consider milk as an important element of their claim to strength and virtue (Ibrahim, 2001). All of these are ideas fundamentally different from our Western perception of milk.

Alcoholic and non-alcoholic beverages have very different functions in the Western world, and it is also here where alcoholism and the concerns over health issues form large parts of the discussion about drinking (Douglas, 2003). Anthropology has for decades—starting with the temperance movement of the late nineteenth century—concentrated on the negative aspects of drinking alcohol. Research into the cultural role of alcohol drinking really only began with Douglas' seminal work. Even in 2006, although Dietler considered it necessary to start by pointing out that anthropology is not overlooking the pathological aspects of drinking, he saw the interest in the social role of alcohol as an outcome of functionalism, hence suggesting that the agentive aspect needs to be studied more intensively.

Drinking together

Alcoholic as well as non-alcoholic drinks can play a role in social and cultic situations, particularly in small-scale societies, where drinking occasions (as well as eating) can be used for labor mobilization and political negotiations through feasts (Dietler, 1996, 2006). Commensal activities and in particular feasting have been discussed intensively over the last decade. There is general scholarly agreement that the discernment between domestic and ritual/cultic or political commensal activities is very difficult in terms of archaeological evidence (Dietler, 1996, 2006; Pollock, 2012a). Most of the archaeological interpretations are based on ethnographic examples of feasting, but the variety of feasting occasions as well as reasons for feasting might differ in past societies. Feasting is understood in this chapter very generally, as defined by Katherine Twiss as "occasions consciously distinguished from everyday meals" (Twiss, 2008: 419). The purpose of feasting is understood as context bound and the meaning of feasting in small-scale low-hierarchy societies is a very different one from state-level societies such as the Late Bronze Age Greece or the Inca Empire (Bray, 2003a; Twiss, 2007).

Mary Douglas' *Constructive Drinking* (2003) shows important cultural aspects of drinking and also the subtle questions of inclusion and exclusion (women and children being excluded from alcoholic beverages is a very typical example). A problematic aspect is that most articles dealing with alcohol in archaeological contexts use ethnographical parallels, which is, however, particularly apt in South America, where the production and consumption of *chicha*, maize beer, has a long tradition going back at least to the Inca Empire, and still is being produced in villages today (Jennings and Bowser, 2009). Such long historical continuity is unusual and certainly not the case in the Near East, where one has to be aware that it is not only the religious prohibition against alcohol that has broken the historical continuity, but also the fact that the archaeological society under scrutiny here is a small-scale prehistoric society, which had a very different social and political setting (than, for example, the Inca Empire), making ethnographical parallels extremely complicated.

In small political units where rank, prestige, and the social position of many members were still being negotiated and changeable, feasts with a competitive character and the possibility to mobilize both labor (small-scale work feasts) and support, could have played an important role in the life cycle of humans. Feasting in small-scale societies can thus certainly both have a character of achieving prestige or paying back work forces (Hayden, 2001). Research about eating and no less drinking occasions shows that the question of inclusion and exclusion in such occasions is very important, followed closely by questions of seating order (e.g. Bott, 2003) and the use of different paraphernalia (who drinks what out of which container).

This is the starting point to discuss drink in an archaeological context, because it is often not possible to actually discern the character of the drink that has been imbibed. Such discernment would require the analysis of the content of vessels and this has become only very recently more common practice in archaeology. The following discussion will thus concentrate on archaeological material evidence for the possible importance of commensal drinking in the Late Chalcolithic of the Southern Levant, without a final statement about which liquid has been consumed, but with some hypothesis as to how research could be formulated in the future to allow further insights into drinking.

Case study

Introduction

The case study is situated in the southern Levant during the Late Chalcolithic period, which spans roughly the time period of 4500–3800 BCE. Its society is organized in small-scale polities, often called chiefdoms (Kerner, 2001; Rowan and Golden, 2009) with few clearly recognizable differences in rank or elite existence, indicating an elite without individuals being set clearly apart. In contemporary Ubaid Mesopotamia, the criteria for the presence of an elite are: existence of public architecture, administrative tools, multi-tiered settlement patterns, mass production of certain types of pottery, and prestige items to signify elite status (Kennedy, 2012, 130).[6] In contrast, in the southern Levant public architecture can be found in cultic buildings in Gilat, Ein Gedi, and Tuleilat Ghassul (Levy, 2006; Seaton, 2008; Ussishkin, 1971), administrative tools in the shape of tokens appear in small numbers (Bourke, 2001: 145), a two-tier settlement pattern can be recognized in some areas, and prestige items undoubtedly exist, possibly even indicating different levels of prestige in the metal finds (Kerner, 2010). The mass production of pottery is less clearly pronounced in the southern Levant, but exists in the shape of the ubiquitous V-shaped bowl, which forms easily 50 percent of the pottery finds in several sites (Burton, 2004; Kerner, 2001: 101ff.). There is little archaeological evidence for clear differences in wealth in the different parts of society, even though differences in grave goods exist (Ilan and Rowan, 2012: 99; Kerner, 2010).

The situation concerning ceramic finds has certain archaeological advantages and disadvantages. One advantage is the amount of excavated sites and the number of potential vessels, which might have been used for serving, eating, and drinking. It is actually the specific amount and variety of certain small vessels in a number of sites that led to this study. The disadvantage is the lack of textual evidence that would allow a secure categorization of drinking and feasting. Moreover the lack of contextual information makes it often impossible to gain a clear picture of distribution patterns of pottery in a site (and thus the consumption pattern in said site) and the lack of content analysis. The nature of this chapter is thus to be understood as a preliminary gathering of ideas.

Material evidence

The basis for assuming that certain vessels can be connected with certain functions is based on ethnographic references (Rice, 1987: 237; Chesson, 2000) and follows certain principles of inherent logic.[7] Large stationary vessels are used for storage. Pots, which can be slightly open but are usually more restricted and made of a porous fabric that can withstand heat, are used for cooking. High, narrow jars, with or without spouts, are used for storing and serving liquid. The vessels for consumption can vary depending on the occasion; while large flat platters are assumed to play a role in communal and feasting occasions of some kind (Chesson, 2000; Kennedy, 2012; Pollock, 2012a); smaller vessels are taken to be a sign for serving and eating from individual vessels. Small vessels with straight sides and a height larger than the diameter are assumed to be for drinking purposes.

The nature of Late Chalcolithic pottery assemblages is dependent on the exact time setting of the concerned layers and sites. Sites, which are not at the very end of the period, show a higher percentage of open compared to restricted vessels. All sites show that certain vessel forms such as straight-sided bowls, cornets, and even cooking pots have bi- or tri-modal size distributions (Kerner, 2001: 109;

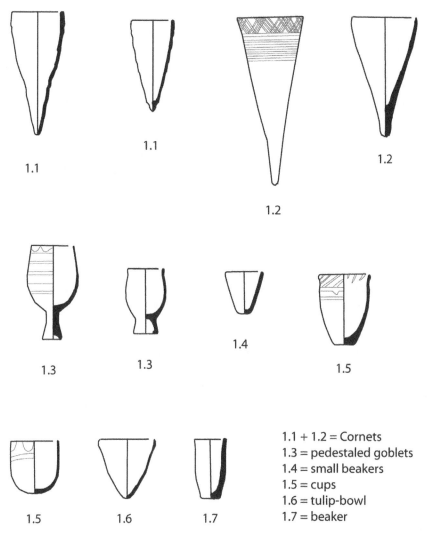

Figure 10.1 Different Late Chalcolithic drinking vessels

1.1 + 1.2 = Cornets
1.3 = pedestaled goblets
1.4 = small beakers
1.5 = cups
1.6 = tulip-bowl
1.7 = beaker

Commenge, 2006: 414). There is a remarkable amount of small vessels, which are also astonishingly varied. The largest percentage of these small vessels is made up of small bowls with V-shaped walls, and to a smaller but significant amount of vessels particularly suited as drinking vessels. The V-shaped bowls (small, straight-sided vessels with diagonal walls) have a diameter up to 14 cm, and could have served both as eating and drinking vessels. It is the only shape that has been finished on the wheel in some sites (Roux and Courty, 1998). The other containers are cornets, pedestaled goblets, chalices, cups/beakers, cups/small tulip bowls, and small tubular beakers or goblets.[8] Cornets have a triangular profile (compatible to ice-cream cones) with a pointed base and can never stand independently. One variety of the cornets has a short (Figure 10.1) base, and the other a long solid base (Figure 10.1: 1.2). The pedestaled goblets (Figure 10.1: 1.3) consist of a straight-sided or slightly rounded cup on a foot of differing height.[9] Chalices are small V-shaped bowls on high hollow bases that come with or without fenestration. Small beakers (Figure 10.1: 1.4) are always higher than wide and their diameter is under 9 cm (with a height below 10 cm; Commenge. 2006: 417). Cups (Figure 10.1: 1.5) (Garfinkel, 1999: 220–1), or small to middle beakers (Commenge, 2006: 418) have rather straight walls and lug-handles, and their diameter is up to 11 cm with a height of 15 cm. Cups (Garfinkel, 1999: Figure 133.27) or tulip-shaped bowls (Commenge, 2006: 416) are small thin-walled vessels (Figure 10.1: 1.6) with small flat bases, on which most of them stand very insecurely. Only some of them are small. Tubular goblets or beakers (Figure 10.1: 1.7) are basically cylindrical with a width of less than 6 cm and a height up to 19.6 cm (Commenge, 2006: 419). They have relationally larger bases that make them stand better. The same is true for the goblets which are small, slightly restricted vessels, and were found in Kissufim Road and Givat Ha-Oranim (Goren and Fabian, 2002: Figure 4.1; Scheftelowitz, 2004: Figure 3.2, 13–16).

Table 10. 1 Distribution of drinking vessels in several sites. N = X number given, other entries are percentages (Burton, 2004; Commenge-Pellerin, 1987, 1990, 2006; Garfinkel, 1999; Scheftelowitz, 2004; Gilead and Goren, 1995)

Site/vessel	Chalice	Footed goblet	Cornet	Tulip bowl	Beaker	Closed goblet
Safadi	0.07		0.03			0.04
Abu Matar	0.3	0.2	0.1			1.2
Zumeili	0.4					0.5
Horvath Beter			N = 65			
Tuleilat Ghassul layer D		Exist	14			
Tuleilat Ghassul layer C		Exist	11			
Tuleilat Ghassul, Area E			50% (N = 63)			
Ein Gedi			40			
Gilat			1% (N = 112)	11.6	1.3	
Shiqmim			N = 1			
Grar		0.5	14			
Meitar			Similar to Grar			
Givat Ha-Oranim			N = 9			N = 5
Abu Hof			21			
Nahal Tillah			0.3			
Abu Hamid						

These vessels appear from sites in the Negev, the Jordan valley, and the Mediterranean coast (Commenge, 2006; Garfinkel, 1999). The geographical distribution (if one keeps in mind that the distribution of excavations is not equal through the region) is thus quite broad, but far from regular (Table 10.1).

Not all varieties of these small vessels exist in all sites. However, vessels with a small volume and an open shape (there are also some small jars with a restricted opening, but they have been left out of the discussion here) exist in most sites. There might be a chronological element to their distribution pattern (sites at the very end of the Late Chalcolithic seem to have no cornets: Burton, 2004: 136), but there is certainly a distinct element in Late Chalcolithic ceramics material that points to a use for serving and most likely drinking.

All these vessels, except the small V-shaped bowls and the tubular beakers, cannot stand individually or have at best a very precarious balance when standing, because their bases are very small, particularly when compared to the volume of the vessel. This point has been discussed before, and devices made from perishable material have occasionally been suggested; however, no archaeological evidence of any such "holders" have been found yet. This is a phenomenon dividing the drinking vessels of that time period from those of earlier and later ones. For a discussion of the function and meaning of these vessels, the context information would be of great importance, but for many this information is only available very limitedly.

Context

The first and most obvious context related characteristic is the lack of the above described vessels in burial contexts. Neither in the intra-village burials in Gilat, nor in the cemeteries of Shiqmim or Kissufim Road, or in the cave sites of Nahal Qanah, Peqi'in, Shoham, or the Warrior cave are any of the above mentioned vessels found (Rowan and Golden, 2009: 45–6). The most common pottery connected to burials (if any at all) is the V-shaped vessel (Commenge, 2006: 337).[10]

Cultic sites such as Ein Gedi, Gilat (Ilan and Rowan, 2012: 103) and the temple complex of Tuleilat Ghassul show high frequencies of cornets (Seaton, 2008: 42). In Tuleilat Ghassul cornets are generally not a frequent item (N = 128), but half of them appear in the Sanctuary complex of area E (N = 63) and a high number in a special building, which also included a wall painting (Koeppel, 1940: 81), that makes it likely for the building to be connected to ritual activities. In the same site a similar distribution pattern can be found for goblets and beakers (Seaton, 2008: 47). In the northern Negev cornets (and other small drinking vessels) exist in the site of Abu Hof, but not in Shiqmim, and only in small numbers in the sites around Beersheba; hence their distribution pattern is difficult to interpret.[11]

In sites such as the small villages of Givat Ha-Oranim (Scheftelowitz, 2004) and Grar (Gilead and Goren, 1995) cornets appear, in the latter site even in quite high numbers. In Givat Ha-Oranim the other group of small vessels is very similar to the goblets in Kissufim. Beakers, tulip-shaped bowls and cups appear again in sites such as Gilat, Ein Gedi (Ussishkin,1980: Figure 7.17, 22; Figure 10.9) and Tuleilat Ghassul (Seaton, 2008: Plate 82, a–c).

Different drinking vessels

In the Late Chalcolithic ceramic repertoire a number of small, upright vessels with small volumes, mostly insecure stand, and slightly different forms have been identified. Through their form, size, and stand, they can all be interpreted as being connected with drinking. Only the group of small V-shaped vessels could as well be used for serving food (and their distribution pattern is far wider than that of the vessels described above). The remaining cornets, cups, beakers, and chalices all differ in shape. While the cornets appear at least in some sites in the hundreds, the other vessels are only known in much smaller numbers (Table 10.1).

Assuming that the practice of daily and special commensality followed a pattern, the question that remains is: what kind of practice structured the distribution pattern of these vessels? Several different explanatory scenarios offer themselves. The different vessels could have a chronological or regional meaning, but there is no clear archaeological evidence for this assumption. It could mean that different consumers used different shaped vessels, that different occasions called for different drinking cups, or that the varied content influenced the choice of vessels.

Rank

Considering the important role of consumption for societal cohesion (Kennedy, 2012: 126), and the importance of paraphernalia in connection with social ranking (e.g. expressed in the Kava ceremonies), a social ranking of different drinking vessels is imaginable. I have suggested earlier that the Late Chalcolithic society might use metal items to announce different levels of prestige (Kerner, 2010: 182), thus a ranked order of drinking vessels could be possible, but that is purely hypothetical. A division could be caused by gender, age or role in the ritual.

Content of drink

Most anthropological studies of drinking are not overly concerned with materiality as they study both the consumers and the consumed goods directly. The information concerning the relationship between the shape of a container and the kind of consumed liquid is thus limited for either historical or ethnographical records.[12]

For archaeology the study of actual material evidence is important to illustrate commensality in past contexts. Archaeological evidence—other than the vessels or the food/drink themselves—that could indicate commensal activities would be particular fireplaces, particular floral, or faunal remains-patterns, and certain instruments, such as drinking tubes (Kennedy, 2012). The kind of liquid that has been drunken from these vessels can at the moment only be hypothesized, as few content analyses have been made, the only exceptions are a recent residue study of cornets by Namdar et al. and a study of the content of different vessels by Burton. The first study analyzed the content of 20 cornets from five sites and seems to indicate a usage as lamps for these particular containers (Namdar et al., 2008). If the cornets would indeed have been used as lamps, many of the considerations here are obsolete, but a number of archaeological facts seem to argue against their use as lamps: there is no evidence for their positioning on walls, which would be expected, when they were meant to light the rooms of the Chalcolithic houses. They also do not appear in particularly large numbers in the subterranean structures that exist in this time period, which would have needed lighting. The possibility that cornets were drinking vessels thus still exists.

The second study analyzed the content of so-called torpedo jars, large cigar-shaped vessels, churns (see below), cornets, and a number of other vessels (Burton, 2004). Gas-chromatography of lipid residues and absorbed biomolecules point toward "grain-based beverages or porridges" in the cornets (Burton, 2004: 589), "levels of fatty acids" indicating milk (products) in churns (Burton, 2004: 595)[13] and olive oil in torpedo jars (Burton, 2004: 598). In the same study the analyzed cooking pots' content indicates more fruit and vegetable.

What liquids might have been drunk then? Water is a first possibility. The fact that water is a very basic drink does not exclude it from a role in any ritual contexts, as it plays the most important role of keeping humans and the land alive. In other archaeological contexts (see Fletcher and Campbell, Chapter 9) water played a role in rituals.

The second possibility would be milk, which would have been widely available, as all milk-providing animals were domesticated at that point in time. Cattle, sheep, and goats have all been identified in the faunal records, with regional differences due to the climatic diversity of the regions in the southern Levant.[14] The available information for a herding economy points (in terms of the caprids) towards a mixed economy, where milk and wool played a role, and not only meat. The "secondary product" revolution (Sherratt, 1981) was in full swing and milk is a very interesting substance, as it has so many connotations indicated in anthropological literature as well as through some archaeological evidence. In northern Cameroon, milk makes you peaceful and is pure unadultered bliss (not just a drink), Massai warriors drink milk to stay strong. Breast-fed milk is the first substance for all human beings and forms the first form of commensality, showing also that food is "embodied" material in more than one sense (Van Esterik, Chapter 3; Sanchez Romero, 2011:

11). In the southern Levant, churns, another ubiquitous shape of vessels, have been connected frequently with milk or milk-related products. The name given to these vessels, churn, already points to the assumed use of it: to churn milk into another product, be it butter or more likely a yoghurt-like product. Churns certainly played a role in rituals, as they exist in three different sizes, of which one, the middle size, is functional and the other two sizes (very large and miniature) are frequently made from a special ceramic paste (Kerner, 2001). The churn appears also in connection with zoomorphic and anthropomorphic figurines, the most famous of them is the "Lady of Gilat." This figurine, clearly marked as a female with small breasts and a pubic triangle, carries a churn on her head and possibly a cornet under her arm. This has been interpreted as a sign of the close connection between fertility and milk, and to a lesser degree between women and milk (Joffee et al., 2001). Milk thus appears to play a role in nutrition and cult. It has at least one vessel form, the churn, that exists in a normal size for the actual manipulation of milk and in a much smaller as well as much larger size, where it might have played a role in rituals connecting milk to the community.

The question of fermented beverages is even more complicated, as little content analysis has been carried out (see above) and no textual or iconological material is available that would allow a clear detection of fermented drinks, either made from grain, grapes, or even milk. No clear evidence for brewing-related artifacts has been found.[15] The intrasocietal significance of Mediterranean crop production has been discussed not only in terms of gruel and bread, but also in terms of fermentation. As Dietler notes, alcohol "is a medium that allows surplus agricultural produce to be converted into labor, prestige, 'social credit,' political power, bride wealth, or durable valuables; and this is a very useful mechanism of indirect conversion which, for example, can be used to circumvent the normal barriers to direct convertibility of subsistence goods to more socially valued items in multi-centric economies" (Dietler, 1990: 369). One aspect of this notion had already been elaborated on by Julian Steward in the discussion "Did man live once by beer alone?," where he pointed out that beer is an important part in discussions about the storage of grain. This was a discussion started by Braidwood, who wondered if the production of beer was actually the guiding motive behind the domestication of grain (Braidwood, 1953). This discussion has only marginally been taken up again in terms of neolithization,[16] but it is interesting to notice that the discussion of maize domestication in the Americas has been following similar ideas (Goldstein, 2003; Jennings and Bower, 2009). The recent discussion of ritual economy by Spielmann takes up the idea that surplus and complexity might be closely related to ritual and the necessary production of consumables for ritual occasions (Spielmann, 2002). Other than grain surplus fermented into an early form of beer, the other possibility in the Near East is the use of grapes (or even other berries, as used in prehistoric Peru; Goldstein et al., 2009). The existence of wine has been illustrated in the Early Bonze Age in Godin Tepe (McGovern, 2010: 61ff.) and slightly earlier in Armenia (Barnard et al., 2011).

Fermented beverages are usually important in political interactions and generally considered to confer higher prestige and to be more essential in politically charged contexts than other drinks (Vencl, 1994: 312; Woolf and Eldrige, 1994).

Conclusion

Drink is not just about a physical necessity, rather the way in which it is prepared, served, and consumed is integral to social practices that affirm, contest, and transform social identities. The case study presented here shows the existence of special drinking vessels that would have to be held in the hand during the occasions, when they were used. This would indicate that they were used during special social events, described here as feasts. These feasts were simultaneously integrative and competitive and played a role in negotiating social hierarchies in small-scale societies, where status and roles were still under discussion and not exclusively defined. These feasts would have included the consumption of liquids that hold a special meaning, either milk as a drink connected to the fertility of the whole society (and understood here purposefully not as a purely female affair) or a fermented, possibly alcoholic drink, that would have played a special role due to its psycho-active abilities. Useful liquids such as milk, oil, and, less likely, wine could have been celebrated during these occasions. The different vessel shapes might have been used for different liquids, but could as well characterize different consumer groups.

A connection between the vessels (particularly cornets) and ritual locations seems to have existed, although their presence in seemingly purely domestic contexts (Grar, Abu Hof, Meitar) could mean that cultic activities spilled over into domestic areas. It could also indicate that cornets would have connected domestic and ritual spheres, and changed their materiality according to the occasion. One should generally assume that there was no absolute division between the ritual and the secular or between feasts and everyday meals.

The feasts might also have been marked by performances undertaken such as the processions illustrated on the wall paintings in Tuleilat Ghassul (Bourke, 2001: Figure 4.3), possibly helped by the psychoactive effects of alcohol (Sherratt, 2007). The social practice of feasting would have offered the people of the Late Chalcolithic an occasion to perform rituals where important food materials (oil, milk, grain) were celebrated, where subtle and less subtle social differences were played out through orders of seating and drinking vessels, and where redistribution through ritual specialists could have been effected. Holding on to their drinks would have been both necessary to successfully negotiate their social roles, but also to actually manage to drink their share.

Part III
The Social and Political Aspects of Commensality

11

How Chicken Rice Informs about Identity

Cynthia Chou

Introduction

It has been said that "[s]tories about eating something somewhere … are really stories about the place and the people there [and that] the reading of a food's story reveals, like any good biography or travelogue, a much bigger story—a cultural geography—of particular times and places" (Freidberg, 2003: 3–4). My subject matter in this chapter concerns the ordinary ritual of everyday life: food and eating, and the role that culinary artifacts play in the construction of a national identity.

The history of what a nation eats bespeaks the history of the nation (Bell and Valentine, 1997: 168). It maps stories of intriguing webs of exploration and power relations, the flow and exchange of people, ideas and goods, as well as the negotiations and contestations of cultural and social practices in times of change and transformation. Aspects of creating local iconic cuisines similarly speak of a place's history as a society. As Avieli (2005: 168) notes, "Iconic dishes, due to various intrinsic qualities of food, are particularly suitable means for the negotiation and expression of complex and contradictory ideas concerning national identity." The food–nationalism equation is indeed almost always a cauldron of contradictions since food that has come to be associated with particular places often stands for complex tales of borrowing, diffusion, invention, and reinvention. Despite these paradoxes, quintessential local cuisines have been created through the unique blending of ingredients from the inside and outside and the very performative actions of the people themselves. The question is thus, "how have people used local iconic cuisines to portray an identity?" By iconic food it is meant specific kinds of food, which instantly express, when consumed or just imagined, links to specific places, groups of people or communities.

This chapter will explore the various and differing ideas expressed by the creation of one such local dish, Hainanese chicken rice, in regard to a multifaceted and at times contested Singaporean national identity. It will also examine how so much of Singapore's history is conveyed in various aspects of this humble dish and how it is a multivocal and powerful representation of the socio-cultural ideas of contemporary Singaporean national identity at an everyday level.

Food, cuisine and national identity

A well-known saying goes, "you are what you eat." While this phrase can be interpreted metaphorically, its literal significance must not be overlooked. Food is a universal basic necessity for the very sustenance of life. No one can do without it. Moreover, it intermingles with different spheres of life—from household to nation, from local to global, and from religion to politics. Food affects the processes and relationships within and between these spheres. Hence, people make food choices. Convictions are stirred into passionate debates in our entanglements concerning how, where, and what to or not to eat. Food and foodways together form an important social barometer to reveal who we are, our origin, and our aspirations. They constitute "a highly condensed social fact" and "a marvellously plastic kind of collective representation" (Appadurai, 1981: 494). They unite people as much as they effectuate divisions, borders, and boundaries. In Fine's *Kitchens* (1996: 1), he makes the astute observation that "the connection between identity and consumption gives food a central role in the creation of community, and we use our diet to convey images of public identity."

That nations are constructed communities is well expounded in Anderson's (1983) much celebrated work *Imagined Communities*, which reflects upon the origin and spread of nationalism. Every modern nation state has, within its territorial boundary, peoples with diverse cultural characteristics. For this reason, nationalist programs deploy particular historical narratives, census, maps, and museums to inculcate a sense of community into its citizenry. Within this discourse, scores of scholars have explored how national communities have emerged through the conscious "invention" of national traditions (Hobsbawm and Ranger, 1983). Considerable insights have been revealed concerning how states utilize their technologies of power—compulsory education, language, flags, monuments, songs, and celebrations—to create national symbols that elicit primordial sentiments of identification among the citizenry (cf. Cohn and Dirks, 1988; Foster, 1991: 244–8). Then again, this national imagination of belongingness propagated by the ruling elites more often than not germinates within it the seeds of its own questioning and cultivates hierarchical distinctions among its citizenry. The propagation of such national identities is clearly open to contest often as much by word as in action. Contrary to official promulgations, such symbols may not necessarily be what evoke the deepest and warmest emotive appeal for the common citizenry on an everyday basis.

Less discussed in academic explorations of national imaginaries are the more powerful and sustaining tools of imagination articulated by ordinary people themselves in their ordinary daily practices that lead to the construction of a community of belongingness. Analysis into imaginaries that have evolved into "second nature ... material practice and lived experience" (Alonso, 1994: 382) such as how the "alimentary tropes" (Alonso, 1994) of cooking, food, eating, and digestion help produce, negotiate, and maintain a sense of nationalism on an everyday basis rarely receive much attention. The pertinent issue here as challenged by Palmer (1998: 180) is to identify these everyday practices and to advance "from this understanding of structural changes that allowed the idea of a cultural community to emerge, toward an understanding of how individuals became consciously aware of the cultural community ... how a sense of nationality is constructed that links individuals to a particular cultural tradition." Until now, little inroads have been made in analyzing the historical importance of the ways by which food and the iconic national dishes perceived by the people themselves have contributed towards the construction and negotiation of national identity.

Wide gaps prevail between the theoretical conceptualization of the nation as an imagined entity and understanding the daily practices that produce, reproduce, and maintain it. Studying and analyzing the seemingly mundane everyday practices of eating is simply not a trivial pursuit but constitutes significant sources for comprehending the movement of society and history. Food has tremendous historical importance (Belasco, 2002: 3). Yet academic texts do not seem to devote much attention to food and eating. In works on history regarding production and trade, or war and peace of the time, food and eating practices are ignored or at best fleetingly mentioned, whereas political and economic states of affairs receive careful deliberation. Without a richer socio-historical account throughout the years, little is understood of the development and evolution of iconic foods that have formed the nation from a bottom-up approach. Historical process is not unilinear. It is the corollary of multiple voices and formations as well as trajectories stemming from interactions and relationships.

Food is a powerful marker and referent of identity. Our choice of food "reflects our thought, including choices of people with whom we wish to identify" (Fiddles, 1991: 33). Food is something that can be indulged alone or in groups, usually with much pleasure and little censorship. Universally available raw ingredients can be combined and cooked in creative and diverse ways to produce an array of cuisines that reflect different forms of societies and cultures. In the words of Lévi-Strauss (2008: 37), "In any cuisine, nothing is simply cooked, but must be cooked in one fashion or the other," with each rather emphatically presenting or expressing a great personal, local and regional variation or creation. Indubitably, the cultural transformation of the universal "raw" ingredients to the distinctly marked "cooked" cuisine takes on further symbolic meanings and relationships connoting corollaries such as economy versus prodigality: or plebian versus aristocrat. These aspects of food and cuisine as a positional marker take on "primary importance in societies which prescribe differences of status" (Lévi-Strauss, 2008: 39). As observed by Bell and Valentine (1997: 168), "food and nation are so commingled in popular discourses that it is often difficult *not* to think one through the other" and "a nation's diet can have a key role to play in nationalistic sentiments" (ibid.: 165).

Food history of Singapore

In everyday conversations among ordinary Singaporeans, or between them and visitors from elsewhere likewise engaging in everyday conversations, food, and eating are always topics of passion in the island. There is no doubt about the central role that food and eating play in reflecting the history, heritage, life, and times of the people. Yet, ironically, there is a paucity of the written account of the island's food history. In recent times, attempts have been made to redress this issue with works such as Kong's (2007) study of hawker centers, Wong's (2009) reflections of the wartime kitchen and Lai's (2010) evolving story of the coffee shop. Although none of these works presents a complete story of the island's food history, each is a crucial individual piece of a jigsaw that will hopefully materialize into a full picture in time to come.

Situated at the crossroads of some of the world's most important maritime lanes, the island of Singapore's advantageous and strategic location has been a crucial contributing factor for a story of the evolution of a rich food history to develop. At this maritime juncture, not only did ideas from major continents flow, intersect, and spread, so did a wealth of food and foodways. The early history of the island—from the seventh century when it was a part of the Srivijaya Empire to the thirteenth century when it became a part of the Malay Sultanate of Johor—has all too easily and erroneously presented, by and large, a story of a placid floating village inhabited by a small population of approximately a thousand persons comprising some 900 "primitive" boat dwelling *orang suku laut* (people of the sea), 20–30 Malays, and an equal number of Chinese. The cultural history of the people is presented as something simplistic with an account of their subsistence derived from a modest existence growing fruits but no rice, and a livelihood of gathering jungle yields, fishing, small-scale trading, and piracy (Turnbull, 1989: 5). Recent archaeological finds and in-depth studies of the *orang suku laut* reveal a more accurate account of the food history and what soldered the lives of the people in communities of that time (cf. Andaya 2010: 173–201; Chou, 2010; Miksic and Low, 2004). These works show that the island already possessed a rich food culture that was inextricably tied to the identity of its local inhabitants, particularly the *orang suku laut*. The identity of these maritime experts was already much intertwined with their unrivalled ability to harvest edible produce from the resource-rich marine environment. Their ability to navigate the seas to harvest every imaginable food from the maritime world provided not only food for home consumption but also delicacies for the neigh-boring world to feast on. Much of the prosperity and hence formation of the Malay sultanates depended on these sea-faring experts to bring in food items much sought after for this lucrative trade (Chou, 2003).

The culture of food and foodways took on new trajectories with the arrival of Western colonialists. In 1819, Sir Stamford Raffles and his contingent from the British East India Company stepped ashore in Singapore. The former pressed for free trade in Singapore to overshadow competing ports under indigenous rulers, such as neighboring Riau, or those under Dutch control, notably Batavia (Jakarta), where traders were subjected to taxes and restrictions. With the opening of a free port came the influx of peoples from all over to trade and work. Droves of Chinese from southern China arrived to work as coolies, artisans, farmers, miners, and itinerant traders; Indians arrived first as sepoys of the Bengal Native Infantry, then as convicts and indentured laborers, and later in the twentieth century as clerks, educationists, and merchants; Malays from the Malay Peninsula and Indonesian archipelago; Armenians, Arabs, and Europeans came as traders; and Eurasians entered the realms of law, medicine, civil service, and trade (Jayapal, 1992: 45–50; Lee, 2008: 21–6; 36–8; Turnbull, 1989: 12–15, 36–8). The population of the island swelled from just over 10,000 in 1824 to more than 60,000 some 25 years later in 1850. The immigrants brought with them an array of new food and foodways. In 1837, the American missionary Howard Malcom (cited in Wise, 1996: 40) enthused over a sumptuous Chinese wedding banquet serving sharks' fins, birds' nests and fish-maw hosted by a wealthy Chinese merchant.

On an everyday level, a busy and lively food scene was unfolding as the immigrant population increased. The first market was constructed in Telok Ayer in 1820, along the waterfront in close proximity to the commercial district and Chinese quarters. By the close of the nineteenth century, five big markets could be found in Telok Ayer, Ellenborough, Rochore, Clyde, and Orchard Roads. The markets were vividly described as offering a profusion of fresh local produce, which included fish, vegetables, fruits, ducks, poultry, and pigs in addition to imported meat from Siam and India, fowls from Cochin China and the Malay Peninsula, and fruits from as afar as China (Knipp et al., 1995: 15). Food vendors did not confine themselves to these markets. In 1865, John Cameron (1865: 65) observed that

> There is probably no city in the world with such a motley crowd of itinerant vendors of wares, fruits, cakes, vegetables. There are Malays, generally with fruit, Chinamen with a mixture of all sorts, and Klings with cakes and different kinds of nuts. Malays and Chinamen always use the shoulder-stick, having equally-balanced loads suspended at either end; the Klings, on the contrary, carry their wares on the head on trays. The travelling cook shops of the Chinese are probably the most extraordinary of the things that are carried about this way. They are suspended on one of the common shoulder-sticks, and consist of a box on one side and a basket on the other, the former containing a fire and small copper cauldron for soup, the latter loaded with rice, vermicelli, cakes, jellies, and condiments; and though I have never tasted any of their dishes, I have been assured that those they serve up at a moment's notice are most savoury, and that their sweets are delicious. Three cents will purchase a substantial meal of three or four dishes from these itinerant restaurateurs.

Eye-witness accounts described the proliferation of food hawkers throughout Singapore in the nineteenth century (Wise, 1996). Hawkers provided cheap meals and snacks such as rice, noodles, and cakes. Before the 1870s, the gender ratio for the immigrant population was highly unbalanced (Turnbull, 1989: 57). Hence, hawker food provided cheap meals to the masses of male laborers who had come to work without their families. Street food, with people squatting together in public spaces to eat, provided a sense of commensality. The combination of street food hawkers and entertainment formed another important aspect in interlacing the social lives of the people. Roving hawkers followed *wayang* (street opera) troupes on their rounds. Certain foods came to be associated with these street opera stalls—*ju her eng chye* (a water convolvulus salad tossed with cuttlefish and jellyfish); *ngo hiang* (a five-spiced pork roll with selections of deep-fried accompaniments dipped into red chili and pink flour sauces); desserts such as sweet potatoes in ginger syrup; *cheng tng* (a refreshing soup of barley, longans, lily buds, gingko nuts, and lotus seeds); and snacks such as *mua chee* (glutinous rice flour balls sprinkled with a peanut sugar mixture) as well as dragon beard candy interwoven with many fine strands of spun sugar.

Although a scrumptious landscape of new food and foodways was proliferating the streets; and hawker food was bringing communities of immigrants together, the British colonialists also used food and eating as a cultural performance to enforce distance between ruler and ruled, and advocate a social hierarchy. In the nineteenth until the early twentieth century, Asians lived socially segregated from the colonialists. In contrast to the Asians, mealtimes for the British in Singapore were a display of conspicuous consumption both at home and in exclusive clubs. Their meals were elaborate Victorian fare with many dishes augmented by Anglo-Asian curries and tropical fruits. In John Thomson's 1865 (cited in Wise, 1996: 77) memoir, he provided glimpses into such dinners whereby soup and fish would first be served, followed by roast beef, mutton, turkey, or capon. Supplementing this would be an array of vegetables, potatoes, and side dishes that included tongue, fowls, and cutlets. Next came various Straits curries and rice accompanied by local piquant sauces, pickles, and spices. Desert was a spread of puddings, preserves, various kinds of imported cheese, and tropical fruits. Sherry and pale ale flowed generously throughout the evening.

Food and eating were strong and regular ways for the British to exercise power. Such opulent fine dining predominated the British colonial society in the nineteenth century, with food prepared by Malay or Chinese servants. Until the 1960s, food was used as a marker for social distinction. Asians were banned from eating, let alone interacting, with the colonials unless on a master–servant basis. Seldom would any Asian visit hotels where wining and dining of the upper echelons of society took place. At premier hotels, which were mainly white establishments, such as the Adelphi, Goodwood, and the Prince Hotel Garni, guests dined on suitable Western menus.

Although Singapore colonial society was largely segregated with different ethnic groups residing within their own enclaves, and much as food and foodways divided the colonials from the Asians, food was also the very vehicle used to cross boundaries. Different communities acquired an appreciation of each others' cuisine so that Chinese condiments of soya sauce or Portuguese chilies became indispensable household items to satisfy the evolving palates across many ethnic communities. The complex blending of Chinese and Malay cooking developed into the Peranakan culinary tradition, while the combination of Portuguese, Dutch, Indian, Malay, and Chinese flavors formed Eurasian food. The disparity between the colonial and Asian, however, did not preclude the percolation of the food the colonials ate to the Asian population. The bridging of this gap was made possible by the vital role played by the Asian cooks, in particular the Hainanese cookboys employed in colonial households. The Hainanese or Hylams arrived long after other larger Chinese immigrant groups had settled on the island because of the relative lateness in the opening of Hainan Island to foreign trade and seafaring activities. Upon arrival, they discovered that other Chinese and their clan associations had already gained control of the more lucrative trades. Hence, as a minority group and one that was at the bottom of the social and economic scales because of their illiteracy, lack of specific skills and difficulties in communicating with Chinese from other dialect backgrounds, there was little they could do but to persevere and try to carve out a niche for themselves in more lowly works such as being sailors, domestic servants, cooks, waiters, butlers, farmers, rubber-tappers, and other unskilled laborers. As time would tell, though, their resilience and creative spirits would serve to their advantage.

Many Hainanese were employed as "cookboys" and "houseboys" by the colonialists, so they began their culinary training in the homes and social clubs of nineteenth-century colonial employers. Very quickly, there came a huge demand for their services as they became known for their loyalty, reliability, and creativity in the kitchen. Their British masters and mistresses depended on them to maintain their colonial lifestyle and to present food that would serve to legitimate and perpetuate their higher social status (Lai, 2010: 8). While they labored to follow instructions from their employers to produce standard British cuisine such as roast chicken, pork chops, pies, and cakes, they also acquired innovative techniques and adeptness to use whatever available condiments to recast the dishes (Tan, 2004: 11). The ability of the Hainanese cookboys to manipulate food and foodways came to symbolize the possibility of crossing boundaries. They made available their knowledge of Western food and opened opportunities for others to learn that the adoption of appropriate eating and food preferences was crucial to the attainment of high social status by demonstrating a cultural affinity with the community of the masters. Wealthy Asian families in aspiring to be socially advantageous would host fashionable and lavish Western-styled receptions or parties serving cucumber sandwiches, meat roasts, and tea instead of rice and *sambal belacan* (shrimp or fish paste condiment).

During World War II, contrary to the popular view that there was not enough to eat, Wong's (2009) documentation of wartime food and variety of recipes using local produce attests to the ingenuity of the people. The memories and autobiographies of how the people themselves recall their food history offers an intimate and vivid account of everyday life that otherwise remains untold in official narratives.

After World War II, an examination of how food and eating patterns moved in different directions has led to a deeper understanding of the changes in the political and social climate of the island. New coffee shops, bakeries, and other food and beverage enterprises were started by many Hainanese cooks who were left jobless with the departure of the British colonialists. That is, the Hainanese cooks had little choice but to use their culinary skills to carve out a new niche for themselves yet again. The emergence of this new food sector very much reflected the rebuilding of Singapore. The snackbar industry serving soda pop and hamburgers was soon cornered by the Hainanese. British colonial menus were replaced by American-inspired menus. Grilled meats peaked in popularity with the opening of American-style steak houses in the 1970s. The emergence of the Soviet Union as a super power in the 1960s led some Hainanese chefs to seek employment in Russian households on the island. Having thus learned to cook Russian food, these Hainanese chefs would in time open a number of highly successful and elegant restaurants specializing in Russian cuisine.

Today, Singapore is experiencing another inflow of immigrants and the everyday foods of the island continue to reflect "a highly condensed social fact" (Appadurai, 1981: 494) mirroring the webs of internal and external social interactions and relationships that the people imagine their nation to be. In this, we find the exploration and quest for self-definition. The promotion of official national icons such as the Vanda Miss Joaquim orchid or the Merlion sculpture has proved to be more popular among tourists rather than among the citizenry in their everyday lives.[1] Instead, it is the continuation of these imaginaries of food and foodways via unofficial national cuisines that continue to capture the imagination of the citizenry. Among the various food favorites contending for the status of the unofficial but most popular national cuisine as perceived by the citizenry themselves is Hainanese chicken rice.

Chicken rice

The dish known as Hainanese chicken rice consists of two parts. First, a chicken is poached in a rich stock of garlic cloves, ginger, chicken fat, and *pandan* (screwpine) leaves. The chicken is then lifted from the stock and immediately soaked in ice-cold water to ensure succulence and tenderness. It is allowed to rest for a while before it is chopped into bite-size pieces and then neatly arranged on a bed of thinly sliced cucumber on a serving plate. Just before it is served, it is drizzled with light soy sauce and sesame oil, and topped with sprigs of coriander leaves. Accompanying the chicken is the rice, which is cooked in a separate chicken stock that gives it a shiny crust and a fragrant aroma. The Chicken Rice dish is served with a bowl of chicken soup, and a trio of sauces: thick dark soy sauce, ginger purée, and a tantalizing garlic cum red chili dip with a touch of vinegar. It is a dish of flavor, aroma, and texture.

Although it is called "Hainanese," it has been documented that "the only chicken rice found in Hainan in China, an island off the southern coast of China, is made with the *Wengcheng* chicken, a bony fowl with very little flesh served with rice thick with oil and accompanied by ground green chilli dip. Hainanese chefs also use pork and chicken bone stock unlike their Singaporean counterparts who avoid the pork base in their chicken rice" (Singapore Infopedia, 2010).

Why has this humble street food appealed to national imaginaries of such a large portion of the citizenry? The much adored local food celebrity, Seetoh (http://www. makansutra.com/Makanzine/aug00/national_day.html) of the Makansutra fame wrote a mischievous but easily identifiable article for the ordinary person on the street:

> National Day is when I eat chicken rice. Why? ...
>
> If I can, I'll vote chicken rice to be my Home Affairs Minister. You see, every time I eat it here, it tells me I am home and the state of affairs about is a-ok! ...
>
> You see, I don't need massive fireworks, dramatic flypast and mobile column displays to remind of how much home means to me.
>
> All I need is chicken rice.
>
> Mmmmm ... I cannot quite articulate what this national dish reveals every time I savour a plate when I return home after a trip abroad, which is quite often. This $3 meal reminds me of my history here. I can hear the noise of the neighbours with their nosey kids waiting impatiently for you to vacate your hawker centre seat for them. I can also see the son of the chicken rice seller, a political science graduate, helping papa out on weekends when he is not on duty in the SAF. I can also smell the thick CBD traffic air whizzing by me—and my mind tells me, it alright, it's home.
>
> The simplicity—rice, chicken and cucumbers—tells me that there is greatness in this humble arrangement. Like the way this country grew up. Though alien in content, the ginger and chilli sauce add that zing that can only complete this Hainanese delight. Cliché—they are like the foreigners calling Singapore home. Polish off that plate and it can only be satisfying.

A narration of the story behind the evolution of the Hainanese chicken rice is but a fine reflection of the material manifestation of an evolving Singapore national identity, bridging the gap between theory and praxis of nationalism.

Wong Yi Guan is said to have been the first to bring the dish in the 1920s to colonial Singapore from Hainan Island. He started as an itinerant hawker plying chicken rice balls wrapped in banana leaves for 1 cent per packet along Hylam Street. Originally, chicken rice was eaten as hand-rolled rice balls (*bui jin* in

Hainanese). The round shape represented harmony and family unity. The practice of shaping chicken rice into balls, though, started to fade from the 1950s, due in part to government laws requiring hawkers to conform to hygiene standards in the preparation and serving of food. After World War II, Wong moved his business into a coffee shop along the same street.

In the 1950s to 1960s, Wong used his chicken rice as a powerful food symbol to express his (and that of fellow Chinese in Singapore) political sympathy for and solidarity with the hometown folks in China who looked forward to bettering their lives under the leadership of the new communist government. He renamed his food "Communist chicken,"—a style which practically became synonymous with chicken rice (National Museum Food Gallery).

Subsequently, the founder of the famous Swee Kee chicken rice along Middle Road was said to have learned to make the dish from Wong.[2] However, the name "Communist Chicken" fell into disuse because the communist insurgencies in Malaya of the time led to the questioning of the loyalty of those Chinese whose political sympathies lay elsewhere. To be part of the new imagined Singapore, one should no longer be consuming "Communist Chicken."

In 1971, the chicken rice dish moved into another realm. The then German chef of the Mandarin Hotel, a premier institution of contemporary Singapore, is attributed to have "created" the dish as a meal that is good enough for royalty. In a 2009 national day article, the following appeared in print in the local paper *Today*.

> When they travel, some people pack their favourite flavours, like sachets of chicken rice mix—just in case their taste buds get homesick …
>
> Before Chatterbox [a coffee house in Mandarin Hotel], several people would share a whole chicken. But Chef Gehrmann, who decided to put it on the hotel menu after he tried it at several hawker stalls in Singapore, presented it as a premium dish. The meat was served in individual portions and presented in a boat-shaped bowl along with rice, soup and sauces like chilli and garlic on a tray.
>
> With a bit of advertising, the Chatterbox chicken rice took off and soon, legions of fans were crowding into the coffeehouse on the ground floor of the hotel. (Ng, 2009: 8)

The hotel offered the dish at half price each year on August 1, the date of the launch in 1971, which is very close to the August 9, the national day of the island state. However, this special offer eventually had to be scrapped not because of its lack of appeal, but rather because the annual celebratory promotion appealed so strongly to the sentiments of the citizenry that too many people turned up each time causing a jam.

It is reported that the Mandarin Hotel sells about 4,000 chickens monthly or 16,000 servings of chicken rice. It follows that there have been nearly 9 million servings since it was launched. The chicken rice dish has won numerous national cuisine awards for the hotel. However, it is ironical that throughout all these years, the chickens have come from the same supplier from Malaysia (Ng, 2009: 8).

Today, Hainanese chicken rice is used to promote Singapore overseas. It is often served at international expositions and global events abroad, and in Singaporean-run restaurants overseas. Hainanese chicken rice is also one of the few local dishes served on the national airline carrier Singapore Airlines.

Because of the Singapore's historical links with Malaysia, it comes as no surprise that Hainanese chicken rice is also a highly favored Malaysian cuisine. At the opening of the Malaysian International Gourmet Festival in 2009, the Malaysian Tourism Minister commented that "Chilli crab is Malaysian. Hainanese chicken rice is Malaysian. We have to lay claim to our food" because some other countries had hijacked various Malaysian national dishes. These remarks led to a furor across the causeway. In this argument on both sides of the causeway, little allowance was given to the fact that both the contemporary nation states of Malaysia and Singapore were once a part of Malaya, and that the cuisine of the people tells their unique history and the heritage they share. For each side, this was a battle to lay claim to a cuisine that had greatly inspired the imaginaries of the construction of their nation state. As arguments were hurled back and forth over the issue of "Can you copyright food?" (http://chutzpah.typepad.com/slow_movement/2009/09/st-can-you-copyright-food-.html), the social history of the people continued writing itself as people on both sides of the Straits continued happily to consume chicken rice. There has been a call that "Hainanese chicken rice" is now so much a part of the Singapore identity that it should be called "Singapore chicken rice."

Conclusion

The historical power of food in shaping the bottom-up cultural memory and identity of belonginess, for the citizenry has not gone unnoticed by those at the top. In the March 2010 debate on the budget statement in the Singapore Parliament, a member of Parliament conceded in the following speech that,

> Food is another important part of our rich cultural heritage—one which has been and will always [be] an attraction to locals and foreigners alike.
>
> We should consider setting up a Singapore Food Museum. There is much room to develop this. This history of our food variety will highlight our links to the world. Our taste buds connect us. Most Singaporeans coming home after a long trip will always say that the first thing they must do is to have their char kway teow or laksa fix. I am sure our second generation new citizens who grow up on hawker food will also have their favourites. At the same time, we are also exposed to many new cuisines and dishes from our new immigrants. (http://www.straitstimes.com/STI/STIMEDIA/pdfs/budget_speech_by_baey_keng.pdf)

The case study of the chicken rice meal represents many things, including: both the articulation with the outside world and the people's own internal integrity and ability to reproduce by their food imaginaries a community of belongingness. Chicken rice as an everyday icon is not abstract but substantive, and, when it is eaten, the nation becomes physically incorporated or embodied by its subjects. By the very fact that the structures of food and cuisine are not fixed and immutable, but in a constant state of transformation, reveals how powerful they serve as ingredients to be studied for relations between the individual and social collective in telling their own history of imagined communities. The transformations in the diet of the people of Singapore and the case study of the chicken rice meal is but just food for thought on larger issues.

12

Feasting on Locusts and Truffles in the Second Millennium BCE

Hanne Nymann

Introduction

In 1889 the founding father of the study of commensality, Robertson Smith, suggested that the act of eating and drinking together could create an atmosphere of mutual obligation among participants (Wright, 2010: 214a). Today, drawing on poststructuralist anthropological theory, the study of food and culture is more than an investigation into how basic biological needs are met; rather, food consumption is viewed as significantly involved in the construction of meaning and identity (Fischler, 1988; Counihan, 1999; Scholliers, 2001; Milano, 2004; Twiss, 2007; Rosenblum, 2010). Identity is seen as a concept that can be negotiated and altered depending on the circumstances. Different types of food can express different types of identity: identities that can be both personal and collective, ascribed and achieved, or manipulated and feigned (Scholliers, 2001; Jenkins, 2008). Eating practices thus not only reproduce identity but also serve to construct it.

A growing body of literature has documented the connection between group identity created through commensality and socio-political development (Dietler, 1996, 2001; Dietler and Hayden, 2001a; Bray, 2003a; Wright, 2010a). Commensality is therefore increasingly recognized as a significant political component of ancient societies and this has become known as "commensal politics." Culinary practices have the potential to define and manipulate social relations, and through that political power (Dietler, 1996: 91).

Owing to the breadth of this theoretical framework, a whole range of complex phenomena can be associated with commensality and identity (Wright, 2010: 213). In order to investigate how these relate, attention must be paid to numerous details: what is eaten, how, where, and with whom? Observations over time are also important; why, for example, do eating habits change or why do previously edible foods suddenly become taboo? Studying all these contextual aspects of food ultimately offers insight into commensal strategies for political control. Studying all of these combined elements in detail would require an extensive corpus of information that is rarely available in historical sources, and ultimately forces a more restricted focus.

This chapter addresses the use of commensality in Old Babylonian Mari during the reign of the Amorrite king Zimri-Lim (c. 1775–61 BCE). The particular focus is on the two foodstuffs, locusts and truffles, apparently much favored by the king. These are examined in the context of how far this type of food actually belonged to a nomadic cuisine instead of being a part of a standard royal cuisine. Zimri-Lim's reasoning in eating these foods is then examined, following the suggestion that his motive may not be purely gastronomic.

Historical framework

In the Old Babylonian Period (2000–1600 BC, henceforth OB) the political landscape of the Ancient Near East consisted of a patchwork of territorial states and mobile groups of varying size and strength, all in constant competition with each other. This ever-changing political arena created numerous conflicts but also a thriving diplomatic scene. One of the more important powers was the Amorrite kingdom of Mari, centered on the city of the same name. The Amorrites were newcomers of non-urban tribal origin from the Syrian plains that had gradually filtered into Mesopotamia proper (modern-day Iraq) and very little is known about them. In reality the term

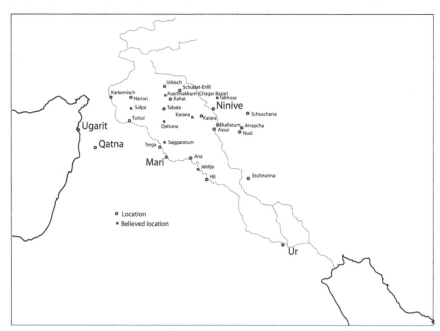

Figure 12.1 The world of the Mari letters (design: author, drawing: H. Barnes)

"Amorrite," coined by the Mesopotamians, does not describe a uniform people but a group consisting of various kin-related tribes, often in internal conflict.

It is not possible to delimit the precise territory for the kingdom of Mari as boundaries were often very fluid but it certainly stretched along the Middle Euphrates up into the Habur area (Figure 12.1). Situated at an important crossing of the Euphrates, the city of Mari (modern-day Tell Hariri) was an infrastructural hub that bridged both west and east, and also linked Upper (or North) Mesopotamia with the ancient southern part. Consequently many foreign dignitaries passed through this region.

Excavations since 1933 have uncovered a circular fortified city and a series of superimposed palaces. The last one of these, a 300-room large palace, had several areas related to the storage and preparation of food and even an icehouse (Margueron, 2004). Several artifacts including innovative cooking molds and decorated serving vessels have also been uncovered (Dalley, 1984: 88). This ceramic has traditionally been ascribed to the luxury of palace life and the refinement of the palace cuisine.

The textual material

A group of c. 20,000 cuneiform tablets was found in a small archive room. The material dates mainly to the period of Zimri-Lim, but some texts belong to his predecessor Yasmah-Addu (Koppen, 2006: 111–13). The Mari archive is one of the largest coherent collections of texts found in the Ancient Near East (Bottéro, 2004: 16) and it contains one of the richest textual evidence for commensality (Wright, 2010a). It is also an influential body of evidence for mobile pastoralism in Ancient Near East (Porter, 2012).[1]

The archive largely consists of brief administrative tablets detailing the distribution of various goods. Exceptions to this are the letters written to the king, some of which are concerned with the procurement of specific foods. In one case a local governor had apparently received a reprimand:

> Ever since I reached Saggaratum five days ago, I have continuously dispatched truffles to my lord. But my lord wrote to me: "You have sent me bad truffles!" But my lord ought not to condemn with regards to these truffles. I have sent my lord what they have picked for me. (Sasson, 1984: 119)

Another official reported about problems procuring locusts:

> … locusts descended on Terqa. Because the weather was too hot, they did not settle. But now I am sending to my lord as many locusts as were caught. (Dalley, 1984: 81)

The Mari tablets are well-studied in Ancient Near Eastern scholarship, although the entire archive still awaits publication in full. Archive tablets only reflect part of the communication (only incoming letters were stored) and the lack of context often blurs the exact meaning. More than one interpretation is therefore possible.[2]

As there is no consensus on the interpretation of the archaeological material (Gates, 1984; Sasson, 2004: 180n. 2) and archaeobotanical and zooarchaeological investigations are sorely missing at Mari, this chapter relies heavily on written records with some degree of ethnographical comparison for identifying foodstuff and diets.

Attestations of truffles and locusts in the Mari archive and in related material will be examined using a contextualized approach where possible. Textual attestations of locusts and truffles are primarily been identified using the *Chicago Assyrian Dictionary* (CAD), supplemented with recent excavation reports.

Cuisine at Mari

The people at Mari had access to a rich and varied diet. The main staples of the Mari kitchen were barley and emmer, whereas legumes like chickpeas and lentils only played a minor role. The cereals were treated in a variety of ways; some were roasted and then ground and mixed with nuts and spices to make an instant porridge flour. The main part, however, went into the making of a wide range of beers and bread. Vegetable species consumed were mostly alliums; onions, leeks, and garlic. Various spices and herbs, whose names are difficult to translate, were used to flavor the food. Meats cooked with oil or lard were mutton, ox, pig, rabbit, gazelle, and a wealth of birds, especially water fowl. The governor of Saggaratum employed professional bird-catchers to provide Zimri-Lim with the unknown TU.TUL bird (Dalley, 1984: 81). Fish was served fresh, dried, salted, or in brine, while dried shrimps imported from the Persian Gulf were used for a fermented sauce not unlike modern-day East Asian fish sauce. Fruits produced in large quantities were dried or made into confections, except for the delicacy of the first harvest that was served fresh:

> ... I am dinning on pears from Nawila; they are delicious! Herewith I have some pears and pistachios (*terebint*) from the Sindjar Mountains, the first fruit of the year send to you. (Koppen, 2006: 118)

Truffles were shipped as soon as officials could lay their hand on them and they were treated as valuable goods:

> ... the one case of truffles and the one tablet which PN sent me, now I am sending the case and the tablet which they brought me on to my lord, both under seal ... (CAD K, 1971: 120)

On one occasion all of six baskets of particular good quality truffles were send to Zimri-Lim (Dalley, 1984: 85).

Locusts were brought to the palace alive and the so-called *Hana*-nomads were particularly capable of finding them:

> To my lord speak! Your servant Zakira-Hammu (says): "About the *erhizzu* locusts concerning which my lord wrote me—over here is where one catches *ergilatum* locusts. There are no *erhizzu* locusts. I sent 5 Haneans, and in Musilanum of the district of Talhaya they took *erhizzu* locusts. And the road is far, and (most of) those *erhizzu* locusts died in the reed box. Now, herewith I have sealed 38 *erhizzu* locusts and sent them to my lord." (Heimpel, 2003: 431)

The locust could apparently be found in many different types or qualities:

> There are *sarsaru*-locusts hidden in the valley ... now I am sending these locusts to my master. (CAD E. 1958: 257)

The meals were created by an extensive kitchen staff that included a variety of cooks, bakers, pastry chefs, and other specialists. One section of the kitchen staff was responsible for preserving food, a job some did with better skills than other:

> Your fish roes in salt water in Qattara have been turning yellow for some time. Now, why don't you dry the fish roes? (Dalley, 1984: 82)

Outside the kitchen proper a dedicated profession took care of fattening animals with barley for final succulence. In one case the animal fattener did such a good job that the beast could hardly walk (Heimpel, 2003: 437).

As for drink, sweet barley beer or mead flavored with various fruits like dates or pomegranates were served in huge quantities, whereas wine was more expensive and restricted to the upper classes. A high-ranking official reveals himself as a connoisseur:

> To Mukannishum speak! Ashqudum says: open my storage room and send 2 jars of red wine, 7 jars of second-quality wine for the king, and 2 jars of wine of good quality for me ... (Heimpel, 2003: 205)

Commensality at Mari

There can be little doubt that a wealth of food was served in the palace; food that represented gastronomy at its finest (Reynold, 2007: 174). Despite this, palatial cuisine did not exclusively cater to the desires of the royal family and its entourage. Instead, a substantial portion of the kitchen production found its way to commensal meals, meals that can only be described as "eminently political acts" (Bottéro, 2004: 103). Evidence of commensality abounds in the Mari archive. Information comes mainly from administrative texts recording the disbursement of food; in total nearly 1,300 dated tablets contain records of communal meals and food layouts (Sasson, 2004: 182).

These meals catered to anything from small groups of local people to large state banquets for foreign kings. Depending on the status of the guests, the meal was often accompanied with distribution of gifts in the form of clothes, perfume and oils.

Different types of meals can be identified according to which person was the host. The king's household was clearly responsible for the majority of gatherings, but the queen and high-ranking palace officials also had their own households that could finance commensal events (Glaeseman, 1978). The occasion was primarily secular although cultic meal sharing also took place (Sasson, 2004: 181–2). Secular meals were imbued with a number of meanings and worked on different levels. Jack Sasson (2004) and Jakob Wright (2010a, 2010b) have amply illustrated how commensality was used actively in foreign politics to secure alliances with other states. However, meals also played a role in domestic politics as they included people from all sectors of society, not just palace staff and visiting dignitaries. The selection process even worked on minute levels, where an official could show his displeasure with a colleague by not sharing any meals with him. Meals were also used to create cohesion in an army that consisted of very diverse groups (Ziegler, 2008 in Wright 2010b: 335). Although these commensally established alliances seemed at times to have been no more than uneasy truces, and some were definitely short lived, meals were considered important in creating bonds.

Zimri-Lim's predecessor Yasmah-Addu had to be reminded by his father on the power of commensality and as suggested by Sasson (2004: 210) it is possible that his disregard of this advice eventually lead to his downfall:

> Rather than opening beer-vats and spending money, satisfy the troops themselves, natives of the region, who might come to Mari and defend the city … They should regularly be at a meal with you. Don't have them eat anything outrageous, yet always do feed them liberally. (Sasson, 2004: 181)

Sadly for us, Shamshi-Adad never specified what kind of food he considered outrageous.

Mesopotamian food culture

Before turning attention to locusts and truffles in more detail and the notion of a nomadic cuisine, some background information on Mesopotamian food is relevant. Food seems to have occupied an important part of Mesopotamian culture, although the evidence usually comes from elite contexts and little is known of daily practices. Despite this, the Mesopotamian diet it is one of the best known in antiquity (Radner,

2008: 475).[3] The educated scribal elite clearly differentiated between biological consumption and gastronomy (Reynolds, 2007: 173).

Communal feasting was a hallmark of Mesopotamian society (Brunke, 2011: 167) and the two distinct markers of civilization, at least as they saw it themselves, were beer and bread. That two refined grain products defined a Mesopotamian cuisine is perhaps not surprising as Mesopotamian economies were heavily agrarian, with an emphasis on cereal cultivation. Despite the importance of agriculture, the Mesopotamian culture nonetheless remained foremost an urban culture and Mesopotamian literature and proverbs contain several references to what they considered non-urban uncivilized barbarians, with strange foodways:

> They have prepared wheat and gú-nunuz (grain) as a confection, but an Amorite will eat it without even recognizing what it contains. (Chiera, 1934, no 3)

Using literature as a historical source is of course problematic (Mieroop, 1999). Earlier scholars somewhat uncritically accepted the simplified and polarized nomad-sedentary relations portrayed here, an approach that has now rightfully been criticized (Szuchman, 2009). Nonetheless, although the identification of the nomadic Amorites as the Other is a literary *topos*, it is a persistent feature that has existed since the end of the third millennium in Mesopotamia (Pappi, 2006: 241). It may simply reflect the views of a certain segment of society—here the old scribal world. As Porter (2012) however points out, writers' views of the world are shaped by their surroundings. A general ill feeling against Amorrites cannot therefore be ruled out.

Apart from this (literary) prejudice against Amorrite food only a few food avoidances or taboos can be found and then often restricted to certain groups or situations for a limited period. The inhabitants of Mesopotamia seemed in general to have had an inquisitive approach to food as exemplified in the letter written by a merchant to a friend:

> Tutu-magir sent me 7 *ushummu* (some kind of rodent) from the city Tur-Ugalla and I sent 6 on to Shamash-Lamassashu, the official. I kept just one to eat myself, and it tasted excellent! Had I known how good they were, I'd not have sent a single one to Shamash-Lamassashu ... (Englund, 1995: 47)

Today, cuisines or culinary traditions often refer to a specific geographical location (Cappati et al., 2003). There are extremely tentative but intriguing hints that such distinct culinary traditions did exist in the Ancient Near East as well (Milano, 2004: 243). One hint comes from an OB recipe collection dating to roughly the same period as the Mari archive (Bottéro, 1995, 2004). In this the writer refers to an Assyrian and an Elamite dish, thus indirectly marking them as distinct cuisines. It is not clear from the recipes exactly what set them apart from the Babylonian recipes.

Locusts and truffles

Locusts have generally been considered standard Mesopotamian fare. Kelhoffer thus considers it a "wide-spread and well-attested delight" (2004: 300) and further that "both rich and poor people ate locusts in a variety of rural and (comparatively more) urban locations" (2004: 302). Harrison (1980: 129) notes that locusts had been eaten in the Near East for millennia, and others have also considered locust eating either a widespread phenomenon or—somewhat contradictory—a sought after delicacy (Borowski, 1998: 159; Reynolds, 2007: 180). These much generalized conclusions rest, however, on very patchy source material that comes from two distinct periods in Mesopotamian history, the OB period and the Neo-Assyrian period. In particular, two Neo-Assyrian reliefs portraying soldiers with what looks like locusts-kebaps, have been utilized as evidence for an uninterrupted and widespread tradition of locust eating. The Neo-Assyrian period, however, dates more than a millennium after the OB period, and occurs in a very different historical and geographical setting. The word *erbu* for locust is actually first attested in the OB period (CAD E, 1958: 256), the period which contains the overwhelming majority of attentions and references to locusts between this and the Neo-Assyrian period are very few.

The textual attestations from the OB period can in fact be divided into five groups. The largest one contains references to locusts as a plague or use locusts as a metaphor for enemy armies, not an edible commodity. They frequently appear in literature (e.g. the epic Lugale), or in incantations and omens. An example is this liver omen: "If the inner side of the liver is curved in at the spot devastated by locusts … there will be pestilence in the Prince's country" (CAD E, 1958: 257). This material originates primarily from southern Mesopotamia. A second, smaller group also refers to locusts as a problem. This material consists mostly of letters from Mari: "on account of the locusts my district could not harvest (anything)" (CAD E, 1958: 257). The third group refers to locust as food. These texts are either from Mari itself or refer to other Amorrite locations like Qattara, Terqa, and Saggaratum, places that are geographically restricted to northern Mesopotamia and the Upper Euphrates area (Figure 12.1). A fourth group consists of texts that refer to locusts as food but unfortunately these texts have not been found in context. This often occurs if the text stems from either early excavations where proper registration was lacking or from the sale of illegally excavated tablets. Without a provenance and thus geographical origin they are difficult to use in an analysis of this type. A final group consists of texts where no clear translation can be established. This is due to philological issues as the word for locusts was also sometimes used for small birds like sparrows: "… and the locusts (?) for which I asked you do not forget[(about them], bring them with you" (CAD E, 1958: 168). It is also worth remembering that modern definitions of what is edible or inedible might differ from past ones. Items identified as food could therefore have been used for other purposes like textiles dyes, cosmetics, or medicines. One medical text thus relates: "you reduce a dust locust to small pieces, you pound it (and) strew it (on him) and he will get well" (CAD E, 1958: 290).

Based on the above groups, two rough geographical areas can then tentatively be identified; a southern Mesopotamian one where locusts were considered a pest and a northern Mesopotamian/Euphratic area where they were considered food. Interestingly, the locusts encountered in the area around the upper Euphrates, the lower Habur and northern Mesopotamia are different from those that visit southern Mesopotamia. As identified by Radner (2004) the latter is the well-known gregarious desert locust that migrates in huge swarms over large areas, eating anything on its way. The former is the less familiar Moroccan locust (Heimpel, 1996). This does not wander and has a limited habitat that today stretches from around Mari up into Turkey. During the mating season in spring the locusts are easy to gather by hand, which then serves as a method of pest control.

The gregarious locust has only been historically attested in the Habur area at three occasions, one of which incidentally took place during Zimri-Lim's fifth and sixth year of reign (Radner, 2004: 11). A local governor, not used to such amounts of locusts, mobilized the population as well as the livestock in a desperate attempt to trample the locusts to death (Heimpel, 2003: 420–2).

Further references to locusts as edible fare come from ethnographic material.[4] For example, the early traveler Burckhardt (1822: 289) reported how Syrian Bedouins collected large quantities of locusts by hand, in the beginning of April where the locusts were occupied with mating.

> After having been roasted a little upon the iron plate, on which bread is baked, they are dried in the sun, and then put into large sacks, with the mixture of a little salt. They are never served up as a dish, but every one takes a handful of them when hungry.

The geographical setting of where locusts were considered edible therefore coincides with the area of the Moroccan locust.

There are considerably fewer attestations of truffles in Mesopotamian material and almost all comes from Mari (Reynolds 2007: 180; CAD K, 1971: 120). Noteworthy, truffles are referred to in Mesopotamian literature as an unappetizing Amorrite fare:

>]He [the Amorrite] ... digs up truffles in the foothills, does not know how to bend the knee, and eats raw flesh. (Black et al., 2006)

The truffle found in Syria and in the rest of the Middle East is related to the better known European one but is less strong in flavor and odor. In contrast to its famous cousin it can grow in arid areas and produces a large amount from February to April (Shavit, 2008: 18). According to Mandaville (2011: 121–2) it is the Bedouin wild food par excellence, associated with the lush abundance of spring and hospitality.

Truffles cannot be grown artificially but have to be collected and require knowledge of places for good truffle harvesting. Today truffles are still particularly abundant around Jebel Bisri in Syria (located between Mari and Tadmor in the Syrian desert, Figure 12.1), an area considered to be the original homeland of the Amorrites (Pappi, 2006: 241).

Nomadic cuisine?

Is it then possible to talk about a specific nomadic cuisine? Except for the above mentioned prejudices, references to nomadic diets are virtually non-existent, and texts from Mari itself seem to indicate that, to a large degree, they did not differ from that of the settled population. In fact, the few references suggest a dependence on grain as there are complaints about nomads raiding grain storages or reports on nomads receiving grain as part of food outlay (e.g. Heimpel, 2003: 412). Mobile groups are notoriously difficult to discuss as they are often invisible in the archaeological record and identifying foodways is even more difficult due to various methodological problems (Riehl, 2006). Truffles have, for example, never been recorded in an archaeological excavation (Riehl 2006: 114).

Despite the lack of archaeological evidence, textual and biological attestations do indicate that locusts and truffles were not a routine part of a Mesopotamian cuisine but rather belonged to the semi-arid area around Upper Euphrates. Furthermore, together with ethnographic considerations, the evidence suggests that the two foodstuffs belonged to a nomadic Amorrite diet.

The Amorrites, and particularly the subgroup called the *Hana*, are in fact often compared to pre-modern Bedouins to the degree that some assyriologists simply translate the word for *Hana* as *Bedu* (see, e.g. Tallon, 1997). This is problematic as the socio-political circumstances of the Amorites cannot be easily equated with that of the Arab Bedouin (Pappi, 2006: 244). Most scholars therefore acknowledge that ethnographic analogies must be used with extreme caution. Analogies can, however, be useful in suggesting possible behavior under similar circumstances (Porter, 2012). In this case, the semi-dry and at times hostile environment fostered a subsistence practice that would have been markedly different from the agrarian Mesopotamian one. Different subsistence practices might have created different culinary traditions.

Limited material makes proper statistical analysis impossible and it is worth remembering that the Mari archive itself cannot be considered a complete archive. What remains today are leftovers of a much larger archive that was looted when the city was destroyed c. 1761 BCE (Koppen, 2006: 112). Also missing are the records of the meals that Zimri-Lim ate when he was away from the palace. This would comprise a substantial amount of time, as a large part of his reign was spent traveling, bringing with him his "alimentary bureaucracy," as Sasson aptly called it (2004: 185).

As for all the other contextual questions—how the locusts and truffles were eaten, where, and with whom?—there are only a few scattered references. Court etiquette seems to have been rather elaborate with each dish being presented individually (Sasson, 2004: 201–2). There is however no mention in the documents of how locusts or truffles were served. So far only one text has been identified that refers to nomads supping in the palace, here in the Mural courtyard together with a group of Elamites (Sasson, 2004: 182). The Mural courtyard has been identified in the archaeological record (Gates, 1984) and seemed a place reserved for important occasions.

The two identities of Zimri-Lim

Why did Zimri-Lim take such an interest in what otherwise would have been a matter for the kitchen steward or pantry chef? Could he have had a preference for truffles and locusts simply because he was very fond of them, as suggested by Stephanie Dalley (1984: 85) and Karen Radner (2004: 19)? It is of course possible. However, an important characteristic of Mesopotamian culture was its continuity and an apparent ability to absorb outsiders. The kings all styled themselves according to millennia old rules and it has generally been assumed that the Amorrite kings rapidly assimilated Mesopotamian material culture (Whiting, 1995: 1239). At a first glance, there is nothing in the material culture that allows the distinction between a king of old Mesopotamian descent and a new one. Likewise, the food served at the kitchen at Mari, with its emphasis on bread and beer, is by all measure proper Mesopotamian food. If, however, it is assumed that locusts and truffles were part of the culinary repertoire of the *Hana*-nomad, did Zimri-Lim as a Mesopotamian king therefore show a lack of decorum by eating what was apparently nomadic fare, a fare generally disliked by Mesopotamians?

A solution might be found in Daniel Fleming's seminal study from 2004 (slightly revised in 2009) on the political landscape of Zimri-Lim's kingdom in which he made two important observations.

First, the OB state of Mari was not a monolithic entity, a highly centralized state whose power derived from control of the production and redistribution of agricultural surplus, as previously thought. Instead, Zimri-Lim ruled over a tribal kingdom whose major components were two different tribes that consisted of both a settled and a mobile population (Fleming, 2009: 236).

Second, a core relationship was the king's interaction with the *Hana*. Zimri-Lim had in fact two distinct identities, one of which was Mesopotamian, and the other that of a *Hana* (Fleming, 2004: 79):

I told my lord the following, "[Certainly,] the Yaminite land is now given to you. Because this land is clothed in Akkadian garment, my lord should give his majesty honor. If you are (firstly) the king of the Hana-nomad, you are secondly also king of Akkad[5] (land)." (Koppen, 2006: 96–7)

Fleming points out that this nomadic or tribal identity is a surprise as the textual evidence, "so obviously assumes an institutionalized urban setting" as known from the rest of Mesopotamia (2009: 332).

The Hana

Who were these *Hana*s? This has been a much debated subject since the discovery of the Mari texts and today there are divergent opinions among scholars how to characterize their society (Heimpel, 2003: 34ff). Here follows the opinion that the *Hana* was the mobile herding segment of one of the two major tribes. Their grazing area was the back country of the Euphrates and lower Habur area (Fleming, 2009: 230). Despite the lack of a clear definition of *Hana* material culture, there is increasing evidence for a culture that differed markedly from their contemporaries (Heimpel, 2003: 30). As discussed above, the textual and ethnographical material indicates that locusts and truffles were foodstuffs related to the same area, with passing references that cumulatively suggest that the *Hana* in particular had the required knowledge to gather this type of food. On one occasion a palace official—not of *Hana* kin—sent some of his own men out to find truffles. Apparently without the skills of the *Hana* the men came back with toadstools instead (Heimpel, 2003: 429). It therefore seems reasonable to suggest that locust and truffles were in fact part of *Hana* diet.

Commensal politics

Owing to the attention the king paid to the details of his food, he has traditionally been considered a gourmet. The texts have therefore been read with an *a priori* assumption that the food reflected *haute* cuisine. The king's elevated position and refined palate was seen as the principal structuring factor in the production of food in the palace kitchen.

However, considering the importance of commensal politics at Mari, another reason might be feasible. Despite both mobile and sedentary groups being integral parts of the social and political structure of the kingdom of Mari, the king at times had little or no control over the various factions (Pappi, 2006: 247–8). As the king did not wield absolute power but had to rely on the leaders of these different groups, he would have been renegotiating and re-establishing his position, often on an individual basis (Fleming, 2009). The incessant travels by the king with his "alimentary bureaucracy" formed a part of this. As direct control often was not possible, Zimri-Lim and his court worked with different strategies to cope with the changing situations. Some groups were bound by contracts, others were coerced, and some simply paid. As for the *Hana* who formed the backbone of Zimri-Lim's army, Fleming (2009: 234) could not find any mechanism for control and therefore suggested their support for Zimri-Lim was on a voluntary basis. As Rosenbaum has stated (2010: 45) there is a connection between eating certain food items and ascribed identity. It is suggested here that Zimri-Lim used commensality as strategy, particularly by ascribing himself with a *Hana* identity through the eating of locusts and truffles, food that belonged to the realm of *Hana* cuisine.

There is unfortunately no smoking gun; no text that clearly states the Zimri-Lim dined on locust "when the *Hana* were in town." He would presumably have met and dined with them on occasions outside the palace, occasions for which there are no documents. One single text refers to *Hana* dining with Yasmah-Addu in an unknown location, and the supper seemed to have consisted mainly of bread (Tallon, 1997: 61). It might be worth remembering in this case that Yasmah-Addu was not of *Hana* descent.

Conclusion

Zimri-Lim's kingdom contained tribal structures that not only coexisted with state structures but also at times were the defining factor. The court relied heavily on local powers and therefore had to develop various strategies to cope with the local institutions. Installing a sense of solidarity through commensality was a common strategy in the nuanced and diverse mechanisms that constituted Mari political life. Social and political identities and aspirations generated distinctive strategies of commensality.

Textual analysis indicates that locusts and truffles were not considered Mesopotamian fare but instead were related to nomadic cuisine and, as food is a venue through which identity is expressed, constructed, and manipulated, Zimri-Lim's apparent fondness for locusts and truffles might have been a conscious or subconscious attempt to construct and maintain a distinct *Hana* identity. By doing so he sought to uphold his authority over his nomadic kin.

As demonstrated here, commensal politics can provide a new approach to otherwise well-known material. Closer examination of individual food items can allow us to discern noticeable variations. Future initiatives would benefit from integrating not only a larger amount of textual material, both diachronic and synchronic (and archaeological material where available), but also to use other avenues of commensal theories to compile a more holistic picture.

13

Commensality and Sharing in an Andean Community in Bolivia

Cornelia A. Nell

In 2008 and 2009 I spent a year in Cabreca, a small Quechua-speaking community in the Bolivian Andes. My main interest has been the area's position in-between the highlands and the valleys of Northern Potosí. As many ethnographies had dealt with the interdependence of the two, the middle had been neglected in ethnographic work but at the same time acknowledged as a zone in its own right. I arrived in Northern Potosí in order to examine this *chawpirana* (*chawpi* Quechua: middle/center, *rana* Quechua: zone) and how the inhabitants position themselves in relation to the people around them.

Cabreca has no electricity, and the next road is a three-hour walk away.[1] There is a wide net of footpaths that connects the inhabitants to the world around them. Cabreca has 58 homes.[2] My hosts were Clemencia and Germán, a middle-aged couple. Their son Javier was 16 at the time of my arrival. As he had left Cabreca to find work and did not return during the year, we never met. I was soon welcomed into the small family and treated as a household member.

Communication, however, was difficult at the beginning. My Quechua knowledge was basic when I arrived, and my new hosts and neighbors were not used to talking to anyone that did not understand their language. While it was difficult to communicate verbally during the first weeks, I understood early through my participant-observation that Cabreca everyday life is devoted to the maintenance of the household and thus largely to food. Agricultural tasks, cooking and eating dominate the daily life—and also special occasions. The production of food, its distribution, its preparation, and its consumption require a lot of time and energy, and thus became part of my own work as a social anthropologist. Anthropologists and other social scientists dealing with the importance of food as a social entity have pointed out how foodways and commensality express identity and belonging or exclusion. The food habits characteristic of Cabreca could thus help me to investigate Cabreca's role as a *chawpirana* place. I will here concentrate on ethnographic material that gives an insight into what commensality and sharing mean in Cabreca.

Everyday foodways

On a typical day my hosts and I would get up at dawn, for most of the year around 5.30 a.m., and immediately start with the breakfast preparations. Many times my host Germán woke me with his Spanish invitation *Vas a cocinar* (you will cook), or my hostess Clemencia did with her Quechua announcement *wayk'ukusunchis* (we will cook for ourselves).[3] We had some heated-up leftovers if there were any, and only then did the actual cooking begin. If there were no leftovers, cooking a meal was the first activity of the day. Mostly we would prepare a meal consisting of maize and potatoes, such as a *lawa*, the very common flour gruel made from ground maize. Grinding the maize on a grinding stone (*kutana*) takes a lot of time and physical effort. But even when there were leftovers from the previous day, the freshly prepared meal was essential to the morning routine. The meal was called *almuirzu*, from the Spanish word for lunch (*almuerzo*). My hosts referred to all hot meals eaten from a plate with a spoon (if available) as *almuirzu*. Only tea, together with some toasted cereals, is called *disayunu* (Spanish *desayuno*—breakfast). However, when people do not have any sugar, they will not have *disayunu* as the sweetness is indispensable. Having tea or coffee without sugar is not an option. Rather we skipped the hot drink and cereals and started the day with the cooked meal.

Sweetness

Sugar is popular and in high demand in Cabreca. Ellen Messer establishes that "[h]igh sugar intakes—where sugar calories are inexpensive relative to other foods—are often associated with the economic need to consume cheap food energy" (Messer, 1986: 637). In Cabreca sugar is not easily obtained. Although not very expensive, it does presuppose that the buyer has some money. Additionally it needs to be transported to Cabreca. And yet it is very much sought-after. The same is valid for sweets. Rather than being pure nourishment, sugar and sweets may be seen as contributing to bodily wellbeing on a different level. Stephanie Bunn relates that in Kyrgyzstan sweet foods are given to people in order "to help sweeten relationships and proceedings" (Bunn, 2010: 113). In Cabreca people will always bring back some sweets from town and give them not only to children but also adults. Sharing them helps to maintain good relationships. Another use of sugar I observed one day was when Clemencia had toothache and insisted on putting some extra sugar in her tea to combat the pain.[4] These uses of sugar, however, have to be seen in the context of sugar, similarly to rice, being a symbol of white food. It is not only white in color itself but also stands for the civilizational valuation of foods.

In order to avoid having to carry the weight of sugar I brought some stevia back to Cabreca from a visit in town.[5] Clemencia was reluctant to try it as she did not know it. Experience had shown her that sugar was very good, and she did not see the need for any replacement at the beginning. However, I offered the stevia again and again, and one day, when she had run out of sugar, she tried it and quickly saw that the sweetening effect was very similar when only a tiny fraction of the quantity of sugar was used. Not only was the stevia much easier to transport to Cabreca, but Clemencia could also carry the small plastic container around with her in her dress. Beside sugar and stevia we had some honey a few times after either Germán or a neighbor had found some honeycombs. The honey was eaten straight from the comb as a treat. This honey was called *misk'i* which is also the Quechua word for sugar, although when talking about sugar Cabrequeños used the Spanish word *azúcar*. However, the Quechua word *misk'i* is also an adjective and used to say that something is sweet or tasty. In the latter case it can be used to describe something that is not sweet at all. This linguistic link between sweetness and liking expresses the preference for sugar and other sweets.

Daily meals

Preparation of the warm meal includes a lot of time-consuming tasks: collecting firewood, fetching water, peeling potatoes, grinding maize, and possibly other ingredients like the hot chili peppers, boiling the water (which takes a long time because of the high altitude), and eventually cooking the dish with the ingredients available. While these tasks are undertaken by the landlady and sometimes with the help of her daughters or other female household members or visitors, other family members might leave to do some little jobs close-by or to visit someone. But they will return to have their *almuirzu*. Only after eating this substantial meal, everybody sets out to work and fulfill their tasks and roles in the household. In our home Clemencia did all the cooking giving me instructions to help her.

The activities and work carried out by the people of Cabreca often require movement. This appears to be a typical feature of the *chawpirana*. Due to its middle altitude at about 2,800 m above sea level and the range of altitude within the *chawpirana* territory the cultivation of both potato and maize is possible. People own fields further up and down from the hamlet and travel between them and their home.[6] When people leave their current home in order to work in a field that is further away or let their livestock graze, they take some lunch away with them. This can be toasted maize or beans (*tustadu*, or less commonly called *jank'a*), boiled maize (*muti*), or boiled potatoes (*papa waiku*), rice or any other solid food. When the workers do not take away lunch with them, someone, mostly little children, might be sent after them later, when something fresh is cooked, to deliver some lunch in a little saucepan or bucket. Also, in certain situations food is prepared in the field, especially during the harvest when potatoes and *oca* are cooked in a pot that has been brought along or in an earth oven (*wathia*).

When people are working around their main residence in the hamlet, they will have lunch there. If a woman is present, she will cook. After a day of work the people of Cabreca come home, and again the woman will cook. This is again a meal like the morning and lunchtime meals, an *almuirzu*, based on potatoes and maize and sometimes rice. Three big meals a day are common. If there is no lunch or lunch is only a dry snack, people require a particularly big dinner with different dishes. Although the varieties of food are very limited, people eat vast quantities of the starch-based meals. At first I thought it impolite to refuse an additional serving and assumed that I was being invited so much because of my status as a guest. Soon I realized that the quantities I was offered were normal for Cabreca people.

Quantities of food

Mikhuylla (eat!) was the imperative I heard regularly during the year. My hosts and I had regular discussions on my "not eating enough"; Clemencia would go as far as to tell me that I would die soon if I did not eat more. We had many arguments, some were humorous, some serious, especially before traveling. One day I had announced I would travel. But when I was invited to join a group of travelers earlier than I had planned to leave, Clemencia got very upset about me not having eaten sufficiently before the journey. She had planned to cook for my provisions later. Germán joined her in supporting the reproachful objections and asked me where I would eat. They both reassured me that people would not invite me to eat and that I would starve to death.

In Cabreca eating disorders are unknown of. Being fat (*gurdu* from Spanish: *gordo,-a*) is a desirable characteristic which indicates wealth, strength, and health. Due to the low-fat diet and active lifestyle all inhabitants are very slim and agile. After my first few weeks in the community a young man pointed out to me that I was not as fat and white anymore as when we first met. The results of the different diet and lifestyle, and of the sun affecting my skin were seen as something negative. His next remark was the question whether my hosts were feeding me enough. At the time I understood this as a humorous comment, but now I believe that his concern might have been serious and connected to the huge importance that is given to appropriate nutrition and to the relationship between my hosts and me established through food. Perhaps what he was asking me was whether there was commensality between us? I reassured him that I was given plenty and thus made a strong statement about my relationship with my hosts, about their generosity and hospitality. It meant that they had accepted me as a household member and were offering me big quantities of food in order to strengthen the bond between us.

Food and sharing

While at the time of my fieldwork a lot of the occurrences during meals that I witnessed daily seemed coincidental, there are indeed a lot of choices that a host takes. Although guests often seemed to be coming along by chance, not everybody was received in the same way and served the same food. Through serving different foods in different quantities and different ways messages were conveyed. And although the choices may sometimes seem arbitrary and decisions are surely not always taken consciously, they serve as means of expressing bonds. Some anthropologists have gone as far as talking about "the non-verbal language of food" (Bourque, 2001: 85; also see Caplan, 1994: 5). I want to agree that food plays a significant role in Cabrequeño communication.

As an anthropologist I asked questions that others had proposed long before to be the matter of the anthropology of food: "What do particular actions involving food (and particular foods) 'say'? To whom? In what context? With what immediate social consequences? To what structural ends?" (Appadurai, 1981: 495) As Mary Douglas demonstrates, "[m]any of the important questions about food habits are moral and social. How many people come to your table? How regularly? Why those names and not others?" (Douglas, 1984: 11). After a short time with my hosts I realized that guests to the household were given food in different forms. In addition I was a guest in many households and received food. These visits did not seem to be guided by some defined code-of-conduct, and nobody ever explicitly explained the etiquette of hosting guests to me. Also I am not talking about a form of commensality that entails sitting down together at a table. Yet the application of unwritten rules provides for much non-verbal interaction between the involved. Cabrequeño foodways have a big importance for the relationships between Cabrequeños and between them and others, e.g. me. Commensality arises from whom one invites and what the guest receives.

The quarrels between me and my hosts on how much I had to eat have to be seen as an indication of our then very different understandings of food. Their understanding is connected to seeing food on the one hand as crucial nutrition, i.e. a means that secures good health and strength (cf. Gudeman and Rivera, 1990: 28), but also as an instrument for negotiating social relationships. When I think about their constant worries now, I realize that they showed that my hosts had accepted me as one of them and were genuinely concerned about my wellbeing and about me having the nourishment they consider necessary. By ensuring that I had sufficient food supplies my hosts demonstrated my belonging to them. In Cabreca, hospitality and generosity are expressed and rewarded through food gifts; and food exchange and reciprocity mark bonds between people, between households. The women of the community play a big role in this. As cooking and serving the food are tasks that are normally the responsibility of the women, they decide not only what they cook but also what exactly and how much everybody eats. Commensality is thus guided by women.

Monica Janowski states that "those who are close kin, and especially those who live together, eat from a common pot almost by definition (although they do not always sit and eat together)" (Janowski, 2007: 4). Although food and family are strongly connected, Janowski also alludes to the problem of what kinship is. In Cabreca it was difficult for me at first to understand the kinship ties between the inhabitants. The terms that I heard did not mean what their direct translation might appear to be. *Subrinus* (from Spanish *sobrino*: nephew) could be one's siblings' sons but also one's cousins' sons. Germán introduced me to many *irmanus* (Spanish *hermano*: brother) who were his cousins (cf. Isbell, 1985; Spedding, 1998). What caused further confusion was that Clemencia said about people: "*kay waway*" ("This is my child") when she wanted to express that a young woman was *like* a daughter to her. Also, some children that would visit from the neighboring community called Clemencia "*jatun mamay*" (my grandmother) while she at the same time was complaining so much about not having any children apart from her only son who had left the community before my arrival. She calls the mother of these children "*waway*" (my child) but also introduced me to that same woman's biological mother. Clemencia always fed these people very well. Their close kin-like relationship was confirmed by sharing food.

Further connections between people that are not family can be established as godparenthood (*compadrazgo*). This is a very strong tie that is chosen by the parents of little children who ask someone to be the godparent of their child.[7] By the end of my time in Cabreca I was the godmother (*comadre*) of three little children. My social ties had been strengthened including all the advantages, obligations, and expectations that *compadrazgo* entails. Not only the godchildren themselves and their parents and siblings but also their relatives were calling me "*comadre*." They would often invite me to food. My initial difficulties in understanding kinship ties are clarified by Mary Weismantel's conclusion that "[f]ood, not blood, is the tie that binds" (Weismantel, 1988: 171). Many of my own relationships in Cabreca and those of Cabrequeños between themselves were established, defined and maintained through gifts of food, sharing food, and requesting food.[8]

Women as allocators of food

In Cabreca everyday life, it is very common to visit other inhabitants of the hamlet, especially in the morning and evening hours. If the hosts are having a meal at the time or have some leftovers, the guest will be served some food. The person that is responsible for serving a guest or any other person is usually the woman that has prepared the meal. This is common in many places, and some discussion on the woman's role has taken place in the anthropological literature on food. The hearth or the kitchen is mostly described as a female domain. In her work on food preparation in an Andean village in Ecuador Emilia Ferraro points out that the "kitchen condenses a wealth of ideological meaning, and although not closed to men, it is openly associated with women and women's socialization" (Ferraro, 2008: 265). In Cabreca, too, the hearth is the place of women and their non-verbal negotiations of relationships.

In the existing discourse on serving practices, hierarchy is one of the topics that is given a lot of attention. On the one hand hierarchy between different women involved in the cooking process is discussed (e.g. Appadurai, 1981: 498). As I lived in a very small household with only one other woman, I did not observe women assuming their position in relation to other women in daily household life. But when visiting others I could often see how one woman tended to be in charge of a second or several other women. This is also true during the communal cooking for *fiestas*. One woman allocates tasks to the others and takes the necessary decisions. Also I often saw young girls doing many of the cooking tasks according to their mothers' instructions.

Andean ethnographies, as well as studies from other rural places, have dealt with the hierarchy between the people served. Nicole Bourque describes how in the Ecuadorian Andes "status is indicated by the order in which people are served, the positions in which people are seated, and even the size and quality of the plates used" (Bourque, 2001: 93). Juana Camacho portrays a hierarchy depicting the father as being served first, followed by the first son and so on until the mother herself receives her dish (Camacho, 2006: 16). This is reminiscent of meal situations in Cabreca. The rules are flexible, but it is always the woman that serves the food who applies them. Appadurai lists the same criteria in South Asia and concludes that these "[d]omestic food transactions express the superiority of men" (Appadurai, 1981: 498; cf. Weismantel, 1988: 28). While Enrique Mayer also distinguishes between male and female roles in the household, he says that in his Peruvian fieldsite "male heads of household were seen as the producers and female heads of household as the allocators or managers" (Mayer, 2002: 11). Although in Cabreca households women take a big role in the production, too, they certainly are the allocators of food. Olivia Harris describes the Andean concept of *chachawarmi* as "the lifelong cooperation that is enjoined between a woman and a man" and notes that it "is clearly seen as a cooperation between unlike categories" (Harris, 2000: 179). However, although the division at the hearth is clear, it is inaccurate to describe the women as subordinate per se as their role as allocators of food and thus agents of commensality is crucial to the social life of the household.

The woman has undeniable supervision of the servings. Only once, when staying with a big extended family in a neighboring community, I experienced father and son undertaking the task of serving everybody present. This was a special meal. Clemencia and I were present as guests, and a goat had died and been cooked, making the meal a bigger one than just a usual evening meal. In the morning, breakfast was served as usual by the landlady. Even when Clemencia was very ill and Germán had to cook, he asked her to serve us when the meal was ready. This was at the beginning of my stay in the household. Later on, when Germán and I were alone at home and about to eat, he always asked me to serve him his big wooden plate. I had become the second female household member. Although this suggests subordination at first sight, the woman may also be seen as having agency when serving food and deciding who to strengthen social bonds with or not. Men are likely to be served first. But there is some flexibility in this. The serving order reveals the hostess's priorities. She may also express her approval or disapproval of a guest through serving others first.

The manipulation of servings

Pat Caplan describes how in Africa and South Asia the fact that women serve the men usually means that women eat less (Caplan, 1994: 16). However, Clemencia, although serving herself last, was also able to keep little treats for herself or for others, which would be served later. There was always enough food for her to decide how much she would eat. And often I had the feeling that she rewarded me with an extra serving of a meal component that she considered tasty whenever I had helped her with some hard work, or when I had brought her some personal present that she liked. Thus the woman in the Cabreca household does not only decide what to cook, but also what exactly every person present gets to eat and how much.

The choice of plate, and if so cutlery, is just as notable as it relates to the sequence of who is being served. There is a certain order of plates. In our household there was one big wooden bowl, a new shiny plastic bowl, an old deformed plastic one, some tin ones with plugged holes in them, and two smaller wooden ones, one of them cracked and leaking. Normally Germán got the big wooden bowl, I was always given the new plastic one, and Clemencia took a smaller wooden one for herself. But when there were visitors, this hierarchy could change. Germán still got the big wooden one. If he was not there, the most important (to Clemencia) visitor would get it. Women with children were often given one plate to share. But sometimes children got their own plate, which showed me that Clemencia meant particularly well with them or was rewarding them. Most people do not have a lot of cutlery. The first people to be served get the spoons that are available.

Everybody receives their dish and starts eating on their own. There is not much of a communal feeling during meals. People sit down wherever they like or are handed over a weaving or cloth to sit on and are allocated a spot. There are no tables and people do not sit together. Often guests sit a bit away from the host family. My *compadres* often asked me to sit up higher on a little wall instead of on the ground with the children. While people talk during the meals, there is no conversation on the contents of the meal. I have never heard anyone paying the cook a compliment. In Cabreca there is not much variation in the preparation of food. Women do not exchange recipes or invent new meals with the limited range of ingredients that they have. Nobody ever mentioned a particularly good chef to me. People never asked me how people prepare certain meals in Europe, but they always wanted to know what products there are. Similarly the stress in Cabreca is on what crops are available. If somebody has bought rice, this is remarkable, not the preparation of it.

When finished, the plate is wiped clean with the fingers and returned to the hostess with the words "thank you" (Spanish *gracias* or Quechua *dius pagarasunki*). The hostess or woman of the house then decides whether to give the person a second and then possibly third serving or not. Very seldom the person is asked whether they would like more. The feeding situation is less formal with household members. Germán would sometimes demand more food or refuse another serving. Clemencia would normally ask the two of us if we wanted more but she would not ask guests. I have observed these serving practices in different households. While there seemed to be certain rules prescribing the course of meals, a lot of it depended on Clemencia's individual decisions at the one time.

Not only is the woman important and essential to a well-functioning household, she also is in the position to "manipulate" the meal in order to get across a certain message and in order to negotiate the relationships that she and the whole household have (cf. Appadurai, 1981: 501). When a woman wants to show disaffection, she can do so through serving food. But she can also show approval by adjusting quantity and quality of the offered dish (Weismantel, 1988: 168). Meat is very rare in the Cabreca diet. When there was some meat, Clemencia could give different amounts to different people.

Receiving food

In the context of sharing and giving food, big quantities or the lack of them qualify the relationship between giver and receiver. Being given a second serving is proof for the host's approval of one's being there. It can also be the expression of gratitude, the remuneration for some favor or work or the preliminary preparation for asking for a favor in return. But, as Bourque points out, over-consumption and big quantities of food are not just evidence for the hosts' generosity but also "acknowledge [...] their ability to provide" (Bourque, 2001: 88). When Cabrequeños have acquired rice or some other bought product from town, they are very keen on sharing it. I always felt that that was not only a sign of generosity, but it also meant that the giver was seen as successful and being talked about.[9] Likewise some people were apologetic about not being able to offer me more referring to their poverty and lack of means.

While others have described receivers to avoid or refuse food offers and withdraw from meals and interpreted it as the denial of the relationship between host and guest (see, e.g. Appadurai, 1981: 501), I have hardly ever witnessed this in Cabreca, definitely not when the food was something that could be carried away. Everybody accepts food offers and shows gratitude. Accepting food does not necessarily mean consuming it at the same time. And the receiver does not have to consume it by themselves, either: "the act of incorporating food does not only involve food entering the body [...] but also the household" (Bourque, 2001: 87–8). Germán often brought some food home that he had been given in another house for work or some favor. Janet Siskind remembers that "[e]ating with people is an affirmation of kinship. Refusing to share food is a denial of all relationship, a statement that the other is an outsider. When people are eating and offer nothing one feels more than hunger, one feels alien and alienated" (Siskind, 1973: 9). While I do not recall feeling alienated and left out much, I know the opposite feeling: in Cabreca being included and offered food makes one an insider and kin even though not a relative of blood.

Food gifts

While I have concentrated here on offering and sharing of cooked meals, the points made are valid for gifts of uncooked staples as well. They, too, are used as a payment method and as a means of negotiating ties. While I did not see people being denied a cooked meal much, I testified how people, and again chiefly the women, decided *not* to give gifts of uncooked food to someone. In our household Clemencia was also the one who decided when to give people food gifts. One day a woman that I had never seen before was visiting with her little child. It was raining, and we were all sitting under the thatched roof. Clemencia served some food, there was meat that day, and I contributed the big boiled potatoes that a neighbor had given me in exchange for some herbal essence to help her stomach ache. When the rain ceased, the woman got ready to leave, strapped the toddler onto her back and slowly left the hut. Germán asked Clemencia in a suppressed voice if she did not want to give her some rice to take away. She refused and told him that that woman had enough and was not poor.

Many times Clemencia told me that certain people were *saqra*, and nearly always it was related to them being mean and greedy or begging for food. Catherine Allen translates the Quechua word *saqra* as "demonic" (1988: 39); while this is true in certain contexts, Henry Stobart's translation "evil, nasty" (Stobart, 2006: 45) comes closer to what I have found it to mean in Cabreca everyday usage: very bad or evil. Clemencia used it all the time to describe her parents-in-law to me. When I asked her why she thought they were *saqra*, she often argued that they had been asking for food or that they had not shared their food with her. She said the same about neighbors that would come to borrow some food. One of my *comadres* is also Clemencia's *comadre*. She has six children and sometimes came to the house to ask for help. Clemencia would often deny that help and afterwards tell me that Ester was *saqra* and that I should not give her anything. I had got to know that family, however, as very poor, and at the same time very generous. Even before I entered the relationship of godparenthood with them, they always invited me and treated me very well. Even the little children would always come and share with me whatever they had on their plate or in their lunch bundle. They always showed great gratitude for the things I gave them.

It is common for a godparent to give their godchild some clothes. In exchange the family of the godchild gives the godparent a rooster. Many times, after I had brought back some clothes from town, the parents of my godchild's parents came to explain to me that they had not been able yet to find a rooster or raise the money to buy one. On the eve of my final leaving they both cried and apologized, and assured me that we would have the rooster on my return. The manifestation of our relationship through this food interaction was crucial to them. This family had not only been inviting me and sharing their food with me from the start, they have had always talked to me when other people were shy or found it too difficult because of my poor language abilities. Clemencia's calling them *saqra* meant a certain dilemma to me. I did not want to compromise my loyalty to "my family," the people that had adopted me, were feeding me and calling me their "daughter." However, I did not want to lose a deeply felt friendship, either.

Many times I asked myself whether Clemencia and to a lesser extent Germán were driven by envy, jealousy, the fear of losing me, and the economic benefits they might see in my living with them or whether they really thought these people were *saqra* and were trying to warn and protect me. Or was something different the reason? The longer I was there, the more I became aware of having a certain role as a household member. Both Clemencia and Germán often lectured me about presents I had given to children. They asked me to demand an egg in exchange for sweets, or sell things rather than give them away. The more such incidences forced me to show loyalty one way or the other, and the more I reflect on these incidences now, the more I realize that at that stage I was part of the household as a whole and that the things that I brought from town were possibly considered everybody's possession. Did I maybe not play my role as a household member well? Mary Weismantel confirms that "[t]o return home after a journey without bringing *wanlla* [gifts] would be unthinkable" (Weismantel, 1988: 140). Whenever I came back from town, I immediately left the things I had specifically brought for our household with Clemencia. Germán did the same whenever he had been to town. I kept a few things that I had bought for other people without showing them to anyone until I delivered them. This compromise allowed me to provide the household with what was expected from me but at the same time have some separate social ties.

Giving food is an important social act. I had to learn whom I was supposed to give gifts and whom not to trust. This was a painful and long process as I often found myself caught between opposing parties. On the one hand I wanted to be loyal to my host family, on the other hand I did not want people to say *"no sabe invitar"* (cf. Harris, 1989: 246): "she doesn't know how to invite, how to be generous and share." Through sharing, a household offers commensality to their guests and thus strengthens the ties between the household members and the guest. Individual household members act according to these ties, and especially the women have a lot of possibilities to show their approval or disapproval of relationships through the distribution of food.

14

Dissolved in Liquor and Life

Drinkers and Drinking Cultures in Mo Yan's Novel *Liquorland*

Astrid Møller-Olsen

The Chinese writer Mo Yan (莫言1955–) is often categorized as belonging to the new historicist trend in fiction (新历史主义小说). This literary current, which evolved in China in the 1970s, viewed fiction and history as related subjects and merged them into a genre characterized by subjective realism, as a reaction to the official and idealised macro-narratives of the Cultural Revolution.[1] Mo Yan often uses food symbolism to exemplify the material connectedness of humans to society, while exposing the cultural web of meaning attached to certain foods and certain situations. In his 1992 novel *Liquorland* (酒国) he writes both symbolically and directly about the function of alcohol[2] in Chinese society.

In this study I have limited my field of research to the role of alcohol in Chinese literary history, with fictional, poetic, and philosophical writings as my main sources. Inspired by Roland Barthes I have discovered three separate alcohol "institutions" relevant to the analysis of *Liquorland*: 1) the commensal drinking culture; 2) the poetic drinking culture; and 3) the heroic drinking culture. Through my analysis I will show how the characters' relationship to the alcohol institutions can be read as a critique, not only of the same institutions, but as part of a broader critique of idealism.

Eating is signifying: Barthes' food institutions

In his 1961 essay "Toward a Psychosociology of Contemporary Food Consumption" the French semiotician and literary critic Roland Barthes demonstrates how food and eating can be described as a system of communication: "Substances, techniques of preparation, habits, all become part of a system, of differences in signification; and as soon as this happens, we have communication by way of food" (Barthes,

2008: 30). Food and food habits are not only products of geographic and economic possibility or nutritional values. Through repetition and cultural sanctioning, certain foods become active symbols with the power to evoke predestined situations and emotions in its consumers. This freezing of the symbolic span of a food product occurs through the normative powers of the mass media, advertising, legislation, scientific discourse, and, of course, through fiction. Fictional characters can be perceived as both symptoms of society build on the "average person," as role models for its populace and can serve as forerunners exposing and breaking the normative boundaries that form a culture.

In Barthes' literary theory certain keywords, or functions, are crucial in forming the fictional characters, whose actions then determinate the course of the narrative. Hence, these key functions have immense effect on the shape of the entire work. Likewise, words and functions attached to certain foods work to determine how we perceive the character of that food, and the function we assign to it in society. Eating is signifying, and different types of food are signs that reach beyond themselves and signify a state of mind and a situation. Thus laden with significance, the food not only becomes inseparable from its function (your colleagues would notice if you had champagne with your packed lunch, and expect there to be a celebratory reason behind it) but possesses the power to invoke the situation associated with it (opening a bottle of champagne, be it in a restaurant or on Mount Everest, produces a celebratory situation). According to Barthes, every situation in modern society can be described through food: at a fitness class you find protein bars and water bottles, at an informal meeting there will be coffee, and at a party alcohol is offered. If you changed the food items and served alcohol at the gym or coffee to people dancing, the whole situation would change.

When food becomes an institution in this way, with its own protocol of function, situation, and behavior, eating becomes a system of communication where every aspect, from producing and buying to cooking and consuming foodstuffs, has social significance. When we meet for coffee, it is for the purpose of having a chat in a relaxed and informal atmosphere, rather than just to drink coffee. The food item has transgressed its identity as an item of consumption and has become a symbol that evokes a specific situation.

Abstract commensality and food in fiction

If we take Barthes' idea of food as an institution which is indistinguishable from certain functions and evocative of certain situations, then studying food is a tangible basis for a more complex analysis of the abstract cultural web which it signifies and to which it owes its own significance. Literary analysis focusing on food and eating might provide less insight into actual cultural practices on a macro-level than socio-logical or anthropological studies, but it has the merit of providing an inside view on how people reflect or refrain from reflecting upon the symbolic and social roles of food. Above all, fictional analysis can serve as a key for investigating the role which food and food institutions play on a personal level in the case of identity building.

Following Barthes' idea of food as a social institution I would argue that commensality, normally defined narrowly as literally eating at the same table, can also be used more broadly as eating at the same symbolic table, partaking in the social connotations of different foods. This broader definition allows us to investigate how the rules of eating and social significance of certain types of food affect us even when we are alone. In this perspective, eating alone is an act of commensality in so far as it refers to a collective understanding and has the power to signify a situation. Because food in fiction is both used to emphasize the symbolic significance of certain foods, and used unreflectingly as a "natural" occurrence, it gives insight into what people contemplate and what they take for granted. The proposition is therefore that, in literature as in life, one never really eats alone; one is always at table with the rules and codes of conduct incorporated into oneself through socialization and education.

When food becomes an institution, or a system of hegemonic cultural understanding, on one side, it becomes a means of revolt and deviation on the other. Participating and sharing the table, means being part of the cultural hegemony, whereas abstaining from or ignoring it becomes an act of resistance. As we shall see in the following, alcohol has this role in China, and Mo Yan's novel shows an effort to break with the institutionalization of the food item, while at the same time relying on it for his own symbolism.

Three Chinese drinking cultures

The Chinese theoretician on China, Lin Yutang (林语堂), has described the Chinese as being more devoted to food than to religion or the pursuit of knowledge (Lin, 1938: 337). Comparative to the immense importance ascribed to food in China, the study of food in Chinese literature has been dealt with only superficially, appearing mostly as a minor aspect, rather than the focal point, of analysis. One of the great exceptions is Gang Yue's *The Mouth That Begs*, which provide in-depth, food focused analyses of some of the most important writers of twentieth century Chinese fiction. Indeed Gang Yue has a whole chapter devoted to the theme of cannibalism in Mo Yan's *Liquorland*,[3] treating the alcoholism of the novel as a sub-function of the corrupt carnival it describes.

Although literary analyses focusing on food are sparser than could be wished for, monographs treating the role of food in Chinese culture in general are more abundant. The same cannot, unfortunately, be said for studies of the role of alcohol in Chinese society. Most food monographs deal with the question of drink only as a question of tea, and research into contemporary alcohol culture in China seems to be a somewhat under prioritized field (Wei, 2005: 740). However, the tradition of the fermenting and distillation of alcohol in China is indeed an old one,[4] and one that seems to be an institution in Barthes' sense of the word. In the following I will present three relevant drinking cultures or functions of alcohol as found in Chinese culture.

One: Drinking at the table

Drinking as part of commensality is the first and main function of alcohol in a Chinese context. One does not drink alone and rarely without eating a little (or a lot) at the same time (Wei, 2005: 737). The most common attitude to drinking can be traced back to Confucius' lesson on temperance in the *Analects* (论语): "惟酒無量，不及亂" ("Only alcohol without limit, not reaching disorderliness"), interpreted to mean that only in the case of alcohol the upright man sets no limits for himself, though not imbibing to the point of becoming disorderly (Analects 10:8. Legge, 2005: 232). This hints at the great prestige, especially for men,[5] connected to the ability to hold great amounts of liquor as well as the great shame in appearing drunk. This attitude to drinking alcohol as a fine balance between inward capacity and outward appearance soaks through both fictional and other descriptions of the majority of drinking experiences in China.

Continuing in Barthes' terms, the commensal drinking institution is inseparable from the situation of the banquet, and it is soaked in a symbolic system of toasting, as a means of communicating friendship and establishing a masculine identity. Rejecting a toast is rejecting friendship, a condition that has led to dangerous situations both historically when the unfavored official had no choice but to accept the poisoned cup of his superior, and today where businessmen and cadres will literally die from alcohol poisoning rather than running the risk of appearing unfriendly at business, or official dinners (Lii, 2005: 49). As the reference to the *Analects* shows, the responsibility for knowing one's own capacity belongs to the individual, so alcoholism remains an under-prioritized problem in China in spite of increasing consumption (Wei, 2005: 739–40).

Two: A toast to the muse

The poetic and heroic drinking cultures are alternative traditions deviant from the mainstream commensal drinking culture in that they encompass the two only characters in Chinese society who are allowed to drink alone: the poet[6] and the hero.

The first drunken poet of China was Tao Qian (陶潜365–427 CE), sometimes styled Tao Yuanming, who renounced officialdom, along with its riches and prestige, to devote himself to poetry and Daoist meditation assisted by loneliness and alcoholic drink. His work and lifestyle inspired later poets, among them the

"Eight Immortals of Drinking" (饮中八仙) of the Tang dynasty (618–907 CE). This tradition of a close connection between alcohol and creativity is well respected in China, and include famous poets such as Du Fu (杜甫) and Li Bai (李白).

Another great drinking poet was Wang Ji (汪机590–664 CE) to whom drinking represented the way to enlightenment and fulfilment of the Daoist principles of natural life style and non-action (无为) through drunken indifference and contentedness. According to Wang, alcohol was healthy for body and mind:

> I am fond of drinking by nature; it is what my body depends on …
> I drink alone behind the closed door, having no need for companions.
> Whenever I get drunk, I feel that my mind is clear, calm, and peaceful,
> that my arteries and veins are open and smooth. [Drinking] not only
> infringes nothing on the world but also gives me personal pleasure;
> therefore I often indulge myself in self-contentment. (Warner, 1998: 350)

Like Tao, Wang also held alcohol to be the source of personal liberation from mundane concerns. The drinking poets shared at least three good reasons for drinking a lot and alone: 1) as an excuse not to enter politics; 2) when drunk, social conventions could be dropped; 3) drinking alcohol provoked an ecstatic state of mind, stimulatory for spontaneous creative exertion.

There is an obvious opposition between the collective, social and systematized commensal drinking culture, where keeping up the façade was essential, and the solitary poet's unreserved drunkenness, rejecting the superficiality of normative society.

Three: Heroism in a bottle and in battle

A third function of alcohol is as a means of increasing one's strength before going into battle. An example of this is found in the literary classic *Tale of the Water Margin* (水浒传 attributed to Shi Nai'an 施耐庵 and Luo Guanzhong 罗贯中 in the thirteenth century CE), in which a type of hero appears,[7] whose unrefined animal strength is boosted by the intake of alcohol. This berserk hero often grapples tigers with his bare hands, and in that way corresponds with the masculine ideal of the mainstream drinking culture. On the other hand he is a loner, often expelled because of his uncontrollable temper, and disregard for the norms and manners of society. He is a kind of hybrid between the strong and loyal macho figure idealized by the commensal drinkers, and the spontaneous and self-guided individualist image of the drinking artist.

Apart from these three drinking cultures to be found the Chinese literary history, another type of drinker is relevant to the reading of *Liquorland*: the drinking detective of the American hard boiled fiction.[8] Rita Rippetoe, in her book *Booze and the Private Eye*, argues that this figure, in many ways a twentieth-century Western equivalent of the tiger-quelling Chinese berserk hero, uses drink to set himself aside from corrupt society. Where society is rotten behind the refined façade, the hardboiled detective protects his honest core by a mask of degenerated immorality. Like the berserk hero he is at bottom honest, loyal, and heroic, but his methods are crude and socially unacceptable.

Rippetoe notes that "[Western] authors have observed that characters can be defined, in part, by what, how much, how, and with whom they drink" (Rippetoe, 2004: 5)—an observation equally valid in a Chinese context as we shall see. She goes on to assert that the essential toughness of the private detective is in part imbedded in his ability to hold liquor, but that the price of this toughness is isolation. Like the Chinese lone drinkers, his masculine capacity for alcohol earns him the admiration of others, but his raw and individualistic habits exclude him from high society.[9]

Apart from these three Chinese drinking cultures, alcohol has played a significant role in religious rituals and in medicine. Furthermore, the relationship between gender and drinking habits in China and Chinese literature is a field of study that appears to me to be both unexplored and extremely interesting. According to some myths it was in fact a woman who invented alcohol.[10] I have come across a few examples of female drinking poets,[11] and, though female heroes are quite numerous, whether or not they drank (and how much) has yet to be looked into.

Brought down by wine and women—Analysis of *Liquorland*

Mo Yan's novel *Liquorland* consists of three narrative strands: 1) the core narrative is a story about the detective Ding Gou'er who is sent to a place called Liquorland to investigate a case of suspected cannibalism among the cadres of the city, supposedly organized by the charismatic and powerful Diamond Jin; 2) encircling this story is a frame narrative which consists of the letter-correspondence between the writer Mo Yan (a fictive replica of the author himself), who is in the process of writing the core narrative; the novel called *Liquorland*, and the liquor researcher and amateur novelist Li Yidou, who wants him as his mentor; 3) this frame narrative is then again broken up by a second, less uniform, narrative strand made up by Li Yidou's more or less coherent stories from his hometown which is also called Liquorland.

The boundary which at the outset of the novel exists between the fictive and the "real" Liquorland is slowly dissolved as the story evolves. Li Yidou and the other "real" inhabitants of Liquorland start entering into the fictive universe of the core narrative, while fictive characters seem to spring to life until the world of reality and the world of fiction finally merge when the author of Liquorland is compelled to visit the "real" Liquorland and there ends up face to face with his own imaginary antagonist Diamond Jin.

As will be observed, this is a rather complicated plot, presented in a modernist split narrative form. However, for the purpose of this chapter the relationship between the protagonists of the two main narratives, Mo Yan and Ding Gou'er and their common antagonist Diamond Jin, will be our main focus. In the following I will compare these three characters and their use of alcohol with the alcohol institutions outlined in the previous passage. However, it is important to keep in mind the entanglement of the different narrative strands, as well as the continuous blurring of the boundaries between fiction and reality.

The commensal drinker: Diamond Jin

Detective Ding Gou'er, the brain child of the character Mo Yan and protagonist of the core narrative, is sent to Liquorland to investigate rumors of the cooking and eating of infants by the local cadres. On his way there he is given a lift by a female trucker, with whom he commences a sexual relationship, only to discover that she is the wife of the leading local cannibal, Diamond Jin. Arriving in Liquorland, he is invited to an official banquet where he becomes so uncontrollably intoxicated that he finds himself eating a dish which looks suspiciously like a steamed baby boy. It is soon obvious that the detective's weakness for women and alcohol renders him quite an unworthy opponent of the great and powerful Diamond Jin, and he ends up shooting the lady trucker in a fit of jealousy, whereafter he falls into a privy and drowns while trying to get away.

The commensal drinking culture, and its masculine ideal of drinking without getting drunk, is present in the mindset of all the characters of the novel, as when Ding tries to decline a toast excusing himself that he is on duty and the other officials rebuke him saying: "[...] drink up drink up drink up, anybody who doesn't drink doesn't deserve to be called a man ..." (46/37).[12] It is Diamond Jin however, and not Ding Gou'er, who is the one that lives up to this ideal. He is a veritable drinking star, capable of inspiring awe, and even love, in his less capacious fellow men:

> He watched Diamond Jin bring the last cup of liquor to his lips and saw a look of melancholy flash in the man's bright black eyes; he was transformed into a good and generous man, one who emanated an aura of sentimentality, lyrical and beautiful [...] There was love in his heart for this man. (51/41)

Alcohol as an institution includes a complicated set of power relations: when the local authorities offer Ding their toast, it becomes impossible for him to turn them down: "We can't show the intimate relationship between official ranks if you won't drink with us, can we? Have a little, just a little, to let us save face" (41/34). This is an example of the symbolic pact of friendship that the toast stands for, and demonstrates the symbolic and social power of drinking and toasting in a Chinese context. Alcohol is here an institution in Barthes' sense of the word, because it contains an identity for the drinker along with a set of rules that must be followed in order to obtain that identity.

Behind the enchanting façade, the drinking star Diamond Jin is the embodiment of corruption and power. Born in the same year as the People's Republic of China (1949), he controls the local propaganda department, and has the ability, like good liquor, to numb the senses and make even the most grotesque actions seem beautiful and right. Rather than being just an evil baby-eating villain, he is temptation incarnate. Falling for him is not only unavoidable, but simply human. Thus there are no raised fingers for those who fall victim to temptation, but there are, as we shall see, consequences.

The drinking anti-hero: Ding Gou'er

Contrary to the traditional heroic drinker, who drinks as a means of increasing his own strength in order to perform heroic, if not strictly moral, deeds, Ding Gou'er is no great drinker and alcohol only makes him weak and selfish. Instead of elevating him to a state of sublime masculinity, alcohol functions to lower Ding into the very depths of corruption and human desire he was sent to expose. Indeed there is a recurring theme of demotion throughout the story: "The decent was meteoric, and I followed my body down the shaft [...] Manhattan's high-rises stretch up to Heaven; Liquorland's reach down to Hell" (86/70).

In his downward movement down under the surface and into the mess of things, Ding's character is comparable both to the Private Eye of American hard boiled fiction and the berserk hero of the Chinese classics. He is a tough man, not caring much for the norms and rules of society, but loyal to his own code of conduct—at least at the outset. Like his American counterpart, and unlike the berserk, Ding doesn't rely on his own physical strength but has a great deal of his masculinity invested in his gun: "After taking it from her and assuring himself that his metal friend, that 'hard-bargainer', was still inside, he stopped sweating" (48/39).

What makes Ding fail to live up to the ideal of the heroic drinking culture is that he simply is not man enough. Through the novel fine liquor is compared to beautiful women (30/25), both being the objects of male desire. It is in sexual and drink-related situations that manhood comes to the test, and in both instances Ding fails utterly and pathetically. Under the influence of alcohol and female charm Ding becomes powerless, and he admits his own unmanly weakness: "[...] I'm a useless sack of shit to have been brought down by a woman ..." (238/185).

Ding Gou'er (丁钩儿) is presented to us as the masculine hero, the tough champion of morality and righteousness, indeed his very name boast his abilities—丁 (ding) meaning "man" and 钩 (gou) meaning "hook"; the human hook to catch all criminals (Yue, 1999: 276), but he ends up exposing himself as a criminal weakling, neither able to hold his liquor or his woman. Diamond Jin, on the other hand, turns out to be the incarnation of the masculine ideal of the commensal drinker: He is immensely popular with both men and women and he can down cup after cup of hard liquor, yet remain sober and civilised enough to recite beautiful ballads. Indeed his very name金刚钻 (Jin Gang Zuan) containing the character 钻 (zuan) meaning both diamond (one of the hardest materials on Earth) and drill, gloss him symbolically as the all penetrating phallus. The characters 金刚 (jingang) possess equally masculine qualities, as they refer to the fierce and muscular mythological figure, often termed Buddha's warrior attendant in English, who stands guard outside temples.

The simultaneous demotion of the heroic drinker and elevation of the corrupt cannibal behind the mainstream ideal drinker seems an ironic exposure of society's glorification of facade and lack of compassion for the real, and sometimes ugly, human conditions underlying it. The story of Ding ends with him drowning in feces: "The pitiless muck sealed his mouth as the irresistible force of gravity drew him under within seconds, the sacred panoply of ideals, justice, respect, honour, and love accompanied a long suffering special investigator to the very bottom of the privy ..." (330/252). In this world even the highest ideals, the finest food and the best liquor end up in the privy after passing through the devastating system of the human interior. The institution of alcohol, though like other idealistic projects not real in itself, is very real in the material reactions and relations it provokes. It is in these material effects, rather than the artificial principles built on top of them, that the novel encourages its reader to submerge him- or herself.

The drunken writer: Mo Yan

The frame narrative starts out as a formal letter correspondence between the famous writer Mo Yan and his self-pronounced student Li Yidou. As the story progresses their relationship become more and more familial, and the master-student hierarchy crumbles as Mo Yan pronounces his unworthiness of Li's pedestal.

In the last part of the novel Li succeeds in talking Mo Yan into visiting Liquorland. As soon as the writer arrives at this real mirror image of his own imagined Liquorland, he begins to fuse with his fictive protagonist Ding Gou'er and the leaky borders between reality and fiction break down entirely. Following in the footsteps of his own creation, Mo Yan accepts an invitation to a welcoming banquet, gets unspeakably drunk, and ends up falling for the masculine charm of the drinking virtuoso Diamond Jin. The novel ends in a rambling stream of consciousness passage presenting a symbolic fusion between the writer Mo Yan, now in the hospital with acute alcohol poisoning, and his alter ego, the detective Ding Gou'er: "[...] smiling like true brothers reunited after a long separation ..." (355/not in Chinese edition).

Li Yidou represents the traditional understanding of the relationship between liquor and literature characteristic of the poetic drinking culture. He compares himself to the ancient drinking poets, admitting, however, that he has not yet reached their skill in neither writing nor drinking. He possesses, however, one advantage that is sure to make him an excellent writer: his unlimited access to liquor as an alcohol researcher.

Li writes in his first letter to Mo Yan that he regards him as one of the great masters of literature, and continues: "What I admire most about you is your spirit, like that of a 'Wine God', who can drink as much as he wants without getting drunk" (22/19). Again we glimpse the Confucian ideal underlying all drinking cultures. Mo Yan, on the other hand, tries with false or real modesty to deflate Li's picture of him as a distinguished mentor in the arts of drinking and writing.

The correspondence reads as a confrontation of the young, aspiring writer's romantic ideals with the practical view of the older, more disillusioned writer. Mo Yan does not reject that alcohol might have a beneficial effect on the writing process, but he has lost his belief in it as a kind of poetic tonic: "I wrote the asinine words 'liquor is literature' and 'people who are strangers to liquor are incapable of talking about literature' when I was good and drunk, and you must not take them to heart" (25/21). As soon as the ecstasy of liquor has left him, he is just an ordinary hung over middle aged man, ugly and afraid to stick out.

Several of the novel's scenes visualize the gap between facade and person already mentioned in the previous paragraph. The Mo Yan character splits into two, as the person behind the literary icon takes of his mask shortly to describe the usefulness and problems associated with being Mo Yan: "Mo Yan is the raingear that protects me from storms [...] a mask I wear to seduce girls from good families. There are times when I feel that this Mo Yan is a heavy burden [...]" (331/253). The "I" takes advantage of the identity of the poetic drinking institution, but is in turn unable to rid itself of it when appearing in public: "Quickly Mo Yan and I merge into one" (332/254). As soon as people raise their eyes and expectations to him, he must become one with his mask and conform to the rules incorporated in that identity.

Through the novel Mo Yan is transformed from being the divine mentor of Li Yidou to being the drunken brother of Ding Gou'er, and through this process becomes the reversed image of the institutionalized drinking poet. To him liquor brings no elevation above the mundane world, no clarity or philosophical insight. Instead it makes him, like Ding Gou'er, sink and dissolve into the common human swamp of subconscious urges and primal instincts. Drinking reveals no truth, only humanity. The idea of a unified, godlike poet always able to drink and always able to write is refuted and replaced with the image of the writer as a human being. To the human writer, drink is not a means of escaping the world, but of joining in it.

Concluding remarks: One cannot drink without getting drunk

Through the novel three of China's drinking cultures are addressed and criticized for their unrealistic and inhumane idealism. The commensal drinker is portrayed as pure facade, under which might lie anything, even corruption and cannibalism. The heroic and poetic drinkers, though more sympathetic and indeed more human, prove unable to live up to the ideal identity associated with their status. The novel exposes the foundations of the various liquor institutions as normatively constructed and ultimately unattainable.

Liquor is presented, not as instant creativeness, strength or masculine success in a bottle, but more as shortcut to making things happen. It is alcohol that destroys the character Mo Yan's image as a famous writer, but at the same time it is from his indulgence in alcohol that his novel emerges. In the words of Ding Gou'er: "[...] liquor is mankind's greatest discovery. Without it there would be no Bible, there would be no Egyptian pyramids, there would be no Great Wall of China, no music, no fortresses, no scaling ladders to storm others fortresses, no nuclear fissions [...]" (308/236). Drinking is not simply good or bad, but simply productive, a catalyst of whatever might lie sprouting in the drinker. It sets things in motion, though not necessarily in the lyrically creative way tradition proscribes.

However critical of the popularly sanctioned drinking cultures, the novel still retains some very basic characteristics of these. On the whole, drinking is still a male project,[13] all the main characters are men and indeed the role of alcohol in the failure or success of proving one's masculinity remains a major theme. Women are not helpless or victimized in any way, but rather than possessing the power to influence the narrative, to succeed or to fail, their power is more like that of a bottle of liquor to which they are constantly compared, to bring a man bliss or destruction.

Although somewhat limited by the incorporated norms of the very institution it tries to break up, the novel can be read as an attempt to redefine the role of liquor in society, and in a broader reading to redefine society's attitude towards life. From having been a means of *idealistic identification* with various civilizing, artistic or heroic ideals, alcohol becomes a remedy for *corporeal awareness* of the human condition and of those desires which create, control, and form it. Liquor can not and should not elevate one to philosophical mountain tops, but rather cause one to sink into the muddy waters of life and into direct, personal and even carnal relations with other people.

In the beginning of this chapter I stated that even eating alone could be named an act of commensality, as common cultural eating practices are incorporated into the individual. My reading of *Liquorland* however, points to the metabolic, rather than the symbolic, act of eating. Eating may be signifying, but it is also consumption of food. The powerful consequences of food symbolism must not lead to forgetfulness of the equally real effects on the physical level.

Seen in the light of the principles of the new historicist trend in fiction outlined in the introduction, the fact that both writer and detective become enmeshed in the very activities they are to investigate/describe, makes their work no less valid. To write a realistic story it is necessary to experience the life you write about. To investigate the underside of society you must let yourself sink down below the surface. The poetic ideal presented in this novel differs from the drinking poet's secluded life of beauty and meditation; on the contrary, it stresses the need for involvement. The conclusion that can be drawn from this new figure of the human writer seems to be that you cannot write about reality without getting your hands dirty and you cannot, no matter what Confucius might say, drink without getting drunk. All else belongs to the artificial idealism of Diamond Jin's propaganda department.

15

Justifications for Foodways and the Study of Commensality[1]

Jordan D. Rosenblum

In 1724, Benjamin Franklin, a founding father of the United States and noted polymath, was traveling aboard a ship, which, due to a lack of wind in its sails, sat idle off the New England coast. At the time, Franklin had resolved to be a vegetarian. However, as he smelled the aroma of freshly caught cod sizzling in his shipmates' frying pans, Franklin began to rethink his dietary regimen. He quickly decided that, since cod are a fish that consume other fish, it seemed logical that he, in turn, could eat them. After positioning himself within the food chain, Franklin concludes: "So convenient a thing it is to be a *reasonable creature*, since it enables one to find or make a reason for everything one has a mind to do" (Franklin, 2005: 31, original emphasis).

I use Franklin's astute observation to frame my current project. I am interested in how cultures critique and defend foodways. While scholars have discussed cross-culturally how and why "We" eat the way "We" do and "They" eat the way "They" do, I do not think that enough attention has been paid to the internal and external justifications for this cuisine. My dataset for this project is the Jewish food laws. In particular, I am interested in how ancient Jews defended the kosher laws and how ancient others—including Greeks, Romans, and early Christians—critiqued these practices. Due to length constraints, I will focus in this chapter only on the apologies for the kosher laws, known in Hebrew as *kashrut*.

While the kosher laws originate in the Hebrew Bible, one cannot understand *kashrut* solely by consulting Leviticus or Deuteronomy. This is because *kashrut* as a foodway developed over time and involved interpretations, expansions, augmentations, and innovations of the biblical texts. Yet, biblical texts are used to justify every interpretation, expansion, augmentation, and innovation. This circularity—namely that *kashrut* extends well beyond the Hebrew Bible but, in doing so, relies upon the authority of the Hebrew Bible—becomes important when one makes an obvious, but all-too-often ignored, observation: namely, that the Hebrew Bible lacks an explicit rationale for the dietary laws contained therein. When the texts themselves do provide some justifications, they are brief and unsatisfying. To offer the most common justifications: the Israelites should not eat specific foods because: 1) God is holy and Israel is a holy people; 2) Israel is a people set apart so it should set apart certain foods; and 3) God says so.

While scholars have attempted to provide them, every discussion of the biblical food laws must start with the fact that these texts do not supply explicit rationales for biblical food selections. This is where Mary Douglas, Marvin Harris, and others have erred. In their attempts to provide a justification for this cuisine, they never account for this basic absence of evidence. However, this can easily be overcome. Once we move beyond the Hebrew Bible, we encounter numerous texts that fill in this gap. In these texts, ancient Jewish exegetes accept the authority of the biblical texts, but seek to offer explicit rationales for biblical legislation. It is in these corpora that we find our first real ancient apologies for the kosher laws.

In this chapter, I will focus on three texts.[2] The first text is from Philo, who was a Jewish philosopher who lived from circa 20 BCE to 50 CE in Alexandria, Egypt. In his day, Alexandria was a major cosmopolitan center of commerce, culture, and education. Writing in Greek, Philo seeks to explain Jewish belief and practice through the lens of Greek philosophy. He thus uses Greek philosophy to articulate the rationality of biblical laws. For Philo, the laws operate on both the literal and allegorical levels, though the latter is understood only by a select few.

With this in mind, we can now turn to the relevant passage from Philo. In explaining the rationale for the biblical legislation concerning not cooking the meat of a kid in its mother's milk, Philo states:

> But so prolific is he [= Moses] in virtue and versatile in giving admirable lessons, that not content with his own prowess, he challenges it to further contest … He now crowns his bounty with the words "Thou shalt not see the a lamb in his mother's milk." For he held that it was grossly improper that the substance which fed the living animal should be used to season and flavour the same after its death, and that while nature provided for its conservation by creating the stream of milk and ordaining that it should pass through the mother's breasts as through conduits, the license of man should rise to such a height as to misuse what had sustained its life to destroy also the body which remains in existence. If indeed anyone thinks good to boil flesh in milk, let him do so without cruelty and keeping clear of impiety. Everywhere there are herds of cattle innumerable, which are milked everyday by cowherds, goat-herds and shepherds, whose chief source of income as cattle rearers is milk, sometimes liquid and sometimes condensed and coagulated into cheese; and since milk is so abundant, the person who boils the flesh of lambs or kids or any other young animal in their mother's milk, shows himself cruelly brutal in character and gelded of compassion, that most vital of emotions and most nearly akin to the rational soul. (*Special Laws* 4: 106–8)[3]

Philo interprets this biblical prohibition as a lesson in ethics. Seasoning the meat of a baby animal with the very milk that once sustained it is reprehensible, since it mixes the domains of life and death. For Philo, such a practice goes beyond the pale and is simply cruel. This does not mean, however, that Philo disapproves of eating meat and milk in general. That prohibition will come later with the rabbis. Here, Philo's concern is not a general meat-and-milk matter, but rather a specific ethical matter reflected in the "cruelly brutal" practice of consuming the milk of a mother together with the meat of her child.

While the Hebrew Bible prohibits cooking a kid in its mother's milk on three separate occasions, it never provides an explicit rationale for doing so.[4] For Philo, however, the justification is clear: an ethical eater is an ethical person. And since an ethical eater would never be so cruel as to season the dead with the liquid that once nourished and sustained it, the ethical person must follow this dietary and moral prescription.

Philo, among other roughly contemporary authors, represents a pivotal moment in the history of Jewish food when he asks an important question: why? Although he understands these biblical regulations as binding, he also seeks to explain *why* these particular rules were commanded. The importance of this shift for the study of Jewish food laws is often missed by scholars. At this moment, Philo, and others like him, seems to be saying: "We agree that God commanded these rules. So what do they mean?"

The ancient rabbis, who lived from roughly 70 to 640 CE in both Roman Palestine and Sassanian Babylon, ask this question, in various ways and on various occasions, and predictably they arrive at various answers.[5] Here, we will discuss two examples; however, many more could be marshaled. In our first example, the rabbis puzzle over what is intended by the wording of Leviticus 11.2, which states: "These are the *living things* that you may eat …"[6] This biblical passage contains a detailed description of the kinds of domesticated quadrupeds that the Israelites are allowed to eat. While the divine commands requiring cud-chewing and split hooves are clear enough for the rabbis, they puzzle over the specific wording of this initial phrase. Why "living things" (often translated simply as "creatures") rather than some other word? For the rabbis, no word in the Hebrew Bible is incidental or accidental. Each word is intentional and instructive. In accordance with this basic hermeneutical principle, the rabbis' job is to determine the intended meaning of each word. This is not to say that they only accept one, singular meaning for a given word; on the contrary, multiple "precise" meanings are accepted, and even celebrated, in rabbinic thought. In *Leviticus Rabbah* 13.2, a fifth-century text edited in Palestine, one possible explanation is offered for that initial phrase in Leviticus 11.2.

Rabbi Tanhum son of Hanilai said: This may be compared with the case of a physician who went to visit two sick persons, one who would live, and another who would die. To the one who would live, he said, "This and that you may not eat." But in regard to the one would die, he said to them,[7] "Whatever he wants [to eat], bring it to him." Thus, of the [other] nations of the world, who are not destined for the life of the World to Come, [it is written in regard to them,] "[Every moving thing that lives shall be food for you]; as the green herbs, I have given you all" [Genesis 9:3]. But to Israel, who are destined for the life of the World to Come, [it is written], "These are the *living things* that you may eat, from among all of the domesticated quadrupeds that are upon the earth" [Leviticus 11.2]. (emphasis added)

To understand this passage, two pieces of information are necessary. First, as previously noted, Leviticus 11.2 uses the Hebrew word *haḥayya*, literally meaning "living things," when it could have used many other words. Further, the wording of Leviticus 11.2 is verbose, stating: "These are the living things which you may eat, from among all of the domesticated quadrupeds that are upon the earth." In contrast, in a parallel passage, Deuteronomy 14.4 omits the word "*haḥayya*" and simply states: "These are the domesticated quadrupeds that you may eat." For the rabbis, these two facts are significant, since they understand each word in the Hebrew Bible to be intentional and, thus, potentially laden with pedagogical meaning. Second, the rabbis believe that there are two worlds: the present world and the World to Come. The World to Come, a future world in which the righteous will be rewarded and the wicked punished, is often used to solve the problem of theodicy, or divine justice.

For the rabbis, then, "living things" appears in Leviticus 11.2 in order to make a theological (and eschatological) point. In order to participate in the World to Come, one must eat only "living" things and not "all" things. Thus, non-Jews who may eat "all" food in this world, as specified in the Noahide commandments given in Genesis 9, do not gain entrance into the World to Come. In contrast, Jews (whom the rabbis call "Israel" here) are commanded to avoid certain foods and only eat "living things." As a result, they are able to enter the World to Come. Since eating is a biological necessity, it is a matter of life or death. For the rabbis, it is also a matter of eternal life or eternal death. Out of their concern for eternal life, therefore, Jews are supposed to avoid certain foods. In the end, however, this ban will be lifted. As *Leviticus Rabbah* 13.3 explains, in the World to Come, the dietary laws will change, with the result that Jews will then be allowed to eat those foods tabooed in this world. Until that time, Jews must follow Leviticus 11.2 and only eat "living things"—the sole (soul?) diet that contains all of the essential vitamins and nutrients necessary for entering the World to Come.

Thus, the rabbis' explication of "living things" in Leviticus 11.2 provides an answer to the "why?" question of special dietary rules: entrance to the World to Come is at stake. *Kashrut*, however, is not only about *what* one eats; it is also concerned about *with whom* one eats.[8] As this is a volume on commensality, I will discuss one final text that expands *kashrut* into the domain of the diner and not just the dinner. *Sifrei Numbers* 131, a text edited in late third-century Roman Palestine, addresses the issue of sharing a table with a non-Jewish woman. This issue arises in the midst of a discussion of a biblical text, Numbers 25.1–3, which details how

Moabite women seduced Israelite men, enticing them to worship Ba'al Pe'or, whom the text considered to be a false god. Interpreting this event, the text states:

> She [a Moabite woman] would say to him [an Israelite man]: "Would you like to drink [some] wine?" He would drink and the wine would burn within him and he would say: "Listen to me [i.e. have intercourse with me]!" She would take out an image of Pe'or from under her bra and say to him: "Rabbi, is it your desire that I listen to you? [If so, then] bow to this!"

Drinking together is the first step down a slippery slope that quickly devolves into idolatry. While wine is associated with idolatry by the rabbis, since it is the only beverage libated in Pagan rituals, a later Talmudic text even extends this prohibition to non-wine intoxicants. And what is the reason given for this extension? "Because of intermarriage."[9] Long before the age of Internet dating, the rabbis knew that a bar was a great place to meet women; they thus add food regulations that limited certain commensal encounters, which they justify on both biblical and social grounds. Biblical warnings concerning whoring after other gods and the sins of idolatry are situated at the rabbinic table,[10] where indiscriminate table-fellowship can lead to illicit sexuality and idolatrous worship. For the rabbis, then, it is better to choose your drink and your drinking companions quite carefully, lest you suffer dire consequences.

So what do these texts add to our discussion in this volume? More than I have space to discuss in depth. However, I will briefly note three main points. First, *kashrut* is the rabbinic cuisine. In using the term "cuisine," I follow Warren Belasco's definition, which defines "cuisine" as:

> a set of socially situated food behaviors with these components: a limited number of "edible" foods (*selectivity*); a preference for particular ways of preparing food (*technique*); a distinctive flavor, textural, and visual characteristics (*aesthetics*); a set of rules for consuming food (*ritual*); and an organized system of producing and distributing the food (*infrastructure*). Embedded in these components are a set of ideas, images, and values (*ideology*) that can be "read" just like any other cultural "text". (2005: 219–20, original emphasis)

In order to understand a cuisine, therefore, one must understand how and why a group chooses to eat the way it does. This is especially the case when that group spills so much ink justifying their cuisine. And, since commensality is but one aspect of cuisine, scholars must make sure to situate it in its larger culinary context. To rationalize what and how to eat is thus both to create and maintain a particular cuisine.[11] As such, whenever a group accounts for why it eats the way it does, it is simultaneously explaining and creating its own cuisine.

Second, commensality is concerned with both diner and dinner. We must remember that the phrase "you are what you eat" has a necessary corollary: "you are with whom you eat." By looking at how the kosher laws are justified, we encounter explicit rationales for why these ancient authors ate the way they did. Before one approaches the table to share it—the very definition of commensality—many social and cultural criteria must be met. In explaining how these culinary and commensal rules are justified, we can deepen our understanding of commensality. As Benjamin Franklin reminds us, as a *"reasonable creature,"* a human can justify any action that he or she chooses to. Therefore, the academic study of commensality must seriously grapple with the rationalizations that are offered in support of particular culinary and commensal practices.

Third, the ancient world has much to teach us about the modern world, and vice versa. As the reader might have noticed, the title for this chapter is a play on the title of Michael Pollan's book *In Defense of Food* (2008). In this book, Pollan seeks to write an "Eater's Manifesto." His previous book *The Omnivore's Dilemma* (2006), raised a series of serious questions about the modern, industrial food system; he thus felt compelled to answer how one could eat ethically. By comparing Pollan's food ethics to Philo's or the rabbis', for example, we can begin to discuss how groups justify their cuisines. Such comparisons prove fruitful to our understanding of commensality, whether the topic of our inquiry is a convivium in ancient Rome or modern Copenhagen.

I shall end as I began, with a quote that grapples with food choices, in particular in relation to vegetarianism. Author Jonathan Safran Foer recently wrote a book entitled *Eating Animals*, in which he discusses the ethics of meat-eating. At one point, he comments: "There are thousands of foods on the planet, and explaining why we eat the relatively small selection we do requires some words. We need to explain that the parsley on the plate is for decoration, that pasta is not a 'breakfast food,' why we eat wings but not eyes, cows but not dogs. Stories establish narratives, and stories establish rules" (2010: 12). When theorizing commensality—which is itself a social practice constructed by narratives and governed by rules—we, as scholars, must listen to these stories.

16

The Role of Food in the Life of Christians in the Roman Empire

Morten Warmind

The Christianization-process of the Roman Empire was not a quick transition, but rather accomplished gradually over several centuries. Although there is a reasonably broad consensus that this was so, it is not always the impression one gets from handbooks and historical overviews of the period. It is not even the contemporary view either, at least to some degree. Many writers in the fourth, fifth, and sixth centuries declare paganism to be dead and gone, but the fact that they do this in century after century is precisely evidence that paganism did not die in one fell swoop. The edict of Theodosius I on February 27, 380 declaring "catholic" (i.e. Nicene) Christianity the only religion of the state, prompting the removal by Gratian of the altar and statue of the goddess Victory from the senate hall in 382 together with other edicts from Theodosius ever more hostile towards paganism in the first half of the 390s can be seen as very important steps, but actually it seems that this chiefly resulted in the removal of paganism from the cities, making it truly "pagan," meaning "rustic" (Williams and Friell, 1995: 120ff.). A telling example, which was also seen as symbolically meaningful by contemporaries, was the destruction of the famous temple of Serapis in Alexandria in 391. However, it is claimed that even high officials have been known to have been non-Christian under Justinian in the early 500s and certainly there was non-Christian teaching taking place in the Academy in Athens when Justinian ordered it closed in 529 (Mitchell, 2007: 129ff.).

Exploring the process of Christianization from the point of view of food seems rather obvious. After all, Christians were defined by or in relationship to food at least in two important senses: They refused to participate in sacrifices or even to eat sacrificed meat. And they were known to participate in a communal meal in secret. A third important aspect of the Christian relationship with food is the denial and abhorrence of it, which became a hallmark of Christian behavior in Syria and Egypt from the third quarter of the third century. These three themes will be explored more thoroughly in this chapter.

Sacrificial meat

In the Mediterranean world in pre-Christian times, butchering and sacrifice were not necessarily clearly distinguished. What now marks the religions of Judaism and Islam as deviant in the modern world, namely that all butchering must take the form of an act of sacrifice, would probably have been closer to the norm in the ancient world. At the very least, the butcher would say a prayer of his own choice before killing a large animal—and the separation of blood and flesh was also the norm.

However, the large public sacrifices of several hundred animals, dedicated to a particular deity, must have made a glut in the butcher shops where the meat would have been sold, if it was not given away. So it would have been both cheap and unavailable to Christians and Jews, who were forbidden to eat sacrificial meat.

The most important result of this is that sacrificial meat was not something unusual, but rather both the norm, and the discount version of meat. And so the injunction against it, which to us does not sound so terribly difficult to comply with, would have put a taint on any Christian's social life. However, avoiding sacrificial meat probably would not have been more difficult or more socially obtrusive than being a vegan is in our times. Maybe even less so, because meat was not a favorite staple food in the ancient world. Fish and most certainly vegetables were a far greater part of the diet in those days. But the matter was an issue for Christians from the very earliest times.

Those familiar with the so-called "First Letter to the Corinthians" of Paul of Tarsus (better known as "Saint Paul") will know that he is uncharacteristically unclear in his injunction against sacrificial food. He writes in Chapter 8 and Chapter 10 (my translation):

> About that which has been offered to idols, we see that we all have knowledge (gnosis). Gnosis inflates, love builds—if anyone thinks to have achieved gnosis about something, he doesn't know it as it should be known; if anyone loves the god, that one is known by him. About the meat which is offered to idols then, we see that there is no idol in the world and no god except one. For even **if** there are so-called gods either in the sky or on the ground as there are many gods and many lords, there is for us one god, the father from whom everything is and we to him, and one lord, Jesus Christos, for whom everything is and we for him. But not in everyone is the gnosis. Those that through habit of dealing with the idols eat as if it were offered to idols and having a weak conscience will be soiled. But our food should not commend us to (bring us closer to) the god, if we do not eat we will not lose anything, if we do eat we will not gain a lot. See that your freedom does not become an obstacle for the weak. For if anyone sees the one who has gnosis sitting in a place of idols and eating, will not the conscience of the one who is weak be built up to eat that which has been offered to idols. The weak person will then be lost because of this your gnosis, the brother for whom Christos died. Thus when sinning against the brothers and harming

their weak conscience, you sin against Christos. Therefore if food makes my brother stumble, I will never eat meat for all eternity, so that my brother shall not be made to stumble. (1 Cor. 8.1–13) You cannot drink of the cup of the lord and of the cup of the demons; you cannot partake of the table of the lord and of the table of the demons. (1 Cor. 10.21) Everything that is for sale in a butcher-shop you can eat, without discerning because of your conscience. The earth and its goods are of the lord. If anyone of the non-believers invites you, and you wish to go there, you may eat everything which is set before you without discerning because of your conscience. If anyone says to you; "this is a sacrifice" do not eat it because of the one who directed your attention to it, and because of conscience. The conscience I speak of is not your own, but that of your neighbor. (1 Cor. 10.25–9)[1]

Paul seems to think that, in a sense, the eating of sacrificial meat should not be forbidden, because this would mean that there were in fact other gods, who could be honored by this eating. And since these gods do not exist, eating is irrelevant. But this is only certain for those who have the gnosis, and those who do not have it, or in whom it is not solid, could be corrupted into thinking that the gods existed. So refrain, for other people's sake, seems to be the conclusion. And the gods do not exist, but demons (apparently) do exist. The exhortation to eat with non-believers under the prudent advice not to ask whether sacrificial meat is served or not shows how important it was to be able to participate in ordinary social life for the Christians in the first century.

It is interesting to note that Paul's standpoint was later seen as untenable by the Church. All later mention of sacrificial meat expressly forbids the consumption. As I stated, this may have made the social life of Christians difficult, but probably not completely impossible. It would have made them conspicuous, but not necessarily as Christians, because several other religious and philosophical schools were following similar rules. Any Christian could simply claim to be a vegetarian.

It is also from Paul that we first learn of the central Christian rite, now known as the Eucharist. Paul connects the meal of the Corinthians with the last supper of Christ, even though his description of the way it is carried out is not at all like the highly ritualized eucharist of the later church. The Christian worshippers apparently bring their own food, and eat it whenever they want, so that Paul observes: "for some are taking their own meal in the eating, (so that) there is one who is hungry and another who is getting drunk" (2 Cor. 11.22).

This seems to resemble an ordinary—if somewhat disorderly—pot-luck supper more than a sacrificial meal—and it resembles not at all the mostly symbolic Eucharist of later times. But it is a meal in remembrance of the last supper—and therefore it is best understood as a precursor of the Eucharist, even though it is technically known as the agape-meal. For one thing, Paul wishes for a more orderly and symbolic meal—indeed for more commensality (v. 33f.: "Thus my brothers, when you come together for the eating, you should wait for each other. If anyone is hungry, he should eat in his home, so that you do not come together to be condemned"), and he may have exaggerated the disorder (Meeks, 1983: 157ff.).

Crimes of the Christians

People outside of Christianity found out about the communal meal. And it seems to have been the things that they knew happened at these occasions which led to the popular dislike of the Christians. It should be noted, by the way, that I have not found a single shred of evidence to suggest that Christianity was ever a very popular religion before it became the religion of the emperors. And even after a century with this status, the army was often necessary to suppress the anger of the people whenever a temple was to be closed. The word "pagan" is the word of the elite minority of city-dwellers showing their contempt for the unlearned populace living in the country and sticking to the old gods.

The meal was, as was usual with the mystery-cults, secret. Women and men participated together. The obscure Christian writer Minucius Felix is the only author who explicitly refers to the "knowledge" about the scandalous meals of the Christians, but another, better known author, Tertullian, refers to the same prejudices implicitly, and to some degree so does the Younger Pliny. In 103 he was an administrator in Bithynia by the Black Sea, and wrote to the emperor Trajan of the meal of the Christians: promiscuum tamen et innoxium, "common and ordinary, however." The "tamen" demonstrates that Pliny knows that the recipient would have expected the meal to be uncommon and extraordinary. About a hundred years later—if not more—Minucius Felix and Tertullian explain what people seem to have "known" already at the time of Pliny. The text of Minucius, a dialogue called "Octavius," is undatable. It is a formal debate between a pagan and a Christian friend of the "I." The protagonists are three noblemen who are killing time together on the beach near Ostia. There is a relaxed, even somewhat playful, atmosphere about the dialogue, which ends in the peaceful conversion of the pagan.

But the descriptions of two instances of Christian eating are not relaxed. The story of the initiation of the Christian is, Minucius has the pagan declare, "as detestable as it is famous" (IX, 5). So everybody "knew" that a baby was covered with dough and placed next to the unsuspecting neophyte. The neophyte is told to strike the dough with a knife and thus involuntarily kills the infant. At the sight of blood the Christians lap it up and consume the entire infant there and then. "This sacrifice unites them under oath, this knowledge of complicit crime induces them to mutual silence" (ibid.).

It seems obvious that this story, which is also alluded to by Tertullian (Apol. VII, 2–9), is behind the expectations of something gruesome and unusual in Pliny's letter.

But there is more, for the meal of love, the agape-feast, is also denounced by the pagan in Minucius' dialogue. It is a banquet where they gather with "children, sisters, mothers—people of both sexes and all ages" (XI, 6). When eating and drinking has inflamed their incestuous passions, a piece of meat is thrown to a dog, which is tied to the only chandelier that gives light to the room. The dog jumps, upsets the chandelier and in the ensuing darkness, each person throws him- or herself at the neighbor, so that a lot of incestuous sex takes place.

Tertullian alludes to these accusations when in his apology he jokingly asks: "What if my mother and sister won't come, or I don't have any?" (ibid., VII, 8).

Much of what was said against the Christians was philosophical, but when it came to imputed "real" crimes, such as infanticide and incest, it was centered on the communal meals. This is an obvious reflection of the importance of the meals as central marker of Christian unity and cross-social coherence. It is interesting to see that commensality, viewed in a certain way, may be understood as (or exaggerated into) an abhorrent social infraction. This demonstrates how commensality is an effective way of marking different groups and making the boundaries distinct.

Since we are in possession of marked and identifiable Christian burial-places, and therefore of bones of designated Christians, it is possible to do more than speculate what the Christians normally might have eaten.

A bone-analysis was carried out on 22 samples of bones from an area in the Saint Callixtus catacombs. The sample which was radiocarbon dated to the period from the mid-third through early fifth century. The analysis led to the result that it could be claimed that freshwater fish was a very prominent part of the diet of the Christian population. This may be a sign of their general poverty, but since there is as yet no contrasting evidence from the general contemporary Roman populace, this is only a conjecture (Rutgers et al., 2009: 1132f.).

Thanks to the price-edict of Diocletian, it is at least certain that freshwater fish was among the cheapest food-items available—if you did not catch them yourself. It is interesting that only beef was cheaper, which would indicate that it was held in even lower esteem as food.

Even if it is tempting to connect the fish-diet with the meat-taboo and possibly with the Christian fish-symbolism as well, such a piece of information demonstrates the complexity of the matter. Until it is known whether the Christian population is markedly different from the general population, it is obviously better to let the question rest.

Christian asceticism

The last factor in the Christianization process where food plays a major role is concerned with restrictions and abstinence. In the context of commensality this may seem odd, but the demonstrative refusal to be part of any kind of commensality is also a sign of the importance of eating together. Furthermore the ascetic practices of the so-called desert fathers became integrated into the understanding of food in the entire Christian Roman empire and hence a part of the European idea of food—as a negative influence on spirituality, even as something necessary, but potentially sinful (Clarke, 2004: 63ff.). This might have had more intrinsic influence on the Protestant countries in the end, but is nevertheless a part of the overall Christian understanding of eating—in Catholic and Orthodox contexts it is reflected ritually in the periodic fasts.

It is unclear to how great an extent the phenomenon of going into the desert and living an ascetic life is tied to Christianity. Much of the evidence would indicate that ascetic practices existed before they became connected with the Christian ideal of forsaking the world. It is said in the Life of Antony (which was probably written shortly after his death in 356) that Antony learned the ascetic life from different older ascetics, and it is also implied that Antony was one of the first Christian ascetics. This would indicate that at least some of Antony's teachers might not have been Christian.

The idea that some foods or food in general is bad for your spiritual health is found in several philosophical and religious disciplines, movements and organizations in many centuries before Antony went into the desert, so it is certainly possible that other ascetics were around, but they were not part of a popular movement.

This certainly changed. By the time the Life was written, the idea of the ascetic life had caught on, and was apparently universally admired as a devout Christian practice. The Life, which was translated into Latin (and thus made readable to most people in the western part of the empire, where monasticism was much less widespread) before 374, declares that there are now many monasteries and many monks. The image in the Life of Antony is striking: "And so, from then on, there were monasteries in the mountains and the desert was made a city by monks, who left their own people and registered themselves for the citizenship in the heavens" (14 as translated in Rapp, 2005: 112).

The ascetics were not only concerned with abstinence from food, and much of the contemporary literature stresses sexual desire and civil ambition as other important dangers to avoid. But in the end, it is food which is the centerpiece of the stories concerning the steadfastness of the hermits.

Antony himself became the model hermit. Giving away his possessions and going into the desert to live was not a simple process, but one of several steps. After a life in a cell behind a closed door for many years, in 311 he came out, went into the town, and tried unsuccessfully to achieve martyrdom. This was at the time of Diocletian's great persecution of Christians. The persecution was abating by then, and halted completely in 313 with the so-called Edict of Milan, which was the first step in the administrative Christianization of the empire. Antony even managed to outlive Constantine and thus he died at a time when Christianity was the religion supported and protected by the emperors, generally respected if not yet universally accepted among the educated (Clarke, 2004: 95ff.).

Ascetics and martyrs

It is possible that the monastic movement in Christianity did more for the acceptance of the religion than it is normally assumed. The feats of the ascetics were famous outside the circles of Christians and caused excitement in the empire as a whole. Saint Augustine recounts how his own complete conversion (in Milan in 386) followed hard after a discussion of the Life of Antony (Confessions 8.6.15).

At a time when martyrs' graves were growing old as evidence for the power and strength of the Christian faith, ascetics seem to have offered a similar—and maybe even more vibrant and less controversial—demonstration of the strength of the Christians. Certainly the visits to martyr's graves became less popular, while the visits to ascetics grew in number in the fourth century (Clarke, 2004: 70). Just as one might sense the sacrifice of a martyr at his or her grave, one might be ascetic "by proxy" by offering support (however probably unwelcome) to an ascetic (1995: 62ff.; Rapp, 2005: 100f.).

The ostentatious refusal of the ascetics to eat more than the barest minimum was a strong counter-image of civic life and convivial feasting as well as an invocation of the Eucharist as the "real" food, which brings about full salvation of body and soul.

Commensality is a key concept in these three instances. The commensality of Christians and non-Christians was of such paramount importance to Saint Paul that eating sacrificial meat was thought by him to be permissible (within a "don't ask, don't tell" context). It is telling that the later authorities on Christian life banned it altogether, thereby making Christians both more removed from and more visible in polite society. Of course it also put rather more emphasis on the "demons" of the non-Christian worship than Paul probably would have thought wise.

In the second instance it seems to be a (mis)understanding of the Eucharistic commensality of Christian brothers and sisters consuming together the body of Christ. These two ritual relationships were confounded with reality and this led to charges of incest and infanticide. According to our sources, this was what people believed, and (I would claim) it is precisely the undeniable fact, that the Christians are eating together in secret (the Eucharist was and is after all a "mysterion" (lit. "secret")), which made them vulnerable to the charges of eating something gruesome and sharing more commensality than was thought proper.

Third, the refusal to eat and the denial of any kind of commensality idealized in Athanasius' Life of Antony serves as a reminder that the absence of something is often as important as its presence. The ideal of denying food demonstrated to everyone just how important it was in life—especially in public, political life.

Thus the concept of commensality becomes a key to understanding an aspect of the life of Christians and the process of Christianization which is often overlooked despite its importance.

17

Ritual Meals and Polemics in Antiquity

Ingvild Sælid Gilhus

Introduction

In the Mediterranean world in the Hellenistic and Roman period, the transformation of religious practices and beliefs "led to the formation of boundary-conscious and knowledge-based religious groups that could be called 'religions'" (Rüpke, 2010: 197). These religions were trans-locally organized and needed to create other measures than geography to mark their space (Smith, 1998; Rüpke, 2010: 205). One of these measures was the development of specific ritual meals and a type of commensality, which contributed to define religious identity. The theme of this chapter is how meals, food, and commensality were used in polemics in the Roman Empire to create religious identities and sustain boundaries between groups. The approach is informed by structuralism and anthropology.

Our sources for ancient meals are to a varying degree texts, images, domestic utensils, crockery, and bones of slaughtered animals. This chapter will mainly concentrate on texts. The textual focus means that we are not studying the social reality of actual meals, but how meals, diet, and commensality were conceived of and described and how these descriptions contributed to create boundaries against external and internal others, which means other religions and religious societies on the one hand and groups within one's own religion or religious society on the other.[1]

Religions, religious societies, and religious groups tend to create "edible identities," which, according to Jordan D. Rosenblum, is a "complex of culturally significant activities surrounding the preparation and ingestion of food that allows diners to make an identity statement by the manner in which they partake of their dinner" (2010a: 7). Polemical descriptions of the ritual meals of competing religious groups, i.e. descriptions of the edible identity of others, were used to create boundaries against them. In some cases polemical descriptions have an extra twist, because they are reports of what others allegedly have said about the religious meals of the author—as when the Christian writers Tertullian (*Ad. Nationes*, 1, 7; *Apologeticus*,

7, 1) and Minucius Felix (*Octavius*, 9, 5) claim that Pagans say that Christians sacrifice children in the Eucharist.

We will concentrate on the interplay between some of the religions and religious societies in the empire in the second to fourth century, especially on the mysteries of Mithras, Manichaeism, and Christianity as well as on traditional Greco-Roman religion. A ritual meal had a special significance in each of these religions and religious societies. A banquet is usually the last step in a sacrifice where one or more animals are slaughtered; the cult room of the adherents of Mithras was a dining room; the Eucharist was a key ritual in Christianity; and one of the most prestigious rituals of the Manicheans took place at the banquet table. The religions and religious societies of the empire were developed together, shared the same cultural context and had much in common.[2] It was therefore important to create and maintain distinctions between them, which was done, among other things, by means of accusations and polemics. Ritual meals and commensality were among the targets.

How were meals, food, and commensality used in polemics in the Roman Empire to create religious identities and sustain social boundaries? How did accusations aiming at the "edible identities" of others mark one group as different from other groups? Discussing these questions also implies commenting on how a religious dimension was established in a meal; what sort of communication with superhuman beings took place; and what the postulated cosmic implications of these meals were.

We will first introduce ancient meals and commensality; present the meanings and functions of ritual meals; describe the construction of external and internal others in polemical settings; and finally discuss how boundaries were created by means of meals and commensality.

Ancient meals and commensality

The culinary triangle in antiquity consisted of cereals, olives, and wine, expressed, for instance, in the gods Demeter/Ceres (Elevsis): grain; Athene: olives; and Dionysos: wine. There were huge differences in diet between the rich and the poor, as well as between men and women. Periods of scarcity of food occurred, but seldom famines (Garnsey, 1983, 1999; Beer, 2010: 21ff.).

Commensality did not usually imply equality. The Roman society was built on hierarchy on all levels. Many meals did not include women, and when they did, for instance in some branches of Christianity, it was sometimes criticized (Corley, 1993: 7ff.). There was a division between people at the table, between those who were declining, sitting, or standing, and by positioning couches according to rank (Smith, 2003: 10–11, 44–5; Malmberg, 2003).

The quality of the food differed as well. Pliny describes a meal where the guests were ranked by being offered three different qualities of wine (*Letter to Avitus* II, 6, cf. Sande, 2011: 25). Lucian warns one of his friends how low he would be in the hierarchy of the dinner table: "In this way you are pushed off into the most unregarded corner and take your place merely to witness the dishes that are passed, gnawing the bones like a dog if they get as far as you ... Your bird, too, is not like the others; your neighbour's is fat and plump, and yours is half a tiny chick, or a tough pigeon—out-and-out rudeness and contumely" (*On Salaried Posts in Great Houses*, 26). According to Lucian, distinctions between people are here made by means of differences in the standard of seating and differences in the quality of the food served. Martial describes a meal with his patron in satirical terms: "Golden with fat, a turtle dove gorges you with its bloated rump; there is set before me a magpie that died in its cage" (Martial III, 60; cf. Sande, 2011: 25).

In other words, a meal and a shared table did not only express companionship, but expressed hierarchy as well. This type of social ranking is commented upon because there was an ideal of social equality in dining together (cf. Smith, 2003: 11), but also because even if one accepted ranking, one did not necessarily accept the criteria for the actual ranking.

In his book, *From Symposium to Eucharist: The Banquet in the Early Christian World* (2003), Dennis E. Smith presents a model, which subsumes all formal meals in the Greco-Roman world under the general category of the Greco-Roman banquet. According to Smith "the banquet was a single social institution that pervaded the culture as a whole" (Smith, 2003: 12). His model includes everyday meals, symposia, funerary banquets, sacrificial meals, mystery meals, everyday Jewish meals, Jewish festival meals, Christian agape, and Christian Eucharist. The model is tidy, but has been criticized for oversimplifying and for underplaying the influence of the biblical sacrificial traditions on Judaism and Christianity (for instance, Lieber, 2006). All the same I think it is fruitful in the present discussion to see the Greco-Roman banquet, as Smith does, as a common and synchronous model in which all formal meals are included, and leave out the question of the origin of the specific meals, i.e. the diachronic dimension (cf. McGowan, 2010: 181). The model of Smith makes each and every meal relate comparatively to all other meals in the model and at the same time it potentially stresses the boundaries between them—both in relation to the preparation, ingredients, commensality, and rituals of the meal, but also in relation to its mythological references, i.e. what myths and narratives the meal explicitly and implicitly refers to, and what its aims are.

Meanings and functions of ritual meals

Eating and commensality have at least two purposes: to sustain biological life and to express and develop social life. Ancient meals in general had a religious dimension (Garnsey, 1999: 132).[3] Sacrifices to the gods usually ended with people eating the sacrificial meat together in the family, at banquets among the ruling elite or in different associations and *collegia*. According to Dio Chrysostom: "What sacrifice has proved pleasing to the gods unless men feast together?" (*Or.* III, 97A). If religion is defined as "communication with culturally postulated superhuman beings," the religious dimension of ancient meals was related to three types of such beings and to different types of communication with them: 1) gods; 2) intermediary beings as angels and demons;[4] and 3) the dead.[5]

Communication with these superhuman beings turned the meal into a ritual, sanctified the whole or part of it, and made it work for added specific non-nutritious purposes. A religion or religious society had usually different types of meals and the communication with superhuman beings could be more or less prominent. In some meals the stress is on a direct interaction with postulated superhuman beings, for instance in an initiation and/or a sacramental meal. In other meals, the inter-action with superhuman beings is minimal, and the stress is rather on the interaction between people who share myths, rituals and values.

The minimum religious element was a libation or a blessing, as a token of devotion to the gods; maximum was when the whole meal was conceived of as communication with these culturally postulated superhuman beings, for instance meals where gods and/or goddesses took part, either by being offered a couch or by having their image present.[6] Gods could preside over the banquet, it could be devoted to them, or the divine substance could be devoured in a sacramental meal.

A ritual meal in antiquity had some general meanings and functions. Some of these meanings and functions are more prominent in some meals than in others.

To promote mundane prosperity

"I give that you may give," *do ut des*, is a Latin phrase that is used to describe the communication with superhuman beings and the circle of prosperity, which the sacrifice and the sacrificial meal were intended to promote. Values that were evoked were agriculture, abundance, health, procreation, patriarchal culture, society, local elites, and the emperor (Gordon, 1990; Jay, 1993; Stowers, 1995). Different types of commensality could be based on sacrifice and expressed in a ritual meal, for instance domestic commensality; kin and communal commensality; ceremonial and religious commensality; and political commensality (cf. Che-Beng Tan, Chapter 2). In a domestic sacrifice the stress was on agriculture, abundance, health and procreation, while in sacrifices and sacrificial meals held on the behalf of cities and states the stress was also on local elites and the emperor (Gordon, 1990; Stowers, 1995).

To promote extra-mundane prosperity

In some ritual meals, rewards lie outside this life, for instance a closer relationship to superhuman beings, a better lot after death and salvation, in other words what could be called supra-biological life was present. These meals could either be sacrificial or non-sacrificial. A sacrificial meal could either be dependent on an actual slaughter of an animal or be based on a symbolic or mythological sacrifice, as was the case in the Christian Eucharist and in the meal of the Manicheans. The meals of the Christians and the Manicheans included further a promise of future salvation, and this was most likely also the case with the Mithraic cult meal. In the Eucharist the salvation of the participants was the goal. In Manicheism the goal was to save the spiritual elements which were trapped in the material world (cf. Pedersen, 1996: 295ff.; BeDuhn, 2000).

To connect past, present and future by means of mythological prototypes

A ritual meal connects past events with the present and points to the future—sometimes, but not always, expressed by means of myths and mythological prototypes. Sacrifices in Rome pointed back to mythical and/or historical proto-types, and to future prosperity, as seen for instance on the *Ara Pacis*, the altar to Peace, which was set up in honor of the emperor Augustus:

> In looking at the altar, Roman viewers did not simply see images of a sacrifice that once happened. They saw a cultural process in which they themselves became involved. This was a process which included the sacrifice Aeneas made long ago, the sacrifice Augustus and the Senate made when the altar was dedicated, the sacrifice that emperor and people would be making every year, the sacrifice in which the viewer had himself participated (maybe last year and the year before) and would make again in the future. (Elsner, 1991: 52)

In the mysteries of Mithras, the ritual meal referred to the sacred meal that Mithras had with Sun after Mithras had butchered the ox (Clauss, 2000: 110; Bjørnebye, 2002). From Konjic in Dalmatia is a picture of an initiation to the highest grade of the mysteries, a Pater and a Heliodromus, in the form of Sol and Mithras lying on a *triclinium*, while people from lower grades, with masks, act as servants (Vermaseren, 1965; Kane, 1975: 318ff.; Clauss, 1986: 270–1).[7] According to Jaime Alvar, "the commensality of Mithraists gains its rationale directly from the commensality of the gods" (Alvar, 2008: 355). The meal pointed, most likely, to a state of bliss to come after death.

Christianity rejected animal sacrifice, but redefined and took over the sacrificial discourse and promoted a sacrificial reading of the gospel. In line with this reading they constructed their most important ritual meal, the Eucharist,[8] as a sacrificial meal. The priest identified the bread and the wine with the body and blood of the savior, communicated with God through the ritual and, together with the community, incorporated the consecrated bread and wine in a ritual that pointed to the saving death of Jesus as well as to the salvation of the participants.[9]

At the "Table" (*trapeza*) of the Manichaeans, the elect consumed their only nourishment during the day. According to Manichaeism the principle of darkness had in the beginning engulfed the principle of light. The Manichean practice aimed at separating the antagonistic elements in the world from the elements of light, and the problem of mixture and embodiment was solved by means of human digestion (BeDuhn, 2000: 125). When the believers ate food that was rich in light, they believed that they released the trapped light and thus participated in its salvation by means of their metabolism (BeDuhn, 2000).

If the ritual meal is predominantly connected to extramundane abundance and supra-biological life, it is usually also expressed in more elaborate myths and alludes more explicitly to mythological prototypes than traditional sacrifices do, where the goal is mainly mundane prosperity. There was a tendency in the first centuries of the common era to develop meals in which the sacrificial element was reinterpreted and where extramundane prosperity and mythological elements and narratives became more important (Gilhus, 2006: 114–38)—as seen in the meals of the Christians, the Manicheans and of those initiated to Mithras.

To create and sustain identity and difference

A ritual meal creates identity as well as division between people, externally in relation to competing cults and religions, and internally at the table when the participants are served by rank, and in relation to groups within the same religion. In this way the meal constructs a power relationship based on the ranking of the participants and on an opposition between those who participate in the ritual meal and those who are excluded.

External others

Meat was not a staple or an important element in the common diet, but partly for that reason it was a key to the sacred diet code, and sacrifices and the sacrificial discourse were the religious *lingua franca* of the Empire. Marcel Detienne and Jean Pierre Vernant have stressed the connection between sacrifice, cuisine and types of commensality (Detienne, 1981: 1–20; Detienne and Vernant, 1989).

According to Detienne and Vernant, eating meat in Greece divided gods, humans, and animals. Animals ate raw meat, while humans cooked it and shared it with the gods in sacrifice. Gods were distinguished from human beings because they savored only the smoke of the sacrificed meat, and they did not consume it in the same way as humans.

Conceptions of meat were used to mark external boundaries to the uncivilized barbarians. The barbarians (whoever they were) were allegedly great meat eaters, ate raw meat, or ate peculiar sorts of meat. One could add that the Roman elite were really omnivores and ate themselves through the kitchen of the nations they had conquered, and would, to paraphrase Peter Farb and George Armelagos, "swallow almost anything that does not swallow them first" (1980). The Roman army, for instance, "ate meat at all times as part of their diet" (Davies, 1971: 126). It is further possible that poor people actually ate wild animals that had died in the arenas (Kyle, 1995). The point is that, independent of what Romans really ate, according to the Greek/Roman view, barbarians ate at tables, which included raw meat, peculiar sorts of meat, or too much meat (cf. Vernant, 1981).

Different religious groups distinguished themselves from each other by means of their diet, table companions, and relationship to sacrifice. Even if some groups did not put sacrificed meat on their tables, or any meat at all, they took part in a sacrificial discourse and in a commensality based on this discourse, either by making reinterpretations of the sacrifice or by eating bloodless meals. Vegetarianism is not necessarily a statement primarily about animals (it could be more like a footnote on them), but it is always a statement about identity and difference, which implies that vegetarianism comments on the relationship to other people.

Types of meat/avoidance of meat were used to mark boundaries between specific religious groups within the empire. The Manichean elite were in the main vegetarians; the Jews kept a diet based on allowed and forbidden food which excluded pork; the Christians did not eat sacrificed meat and sometimes ate neither meat from strangled beasts nor blood. Other types of food contributed to make and maintain identities as well. The Christians ate bread and drank wine in the Eucharist and interpreted those ingredients as the body and blood of their savior; the Mithraists probably consumed bread and water in their ritual initiation, while the Manichean Elect ate a diet of fruit, vegetables, bread, and water (Pedersen, 1996: 285) and saved the spiritual elements in the world by consuming them.

Great effort went into constructing self-other dichotomies by means of food and commensality. Christian groups made boundaries against Pagans by neither partaking in the sacrificial meal nor eating meat that had been sacrificed. The impurity of sacrificed meat is commented on, for instance by Lactantius who wrote about emperor Maximian (c. 315): "It was also an invention of his to cause all animals used for food to be slaughtered not by cooks, but by priests at the altars; so that nothing was ever served up, unless fortasted, consecrated, and sprinkled with wine, according to the rites of paganism; and whoever was invited to an entertainment must needs have returned from it, impure and defiled" (*Of the Manner in which the Persecutors died*, 37, 2). There was a continuous use of paganism and sacrifice in Christian apologetics. According to Alan Cameron, "paganism lasted much longer for Christians than pagans. And for Christians, paganism always implied sacrifice" (Cameron, 2011: 67).

Similar to Judaism after the fall of the temple (70 CE), Christians did not sacrifice, but differed from the Jews by not keeping the Jewish dietary laws, and from the Manichean elite by eating meat. In fact it was important for Christians to eat meat to show that they were not Manicheans (cf. Grumett and Muers, 2010: 89–95).

The boundaries between Christians and external others as Pagans, Jews, and Manicheans were manageable and easy to combine. Christians might at the same time make external others out of the adherents of these religions simply by eating all types of meat except meat that had been sacrificed. But reality is not that tidy, and the boundaries were blurred: There were Christians who ate meat even if they knew that it had been sacrificed; Christians who kept the whole or part of the dietary law; and Christians who avoided meat. Even if killing animals and eating meat in the Bible are closely connected to man's god-given control over nature, even if it is implied in the gospels that Jesus ate meat, and even if Augustine made the Stoic notion of the irrationality of animals decisive for their treatment (Sorabji, 1993: 201ff.), meat was a contested as well as a symbolically and emotionally loaded type of food.

The boundaries between Jews and Christians as well as between Christians and Manicheans were sometimes blurred. Mani included Jesus in his religious practice and mythology in ways that were not acceptable to the Church. Manicheans saw themselves as Christians and sometimes described their sacred meal as the true Eucharist (Pedersen, 1996: 290). In the words of Epiphanius (ca. 374), the pious and sarcastic bishop of Salamis: "They pretendedly speak of Christ, but worship the sun and the moon, and evoke stars, powers and daemons" (*Panarion*, V, 66, 1). A considerable cultural work to maintain and strengthen the boundaries between Christianity and Manichaeism took place, and polemics against the edible identity of the Manicheans was part of this work. The relationship to animals and meat was in focus.

Epiphanius refers to one of Mani's disciples, Turbo, and comments on Manicheans who eat plants to save the light and who refuse to eat meat:

> To venture a joke, to refute him [i.e. Turbo] in terms of his own mythology I may say that if the seeds of lentils, beans, chick-peas and the rest are souls, but the soul of a bull is the same, then, on his premises, people who eat meat have more to their credit than ascetics do. For as his rigmarole goes, he is afraid that if he eats living things—animals and the rest—he will become like them. But [the truth is] the opposite! Sure, in his worthless quibble if fifty, or even a hundred men assemble and they all dine on one bull, they are all guilty of murder together. But still, we must say in refutation that the fifty, or the hundred, become guilty [of the murder] of one soul, while someone who eats the grains of seeds will be guilty of ingesting thirty or forty souls at one gulp! And all his teachings are worthless and absurd. (*Panarion*, V, 34, 2–4)

Augustine, who had been a Manichaean for nine years before he converted to Christianity, wrote several treatises and letters against this religion and comments on their ritual table and eating habits, especially on their vegetarian diet and the rationale behind it, which Augustine, like Epiphanius, found to be inconsistent and blameworthy.

Augustine repeatedly returns to moral dilemmas in the Manichean treatment of plants versus animals. He presents, for instance, an example with a hungry raven, which is about to eat a fig: "In accord with your opinion, do you not suppose that the fig itself speaks and pleads with you in a pitiful fashion that you yourself should pick and bury it in you holy belly to be purified and resuscitated, rather that the raven should devour and mingle it with its dark body and from there send it on into other forms to be bound and tormented in them?" (*The Catholic Way of Life and the Manichean Way of Life*, II, 57). Here, the fig is assumed to cry desperately out to the Elect and to beg to be plucked and saved from the raven. But the Elect are never allowed to pluck food for himself, so the fig has to suffer. In this way the Manichean dilemma is made into mockery.

Internal others

In addition to the boundaries against external others there was a tapestry of criss-crossing lines drawn between groups *within* the religions and religious societies of the Roman Empire (cf. Rosenblum, 2010b).

The Mithraic mysteries included seven grades, and images show how those who belonged to the lower grades served those who belonged to higher grades at the table. The Manicheans made a division between *auditores*, those who listen, and *electi*, the elected ones. These groups ate different sort of food, and the Hearers brought food to the Elect. Augustine makes a point out of not knowing exactly how the meal of the Elect is conducted, even if he belonged to the Hearers for nearly a decade, so apparently the Elect ate separate from the Hearers.

Christians used diet, ritual meals, and commensality to better define themselves and make internal boundaries against other Christian groups and individuals. One distinction was between those who lived in families and those who lived ascetic lives. According to Richard Valantasis, asceticism "may be defined as performances designed to inaugurate an alternative culture, to enable different social relations, and to create a new identity" (Valantasis, 1995: 548). Christian asceticism implied to alienate oneself partly from non-ascetic Christians, develop a new and alternative Christian identity on a higher level and express it by means of a frugal diet.

The opposition between Christian orthodoxy and heresy, whoever acted out the two positions, found its outlet in hostile demarcations against proximate others. These demarcations were also expressed by means of edible identities, and the Eucharist and Eucharistic imagery were used to map differences between Christian groups. One example is Antony, who according to his biographer, Athanasius, saw in a vision the Eucharist table, which was surrounded by mules that kicked it violently. According to his interpretation the mules were the Arians who attacked the church (Athanasius *Vita Antonii*, 82).

The Eucharist was also used to connect groups in an extended commensality. In the churches in Rome in the second century, Eusebius, quoting Irenaeus, says that portions of the Eucharist bread were sent from one congregation to another (*Church History*, 5, 24, 15). This could be seen as a case of virtual commensality. Einar Thomassen makes the pertinent point that such "a desire for coming together, coupled with a recognition of shared obligations, is not attested for pagan cults associations such as the mysteries of Isis or Mithras, nor, though this is perhaps more debatable, for the synagogues. None of these other religions was, in any case, evolving larger organizational structures" (Thomassen, 2004: 249–50). According to Peter Lampe, in late antiquity, the bishop sent Eucharistic gifts from the mass to the titular priests (Lampe, 2003: 386) in a similar extended show of "virtual Christian commensality."

Defining boundaries

Some frequently used techniques to define boundaries in relation to ritual meals and commensality were to accuse competing religions and groups of 1) unclean eating; 2) overeating, fatal edible identities, and deviant meals; and 3) sexualized commensality; and, further, to 4) explain similarities by means of mythological difference.

Unclean eating

The clean/unclean divide is frequently used to make distinctions and hierarchy between religious groups. According to the *Cologne Mani-Codex* (1979), which describes the life of Mani, Mani belonged to the sect of Elcesaites, a Jewish-Christian Baptist sect, where the adherents cleansed their food by washing it. In this text, Mani is critical to the cleansing ritual and claims that it does not make any difference whether the digested food had been cleansed before it was eaten or not. "You can see how, whenever someone cleanses his food and partakes of that [food] which has just been washed, it seems to us that from it still come blood and bile and flatulence and excrements of shame and (the) defilement of the body," (81, 5–13). It is also a difference in what one eats. The Mani-Codex renders the Baptists' opposition against Mani in this way: "you even wish to eat wheat bread and vegetables which we do not eat" (91, 11–14). Mani retorts, according to the codex, that this is the type of bread that Jesus gave to his disciples. The point of the codex is further, with appeal to the example of Jesus, that the food of the Elect should always be received as a gift—the Elect should never take part in any food production (80–2). In line with this attitude, before they eat bread, the Elect should say: "I neither reaped you, nor ground you, nor poured you, nor put you into an oven; someone else did these things, and brought you to me. I eat without guilt" (*Acta Archelai*, quoted by Epiphanius in *Panarion*, V, 28,7). To the one who gave him the bread the Elect would say that he had prayed for him.

The idea that impurity is clinging to food in its natural state and that measures should be taken to counteract the impurity and thus divide the preparation of food outside the group from how it is prepared within the group—the clean from the unclean—are common for the Elcesaites, as they are described in the Mani-Codex, and for the Manicheans. However, the measures that are taken to counteract the impurity differ and are used to create an edible identity that distinguishes the Manicheans from the Elcesaites. The Manichean text defines the boundaries against the Elcesaites by explaining why their measures against impurity do not work.

When a new religion or cult grows out of an old one, it creates a new edible identity, as was the case when Christianity grew out of Judaism, and its adherents no longer followed the Jewish dietary law, and, as was the case when Manichaeism kept their distance to the Elcesaites by introducing new measures for pure eating. In both cases impurity was an issue. The Christian strategy, opposed to both Judaism and Manichaeism, and a demarcation against them, was to do away with the clean/unclean divide.

Overeating, fatal edible identities, and deviant ritual meals

The struggle between the various religions and religious groups was also a competition in asceticism.

While the Manichean *Kephalaia* stresses that the Elect ate their alms in a state of hunger and thirst (191, 16–19; 213, cf. Pedersen, 1996: 282), the accusation of gluttony was sometimes made against them. Augustine accuses Manicheans of stuffing themselves with voluptuous vegetarian food, delightfully spiced, and describes a Manichean as one, "who have devoured mushrooms, rice, truffles, pastries, grape juice, peppers, and curry, who with distended belly burps his condiments with a feeling of self-satisfaction and who daily requires such a menu" (*The Catholic Way of Life and the Manichean Way of Life*, II, 30). The contrast is the one "who eats vegetables that have been cooked and flavoured with bacon, but not more than enough for quieting his hunger" (ibid., II, 29, 30).

Augustine further combines the theme of ritual overeating with the theme of a "fatal edible identity": When too many gifts were lavished on the table of the Elect, and they did not manage to eat anymore, the superfluous food was given to children. Augustine knows a rumor of cases where these children had been forced to overeat so that they died (*The Catholic Way of Life and the Manichean Way of Life*, II, 52).

To accuse the external other of eating deviant ritual meals was also a way of constructing the other as completely different from oneself. Augustine suggests that Manicheans, who said that they set the souls free when they ate grain, beans, lentils and other seed, also consumed sperm of animals in their ritual meals: "And because such seed [sperm of animals] cannot be brought to you by your Hearers to be purified, who would not suspect that you yourselves perform such a secret purification among yourselves and conceal it from them for fear that they might abandon you?" (*The Catholic Way of Life and the Manichean Way of Life*, II, 66). Augustine is vague about if he really believes it, but says that it is easy for people to think along such lines because of the teaching of the Manicheans.

In a similar vein, the opposition between orthodoxy and heresy (internal others) could be expressed by accusations of eating deviant meals, as when Epiphanius accuses Gnostic groups of using sperm and menstrual blood in their Eucharist (*Panarion*, 26, 1–9).

An extreme form of deviant meals is ritual cannibalism. Tertullian and Minucius Felix mention examples of Pagan accusations against Christians of sacrificing and eating children in their ritual meal (*Ad. Nationes*, 1, 7; *Apologeticus*, 7, 1; *Octavius*, 9, 5). These accusations might have been based on a pagan anxiety about religious groups that were seen as threats to society (McGowan, 1994). The accusations were used for internal reasons by Christian authors to show how mistaken the enemies of Christianity were in their conceptions of this religion and to boost the morale in their own ranks. In both cases the idea of cannibalism was used to mark the boundaries between Christianity and Paganism.

Sexualized commensality

Jack Goody has pointed at the cultural relationship that exists between food and sex on the one hand, and between food and health on the other (Goody, 1982: 114, 191–2). This has some resonance in ancient humor theory, which was applied to promote health and correct diet, and where red meat was thought to generate heat in the body and to fuel sexual impulses.

The Egyptian desert fathers (*Apopthegmata patrum*) saw the intake of food as directly related to the creating of human desire, and it was therefore important to reduce eating to a minimum (cf. Freiberger, 2009: 197). In the monasteries, a frugal diet consisting of bread, water, vegetables, and fruit, preferably in small portions, and usually only once or twice a day, should help to keep the brothers and sisters on the ascetic path. Some saw eating meat as a result of the fall of Adam and Eve, and wanted to return to the prelapsarian state and keep a diet without meat and sex (cf. Shaw, 1998: 197–8). By means of their ascetic diet and sexless life, they referred to, re-enacted and anticipated the ideal life in Paradise before the fall. That meat was considered to generate heat in the body and thus fuel sexual lust seems to have been a legitimate reason to avoid it—"a key maker of Christian monastic identity was abstinence from red meat" (Grumett and Muery, 2011: 9–10, cf. 5–6 and 18).[10]

Accusations of sexualized commensality are frequently found in Christian authors aiming at other religions or competing Christian groups. In Greece and Rome banquets seem usually to have been attended by men as the primary participants and sometimes by women in the form of courtesans and prostitutes (Corley,

1993). Decent women usually did not eat together with men at banquets. This tradition did change during the Empire and also among some of the religious groups, which in its turn led to accusations of indecent and lewd behavior. Such slander was levelled both against Jewish and Christians by Graeco-Roman authors (Corley, 1993: 75f.). Minucius Felix refers to this type of criticism against Christians: "On the day appointed they gather at a banquet with all their children, sisters, and mothers, people of either sex and every age ... in the shameless dark lustful embraces are indiscriminately exchanged; and all alike, if not in act, yet by complicity, are involved in incest, as anything that occurs by the act of individuals results from the common intention" (*Octavius*, 9, 6).

Explaining similarities by means of mythological difference

It is not only a question of what people eat, but also of how they interpret what they eat. The bread and wine of the Eucharist could be interpreted as signs and images or as an actual presence of Jesus. Shenoute (347–465 CE) the monk and spiritual father of three monasteries in Upper Egypt, defends the real presence of Christ in the Eucharist, but knows "blasphemers" who say: "How are bread and wine the body and the blood of the Lord?" (*As It Happened One Day* 84, cf. Davies, 2008: 80–1).

When the goal is to create a specific edible identity, similarities between competing groups might be conceived of as threatening and to need an explanation. The Christian apologists Justin and Tertullian both comment on similarities between central aspects of Mithraism and Christianity, especially the ritual meal of those who are initiated to Mithras and the ritual meal of those who are initiated to Christianity (Beskow, 1994).[11] Both interpret the perceived similarities between the meals as the work of the devil (cf. Clauss 1986): According to Justin, it is the Eucharist, which "the wicked devils have imitated in the mysteries of Mithras, commanding the same thing to be done. For, that bread and a cup of water are placed with certain incantations in the mystic rites of one who is being imitated, you either know or can learn" (*First Apology*, 1993, 66). Tertullian puts it in this way: "Mithras there, (in the kingdom of Satan), sets his marks on the foreheads of his soldiers; celebrates also the oblation of bread, and introduces an image of a resurrection, and before a sword wreathes a crown" (Tertullian, *The Prescription against Heretics*, 40, 3–4, cf. *De corona*, 15).

The similarities between the two meals seem to have been striking and an explanation was needed. It is given by introducing the idea of the Mithraic initiation being a devilish imitation of the Eucharist. In the Eucharist the participants communicate with God, in the Mithraic meal they communicate with Satan.

Conclusion

Boundaries between different religions and religious groups are created by means of dichotomies. In relation to food, commensality and edible identities, dichotomies are made between sacrifice and non-sacrifice; sacrifice and metaphorical sacrifice; meat and vegetarian diet; frugal diet and overeating; commensality and solitary eating; equality and hierarchy; purity and pollution. By use of such dichotomies as well as by means of mythological references and explanations religions and religious groups in the multi-religious society of the Roman Empire made and maintained boundaries against external others as well as boundaries against internal others and thus created the specific edible identity of each and every group.

The social, cultural, and religious constructions of edible identities led to an interaction between external others and internal others in a complex and continually changing web. Regulation of diet further intersected with other types of regulations especially connected to use of periods of fasting, silence, type of clothing, sleep deprivation, and sex, which made the web even more complex. How strong the crisscrossing lines between religions and religious groups were polemically marked was dependent on the relationship to other religions and religious groups and to the wider society.

Acknowledgment

I wish to thank my colleagues in Ancient Studies at the University of Bergen for their helpful comments.

Notes

1. Introduction

1. The suggestions concerning the food pyramid have changed over the last 20 years, e.g. concerning the amount of suggested intake of milk-products and grain in the 1992 food pyramid, compared to the 2012 food plate.
2. The World Health Organization (WHO, 2011a) report shows that 50 percent of all child deaths in the eastern Mediterranean region are related to malnutrition, while at the same time, in some countries of the region, 70 percent of adults aged above 15 are overweight to obese.

2. Commensality and the Organization of Social Relations

1. An early ethnography that includes a discussion of commensalism is that of Richards (1932: 174–82), who used the term "commensualism."
2. I shall use my research experiences over the years in Malaysia and China to illustrate my discussion, and the ethnic groups mentioned include, in Malaysia, the Chinese, Malays, Orang Asli (aborigines in Peninsular Malaysia), Badeng Kenyah, Kelabit, etc. and in China, Minnan Chinese, the Yi, Ersu, etc.
3. Commercial *puhn choi* may use expensive ingredients and the price for each "basin" differs. For example, one that includes abalone, scallops, and sea cucumber (*trepang*) will be more expensive.
4. I thank Professor Sidney Mintz for drawing my attention to this good work.
5. This term was mentioned quite frequently at the conference Food: Commensality and Social Organization Workshop, organized by the Department of Cross Cultural and Regional Studies, University of Copenhagen, October 6–10, 2011. I presented my paper, which has been revised here, at this conference. I thank the fellow participants for alerting me to this useful concept, which is mentioned in Sobal (2000). I am grateful to Dr. Cynthia Chou, Dr. Susanne Kerner, and Dr. Morten Warmind for inviting me to the conference and thus provided me the opportunity to reflect more deeply the significance of commensality in the organization of social relations.
6. On July 3–13, 2011, I led some M.A. students to Turkey and we were treated to mixed *kebap* in Bursa by a local businessman. I thank Mr. Mujdat Yelbay of

the Anatolia Cultural Dialogue Center (Hong Kong), who accompanied us, for explaining to me the social significance of *marube*.

3. Commensal Circles and the Common Pot

1. Colostrum is the thick, yellow protein-rich milk-like fluid produced in late pregnancy and at birth, before mature breastmilk comes in.
2. In a 1999 paper, I argued that multilateral food policy addressed the right to food as a human right, and the provision of food through food aid, but ignored the powerful need to share food and feed others. This conference addressed the expression of this need through examining social commensality.

4. Commensality between the Young

1. This chapter has been written as part of my ongoing Ph.D. project, that is about how the pleasure of and the competence in cooking are developed among youth, and how this pleasure can be amplified and how this competence can be improved. By young I mean 18–24 year olds, who have left home, but do not yet have their own family. The project will run in two phases: 1. A literature based study, for forming hypothesis and the research design. 2. An empirical study among occupants of student hostels and flats for young people. The empirical part of my project will apply my Foodscape-perspective—starting with an observational study (video-based-interaction analysis) that aims at embracing the young people's activities in the kitchen area as a physical, social and mental phenomenon, and on the basis of this observational study, the design of the individual in-depth interviews is created.
2. It should be emphasized that the concept of Foodscape is far from unequivocally applied by the different researchers who use it in their investigation of the interaction between food and people. The following examples include some of the differences:

   - Foodscape is the *physical context* in which food choices are made (Burgoine et al., 2009).
   - We employ the term Foodscape to describe a *social construction* that captures and constitutes cultural ideals of how food relates to specific places, people and food systems (Johnston et al., 2009).
   - Foodscapes represent the view of a particular food object, as seen in the total sum appearance of the *food's visual features* (Sobal and Wasink, 2007).

- Foodscape is the *multiplicity of sites where food is displayed* for purchase, and where it may also be consumed (Winston, 2004).
- Foodscapes are *processes*, where elements relate to each other and generate relationships and affect (Brembeck and Johansson 2010, inspired by the thought of Deleuze).
- Foodscapes are *cultural, economic, historical, personal, political, or social landscapes that, in one way or another, are about food* (Adema, 2007).

As this shows, different uses of the concept Foodscape are brought into play: some scholars understand it as a "processes of signification," while others understand it as "products of signification," some see it as pure "materiality," while others see it as "social constructs."

5. Activism through Commensality: Food and Politics in a Temporary Vegan Zone

1. This chapter is based on the author's Master's dissertation as defended at the Institute of Social Sciences (ICS) of the University of Lisbon in 2010 and can be retrieved at: http://repositorio.ul.pt/handle/10451/307
2. The GAIA website: can be found at: http://www.gaia.org.pt/
3. In a footnote Scott specifies: "Public here refers to action that is openly avowed to the other party in the power relationship, and transcript is used almost in its juridical sense (procès verbal) of a complete record of what is said. This complete record, however, would also include non-speech acts such as gestures and expressions" (Scott, 1990: 2).
4. "I prefer the Latin term 'communitas' to 'community', to distinguish this modality of social relationship from an 'area of common living.' ... It is rather a matter of giving recognition to an essential and generic human bond, without which there could be no society" (Turner, 1997 [1969]: 96, 97).

6. Cooking in the Fourth Millennium BCE: Investigating the Social via the Material

1. We would like to thank the organizers of the workshop, Cynthia Chou, Susanne Kerner, and Morten Warmind, for inspiring three days about (and with) commensality. We are also grateful to the following institutions and persons:

Susan Pollock and Marcella Frangipane for their support in the compilation of this chapter; Gabriela Castro Gassner, Jacob Dahl, and Dan Lawrence for their comments; and the Oriental Institute Museum, Chicago for access to Chogha Mish material. Carolin Jauss' Ph.D. research is funded by the Excellence Cluster TOPOI, Freie Universität Berlin.

2. "Nearly 2 million people die prematurely from illness attributable to indoor air pollution [...] Exposure is particularly high among women and young children, who spend the most time near the domestic hearth." http://www.who.int/mediacentre/factsheets/fs292/en/index.html# (WHO, 2011b). Burning biomass also causes negative environmental effects on global warming and deforestation (WHO, 2011c).

3. The field of practice theories is very heterogeneous (Schatzki, 2006: 2) and covers different approaches that focus on different notions of practice. Fundamental works include Bourdieu, 1972; Butler, 1990; Giddens, 1984; Reckwitz, 2000; Schatzki, 1996, 2002; Schatzki et al., 2006.

4. This analysis is based on published data as well as original material examined at the Oriental Institute Museum, Chicago within the framework of Carolin Jauss' Ph.D. research. The material is supposed to capture the character of the ceramic assemblage according to shape types, established by the excavators, and can be considered a representative cross section. However no quantitative data on vessel counts are available. Not all objects are preserved in a complete profile; consequently not all aspects could be analyzed for the whole group.

5. More detailed analyses on the production techniques of this pottery are needed.

6. Ninety-one objects are included in this study. Forty-eight of them were examined at the Oriental Institute Museum, Chicago; for 43 only published data are included in this analysis. Because of heterogeneous data and preservation, some aspects could be analyzed only for a part of the assemblage.

7. Not considering miniature vessels with a height less than 8 cm.

8. A more precise description of sooting patterns based on a cooking experiment will be published in Jauss, submitted.

9. Two pots were analyzed according to use wear at the Oriental Institute Museum, Chicago. Sooting is also visible on photos or recorded in descriptions of published vessels.

10. Henrickson and McDonald, 1983: 613: Rim-to-base height ranges from 6 cm to 41.5 cm (mean 17.8 cm). Maximum diameter runs from 12.7 cm to 56 cm (mean 24.1 cm).

11. Most vessels come from the architectural "phase 2."

12. It seems possible that there were more people working than living in this area. Further research also on other kinds of vessels used in the area might shed light on this question.

13. The excavators assume that fireplaces were chiefly used for cooking but could also have served for firing pottery, although they don't give any supporting

evidence for either hypothesis (Delougaz et al., 1996: 29). As the characteristics described are suitable for open hearths, and therefore potentially for cooking, we assume this possibility for the present analysis.

14. No precise location and number are published for these fireplaces.

15. The texts are dating to Susa Acropole level 16, which means that they were slightly younger than the record of Chogha Mish analyzed here, which shows most parallels with Susa Acropole levels 18 and 17 (Alizadeh, 2008: 24).

16. Residue analysis could provide data to test this hypothesis.

17. Chogha Mish is located quite close to the first foothills of the Zagros. In a personal communication Susan Pollock pointed to the instance that in modern time the site is partially settled by nomads with their flocks in winter, which indicates that Chogha Mish would be a good location for exchanging and processing pastoral products, including dairy products (Susan Pollock, personal communication, 2011).

18. The results on the Arslantepe materials are part of Maria Bianca D'Anna's Ph.D. research. The cooking pots presented here are complete or nearly complete vessels found *in situ*. Other pieces from secondary or tertiary contexts were not considered for the present study.

19. "In period VI A commensality seems to have played an important role in substantiating social identities among elite and non-elite members of Arslantepe society. The case of meal/ration distributions is the more extended, inclusive case of formal commensality, which is anyhow characterized by a high degree of depersonalization and embodies labor alienation. On the other extreme, the rituals carried out in Temple B constituted a restricted form of commensality, in which large amounts of food and possibly special drinks were shared by a limited number of people" (D'Anna, 2012: 116).

20. The small rooms A46 and A36 in Temple A; the "public" stocking areas A364 and A365; and in the "private" storeroom A946 (D'Anna, 2010: 175–81; D'Anna and Piccione, 2010: 238–40).

21. As noted above, in Temple A cooking pots were stocked with other vessels in the two small side rooms, where no hearth was present. The evidence suggests that at the time of its destruction Temple A was probably no longer used for rituals. The presence of a large number of small cooking pots that overlap with the cooking pot assemblage found in the residential buildings in terms of mean capacity and standard deviation would support this hypothesis and also marks a difference with the assemblage found in Temple B.

22. The remains of complete cereal caryopses is in general very scanty in all period VI A buildings, as in A340 too (Follieri and Coccolini, 1983; Balossi Restelli et al., 2010: 110–11).

23. A closer look at the role of cooks in Chogha Mish will be published in Jauss, submitted.

8. Medieval and Modern Banquets: Commensality and Social Categorization

1. I am grateful to Dr. Elliott Shore, Executive Director, Association of Research Libraries, for this reference. Johnson didn't actually make this remark about benevolence, but it would have been in character. I greatly appreciate the observations of Dr. Gordon Turnbull, Editor of the James Boswell Editions, Yale University, on the history of the word "commensality" and the background to the pseudo-Johnsonian statement.
2. My thanks to Yve Le Grand for the Hirschman reference. Within a generally positive discussion of commensality, Fischler (2001: 538–9) acknowledges there are occasions when dining together can be stratified, tense, or dangerous.
3. See the articles collected in De Vooght 2011, especially Lair 2011. Napoleon III lived in splendid quarters and was an ambitious builder and reconstructor, but his dinners were prosaic.
4. Menus of annual meetings of the Shakespeare Society of Philadelphia in the Library Company of Philadelphia, Ephemera Iu 15 5763E.1, nos. 85 (1858); 87 (1860), 88 (1864), 89 (1869), 90 (1870); 91 (1873); 92 (1876). All the dishes are accompanied by appropriate quotations from Shakespeare's plays and poems. Menus for annual banquets of the Associated Pioneers of the Territorial Days of California (held at various restaurants in New York City), University of California, Berkeley, Bancroft Library F856.A84 (1881–2, 1888); XF 856 A8 31880 (1887); San Francisco, California Historical Society, CA Misc. Ass. Pioneers of the Territorial Days of CA (NYC) (1886, 1889, 1890).
5. El Bulli, menu from April 5, 2011. "Hard to decode," that is, from the words alone. As Marion Nestle pointed out in a talk given at New York University on October 28, 2011, it is easy to enter in a search engine the seemingly mysterious name of an El Bulli dish along with the name of the restaurant to find photographs and descriptions. Thus in fact "everyone" knows that "Box2 is an assortment of candies" and that "Pond2 is a thin layer of ice with mint, green tea, and spices embedded in it."

10. Drink and Commensality, or How to Hold onto Your Drink in the Chalcolithic

1. The Chinese politician Lin Biao has been reported to be so phobic about the intake of liquid that his needs had to be fulfilled by cooked food (Li, 1996: 454).
2. The social construct is often embodied in social exclusion, where self-declared wine connoisseurs describe wine tastes and smells in terms of "wet socks," etc.

and decree that certain wines can only be drunken at certain occasions. The cultural (and that can be family as well as regional or other traditions) taste explains why the coffee consumption in Denmark is 11.53 lb compared to 0.7 lb of tea per person in 1965, while the consumption at the same time in Germany is 4.86 lb of coffee to 0.33 lb of tea (Stocks, 1970); two countries quite compatible in terms of climate and wealth). The aspect of personal taste and its correlation to tradition and socialization are also different topics.

3. That taste in the historical periods of Mesopotamia (3rd-1st. mill. BCE) was different, can be assumed from the less than satisfying experience most people find tasting beer brewed after ancient receipes.

4. http://www.tagesspiegel.de/weltspiegel/alkoholexzesse-unter-jugendlichen-maedchen-saufen-sich-immer-haeufiger-ins-koma/9224158.html. http://www.theguardian.com/lifeandstyle/2008/aug/27/foodanddrink.france

5. There is, for example, a change noticeable in the cultural context of alcohol and coffee during the industrial revolution: while the first moved from the sphere of worktime to playtime, the latter made the opposite movement (Gusfield, 2003).

6. The fact that the nature of the public architecture—monumental in Mesopotamia and far more ordinary in the Levant—and the kind of prestige items are very different is for the discussion here without relevance.

7. It is understood here that special shapes are difficult to understand and interpret, which can be seen during any experiment in an archaeological class, where slightly more specialized containers (such as a fat-divider) or containers used in particular ritual contexts (frankincense containers used in the Catholic Church) are not being recognized by students.

8. The different terminologies are not consistently used throughout the various excavation reports.

9. The best made examples show a certain similarity to a "Römer" wine glass.

10. The few goblets from Kissufim are different from the above described drinking vessels (Goren and Fabian, 2002: Figure 4.1).

11. In Safadi they appear in one sub-terranean structure and otherwise on surface levels (Commenge-Pellerin, 1990: Figures 36.1–6, 10–11); in Matar the distribution is similar (Commenge-Pellerin, 1987: Figure 22.4–7).

12. Modern developments in the Western world, where even one kind of drink, wine, requires at least four to five very finely differentiated glass shapes (white wine, red wine, burgundy, sweet white wine, port, madeira) is certainly a case that cannot be transferred back in history, as it is both due to capitalist economic conditions of selling several sets of wine glasses to the same household, and the fact that the knowledge of the right wine glass allows subtle social distinctions. So it is clearly a system to exclude people (who drink their wine from plastic cups).

13. The use as milk containers is a function which has long been assumed because of ethnographical comparisons to these unusually shaped pots.

14. The more arid areas of the central Negev show a higher use of caprids than the wetter areas along the Mediterranean coast or along the eastern mountains.
15. The case is much clearer in later time periods such as in Tell Bazi in the Late Bronze Age, where jars of different sizes have been shown to have contained beer (Otto, 2012: 188).
16. Discussions about feasting in the Neolithic are generally more concentrated on meat consumption (e.g. Gorring-Morris and Belfer-Cohen, 2011, Fletcher and Campbell, Chapter 9) due to the nature of the evidence. But Katz and Voigt (1986) and Haaland (2007) follow the line of argument that early cereal domestication could have led to early beer.

11. How Chicken Rice Informs about Identity

1. The orchid Vanda Miss Joaquim was made the national flower of Singapore in 1981. In contrast to other national flowers, it is noteworthy that the Vanda Miss Joaquim is a hybrid. It was the first Singapore hybrid plant to be registered (*Singapore: The Encyclopedia*, 2006: 578). The merlion is a mythical creature which possesses a lion's head and the body of a fish. The idea of using a merlion to symbolize Singapore as the "Lion City" was mooted in 1964 by the then Singapore Tourist Promotion Board. In 1972, Lim Nang Seng was commissioned to create Singapore's Merlion sculpture (*Singapore: The Encyclopedia*, 2006: 349).
2. Swee Kee is a famous Hainanese coffee shop in Singapore. However, there is much debate over whether it was Swee Kee or still another Hainanese coffee shop Yet Kon Hainanese that first served chicken rice.

12. Feasting on Locusts and Truffles in the Second Millennium BCE

1. Page numbers cannot be supplied for Porter (2012) as the version read is a Kindle e-book.
2. A thorough discussion of this problem can be found in Sasson (1998).
3. Reynolds (2007) provides a good overview of food and drink in the OB period.
4. More examples can be found in Lepp (2009).
5. Akkad = Mesopotamia

13. Commensality and Sharing in an Andean Community in Bolivia

1. The road one reaches connects the mining town Colquechaca with Surumi, a place of pilgrimage. However, there is not much traffic on this road, and people frequently walk the remaining way to Colquechaca, a walk that took me about 14 hours.

2. This does not mean that there are 58 active households in the community at any one time because mobility is one of its characteristics. People constantly move about.

3. Germán like some other Cabrequeños speaks very little Spanish and sometimes used it when talking to me, while Clemencia, like most older inhabitants and women, does not know any Spanish at all.

4. Examining the history of sugar Sydney Mintz lists a mentioning of the "value of sugar as *dentifrice*" by the Englishman Dr. Frederick Slare from 1715 (Mintz, 1985: 107).

5. Stevia is a plant the leaves of which are used as a sweetener. It is sold in the form of a white powder.

6. These fields can also become a temporary home for a few days or even weeks. A shelter is erected and the whole household moves.

7. Other forms of *compadrazgo* occur, e.g. when people choose godparents for their marriage, or for the ritual of a child's first haircut.

8. It is important, however, to acknowledge that blood relations are important in the Andes in some contexts. Due to the length and focus of this chapter, I am not dealing with them here.

9. Sometimes the opposite seemed to occur as well, i.e. special products were hidden away or denied.

14. Dissolved in Liquor and Life: Drinkers and Drinking Cultures in Mo Yan's Novel *Liquorland*

1. For further reading on Chinese new historicism see Choy 2008 and Lin 2005.

2. The character 酒 translates to mean alcohol in the broadest sense, incorporating everything from beer to hard liquor. It is the latter, however, that plays the major part in the novel.

3. Cannibalism is a highly charged subject in Chinese literature, see Møller-Olsen 2011.

4. The earliest archaeological find of fermented beverages was discovered in Jiahu 賈湖, a Neolithic dwelling in Henan, and dates about 7000–5600 BCE (McGovern, 2009: 42).

5. Women are sometimes praised for their capacity for liquor as well, but it is not expected of them in the same way as it is of a man. The psychology behind this masculine idealization of the great drinker might be connected to the relatively low alcohol tolerance of many Chinese, and yet similar masculine attitudes towards drink are found in many other cultures.

6. And, by extension, the artist in general, but poets are the main interest for this study.

7. Examples of the berserk heroes from this source include the monk Li Zhishen 鲁智深 and Li Kui 李逵 the pugilist.

8. Detective Hunter, a Hollywood descendant of the hard boiled Private Eye of the 1930s, was very popular in China at the time the writing of *Liquorland*, and Mo Yan has pointed to him as inspiration for Ding Gou'er (Yue, 1999: 281).

9. Though mainly concerned with male PIs, Rippetoe also has one chapter on alcohol and female detectives, see Rippetoe, 2004: 158–75. For more on gender and alcohol in American literature see Crowley, 1994.

10. Namely the daughter of the legendary ruler Da Yu (大禹 2200–2100 BCE).

11. An early female poet writing about liquor was Li Qing Zhao (李清照 1084–1151 CE).

12. In subsequent citations from the novel the first page number refers to the English translation (Mo, 2000), the second to the Chinese original (Mo, 1992).

13. With the exception of the female mayor of Liquorland who is only mentioned in passing, but whose renowned ability to "hold her liquor" serves to make Mo Yan's unmanly inability to hold his even more embarrassing (352/273).

15. Justifications for Foodways and the Study of Commensality

1. I would like to thank Israel Haas for his invaluable advice and assistance in preparing this chapter. Any errors that remain should be credited to the author alone.

2. My discussion of the first two texts draws on a forthcoming essay (Rosenblum, forthcoming).

3. Translation by Colson (1939: 249–51).

4. See Exodus 23.19; 34.26; Deuteronomy 14.21.

5. "The ancient rabbis" refer to the first two groups of rabbis (the Tannaim and the Amoraim). For a brief summary of their history and literature, see Strack and Stemberger (1996). Subsequent rabbis trace their lineage, authority, texts, and practices from these early rabbinic circles.

6. All translations from Hebrew are my own.

7. The plural pronoun here either anticipates the application of the parable, as the dying person is compared to the other nations, or is addressed to the ones taking care of the patient.

8. See Rosenblum (2010a: 91–101; 2010b: 18–29).

9. See *b. Avodah Zarah* 31b.

10. Israelites are supposed to be in a monogamous relationship with God. Thus, when they worship other gods, they have gone a-whoring and committed adultery. For an example of this theology, see Hosea. Idolatry is therefore a practice that is sexualized beginning in the biblical corpus itself.

11. Here, I am influenced by Catherine Bell (1992).

16. The Role of Food in the Life of Christians in the Roman Empire

1. Note on the translation: There is a certain tradition of translation when dealing with NT-texts. I have tried to avoid this and to be as precise as possible, rather than elegant. I have consistently referred to "the god," rather than "God," because that is what the text says. I have kept "Christos" because I believe it did not yet mean "Christ" as we understand that word. But because Paul does not use an article it should not be translated as "the anointed one," which is what it originally meant. At this time it seems to be between these two meanings.

17. Ritual Meals and Polemics in Antiquity

1. The terms "external other" and "internal other" are borrowed from Rosenblum (2010a: 141) and Hayes (2007).

2. Jaime Alvar uses the term "commensality" to describe the common religious and cultural context in the Empire (Alvar, 2008: 417–21).

3. Commensality is sharing a table (*mensa*) with companions. ("Companions" are literally those who share bread, *panis*.) You eat with those that are part of your group, and each person is usually a member of different groups, a family group as well as groups related to a trade, to society or to religion.

4. Porphyry claimed that animals were offered up to good and bad *daimones* and not to the highest god or to the celestial gods (*Abst.* 2.34–36), a view shared with other philosophers (Rives, 2011: 195).

5. The dead were fed with libations of milk, wine, water, honey, and oil that were poured out on the graves. Sometimes a holocaust animal sacrifice was made,

(that is a sacrifice were the victim is totally consumed by fire), usually of a pig, and blood sating might take place (*haimakouria*) (Ogden, 2001: 7). This type of communication with the dead implied to keep a distance between them and the living, in this case there was no commensality with ghosts.

6. *Theoxenion* (Greek) and *lectisternium* (Latin).

7. *Corpus Inscriptionum et Monumentorum Religionis Mithriacae* 1956–60.

8. Eucharist means "thanksgiving" and is used as a technical term from the second century CE, as seen for instance in Ignatius and Justin. Not all Christian groups supported a sacrificial interpretation of Christianity. In the newfound *Gospel of Judas* the 12 disciples are cast as representatives of a competing branch of Christianity from the Christianity that is promoted by the *Gospel of Judas*. The gospel speaks against the ruling sacrificial interpretations of Christianity, according to Louis Painchaud, "there is good reason to believe that the *Gospel of Judas* is a polemical text, reacting against the sacrificial ideology that grew and established itself in the Christianity of the second century. The *Gospel of Judas* views this ideology as a perpetuation of the Jewish sacrificial cult, which is seen as being addressed to the archon of Saklas, and which Jesus wished his disciples to abolish" (Painchaud, 2008: 184; cf. Petersen, 2012).

9. According to Justin: "And this food is called among us *eucharistia* [the Eucharist] … For not as common bread and common drink do we receive these; but in like manner as Jesus Christ our Saviour, having been made flesh by the Word of God, had both flesh and blood for our salvation, so likewise have we been taught that the food which is blessed by the prayer of His word, and from which our blood and flesh by transmutation are nourished, is the flesh and blood of that Jesus who was made flesh" (Justin, *First Apology*, 66).

10. The close connection between meat and sex is, for instance, seen in the canons of the Synod of Gangra (c. 350) where the first two canons anathematize anyone who condemns lawful marriage and anyone who condemns those who eat meat that has been slaughtered in the prescribed way (cf. Shaw, 1998: 233). The condemnations of eating meat and of being sexually active appear in tandem and mark the boundaries to other not-so-ascetic groups.

11. Clauss points out that Tertullian seems to know the Mithras mysteries very well and suggests that he as the son of a centurion could have been initiated in the mysteries (Clauss, 1986: 268; Beskow, 1994: 51).

References

Adema, P. 2007. "Foodscape: An Emulsion of Food and Landscape." *Gastronomica: The Journal of Food and Culture* 7(1): 3.

Adolph, A. 2009. *Food and Femininity in Twentieth-Century British Women's Fiction*. Farnham: Ashgate Publishing.

Agresta, A. 2011. "Meaning and Social Use of an Urban Garden: The Medici Palace Garden in the Fifteenth Century." Unpublished paper presented at Yale University.

Akre, J. 2009. "From Grand Design to Change on the Ground: Going to Scale with a Global Feeding Strategy." In F. Dykes and V. Moran (eds), *Infant and Young Child Feeding: Challenges to Implementing a Global Strategy*. Oxford: Wiley-Blackwell.

Albala, K. 2007. *The Banquet: Dining in the Great Courts of Late Renaissance Europe*. Urbana, IL: University of Illinois Press.

Alizadeh, A. 2008. *Chogha Mish II. The Development of a Prehistoric Regional Center in Lowland Susiana, Southwestern Iran. Final Report on the Last Six Seasons of Excavations, 1972–1978*. Oriental Institute Publications 130. Chicago, IL: The Oriental Institute of the University of Chicago.

Allen, C. 1988. *The Hold Life Has: Coca and Cultural Identity in an Andean Community*. Washington, DC and London: Smithsonian Institution Press.

Alonso, A. M. 1994. "The Politics of Space, Time, and Substance: State Formation, Nationalism and Ethnicity." *Annual Review of Anthropology* 23: 379–405.

Altenburg, D., Jarmut, J., and Steinhoff, H.-H. (eds) 1991. *Feste und Feiern im Mittelalter*. Sigmaringen: J. Thorbecke.

Alvar, J. 2008. *Romanising Oriental Gods. Myth, Salvation and Ethics in the Cults of Cybele, Isis and Mithras*. Leiden: Brill.

Amundsen, C. P. 2008. *Culture Contact, Ehnicity and Food Practices of Coastal Finnmark, Norway (1200 to 1600 A.D.)*. Ph.D. dissertation, Department of Anthropology, City University of New York, New York.

Andaya, L. Y. 2010. *Leaves of the Same Tree: Trade and Ethnicity in the Straits of Melaka*. Singapore: National University of Singapore Press.

Anderson, B. 1983. *Imagined Communities: Reflections on the Origin and Spread of Nationalism*. London: Verso.

Anderson, E. N. 2005. *Everyone Eats: Understanding Food and Culture*. New York: New York University Press.

Anigbo, O. A. C. 1987. *Commensality and Human Relationship among the Igbo.* Nsukka: University of Nigeria Press.

—1996. "Commensality as Cultural Performance: The Struggle for Leadership in an Igbo Village." In D. Parkin, L. Caplan, and H. Fisher (eds), *The Politics of Cultural Performance*, pp. 101–14. Oxford: Berghahn Books. Anonymous. 1826. [Note on meals offered by the Speaker of the House of Commons]. *New Monthly Magazine and Literary Journal* 22: 326.

—2007. (Attributed to "Dealbook"). "Inside Stephen Schwarzman's Birthday Bash." Available from http://dealbook.ny-times.com/2007/02/14/inside-stephen-schwarzmans-birthday-bash/

Appadurai, Arjun. 1981. "GastroPolitics in Hindu South Asia." *American Ethnologist* 8: 494–511.

Aranda Jiménez, G. and Monton-Subias, S. 2011. "Feasting Death: Funerary Rituals in the Bronze Age Societies of South-Eastern Iberia." In G. Aranda Jiménez, S. Montón-Subías, and M. Sánchez-Romero (eds), *Guess Who's Coming to Dinner: Feasting Rituals in the Prehistoric Societies of Europe and the Near East*, pp. 130–57. Oxford: Oxbow.

Aranda Jiménez, G., Montón-Subías, S., and Sánchez-Romero, M. (eds) 2011. *Guess Who's Coming to Dinner: Feasting Rituals in the Prehistoric Societies of Europe and the Near East.* Oxford: Oxbow.

Athanasius. 1991. "Vita Antonii." In P. Schaff and H. Wace (eds), *Athanasius: Select Works and Letters.* A Select Library of The Nicene and Post-Nicene Fathers, II, 4. Edinburgh: T&T Clark, 1991 [reprint].

Augustine of Hippo. 2006. "The Catholic Way of Life and the Manichean Way of Life." In: *The Manichean Debate.* Introduction and Notes by R. Teske. (S. J. Works of Saint Augustine: A Translation for the 21st Century I/19). Hyde Park: New City Press.

—1977–9. "Confessiones." In *St. Augustine's Confessions*, trans. William Watts, pp. 188–221. Loeb Classical Library. Cambridge, MA and London: Harvard University Press & William Heinemann.

Aurell, M., Dumoulin, O., and Thelamon, F. (eds) 1992. *La sociabilité à table. Commensalité et convivialité à travers les âges.* Rouen: Université de Rouen.

Australian National Botanic Gardens (2012). "Desert Truffles—Middle East and Mediterranean."

Avieli, N. 2005. Vietnamese New Year rice cakes: iconic festive dishes and contested national identity. *Ethnology* 44(2): 167–87.

Balossi Restelli, F., Sadori, L., and Masi, A. 2010. "Agriculture at Arslantepe at the End of the 4th Millennium BC. Did the Centralised Political Institutions Have an Influence on Farming Practices?" In M. Frangipane (ed.) *Economic Centralisation in Formative States. The Archaeological Reconstruction of the*

Economic System in 4th Millennium Arslantepe. Studi di Preistoria Orientale 3, pp. 103–17. Rome: Sapienza Università di Roma.

Banquets et manières de table au Moyen Âge. 1996. Aix-en-Provence: Université de Provence.

Barnard, H., Dooley, A. N., Areshian, G., Gasparyan, and B., and Faull, K. F. 2011. "Chemical evidence for wine production around 4000 B.C.E. in the late Chalcolithic near Eastern Highlands." *Journal of Archaeological Science* 38: 977–84.

Baroni, L., Cenci, L., Tettamanti, M., and Berati, M. 2006. "Evaluating the Environmental Impact of Various Dietary Patterns Combined with Different Food Production Systems." *European Journal of Clinical Nutrition* 61(2): 27–86.

Barthes, R. 2008. "Toward a Psychosociology of Contemporary Food Consumption." In C. Counihan and P. Van Esterik (eds), *Food and Culture: A Reader*, (2nd edn) pp. 28–35. New York: Routledge.

Beardsworth, A. and Keil, T. 1997. *Sociology on the Menu: An Invitation to the Study of Food and Society*. London: Routledge.

Beck, M. E. and Hill, M. E. 2004. Rubbish, Relatives and Residence: The Family Use of Middens. *Journal of Archaeological Method and Theory* 11(3): 297–333.

BeDuhn, J. D. 2000. *The Manichaean Body. In Discipline and Ritual*. Baltimore, MD and London: The Johns Hopkins University Press.

Beer, M. 2010. *Taste or Taboo: Dietary Choices in Antiquity*. London: Prospect Books.

Belasco, W. 2002. Food Matters: Perspectives on an Emerging Field. In Warren Belasco and Philip Scranton (eds), *Food Nations: Selling Taste in Consumer Societies*, pp. 2–23. New York and London: Routledge.

—2005. Food and the Counterculture: A Story of Bread and Politics. In J. L. Watson and M. L. Caldwell (eds), *The Cultural Politics of Food and Eating: A Reader*, pp. 219–20. Malden, MA: Blackwell Publishing.

Belasco, W. J. 2006. *Meals to Come—A History of the Future of Food*. Berkeley, CA and London: University of California Press.

Bell, C. 1992. *Ritual Theory, Ritual Practice*. Oxford: Oxford University Press.

Bell, D, and Gill V. (eds). 1997. *Consuming Geographies: We Are Where We Eat*. London and New York: Routledge.

Bellan-Boyer, L. 2003. Conspicuous in their Absence: Women in Early Christianity. *Cross Currents* 53(1): 48–63.

Benson, G. 1919. *Later Medieval York: The City and Country from 1100 to 1603*. York: Coutas and Volans.

Bernbeck, R. 2008. Taming Time and Timing the Tamed. In J. Córdoba, M. Molist, C. Pérez, I. Rubio and S. Martínez (eds), *Proceedings of the 5th International Congress on the Archaeology of the Ancient Near East Madrid, April 3–8 2006*

III, pp. 709–28. Madrid: Centro Superior de Estudios sobre el Oriente Próximo y Egipto.

—and Pollock, S. 2002. Reflections on the Historiography of 4th Millennium Mesopotamia. In A. Hausleiter et al. (eds), *Material Culture and Mental Spheres. Rezeption archäologischer Denkrichtungen in der vorderasiatischen Archäologie. Internationales Symposium für Hans J. Nissen, Berlin, 23–24 Juni 2000.* Alter Orient und Altes Testament 293, pp. 171–204. Münster: Ugarit-Verlag.

—and Pollock, S. 2003. The Biography of an Early Halaf Village: Fıstıklı Höyük 1999–2000. *Istanbuler Mitteilungen* 53: 9–77.

Beskow. P. 1994. Tertullian on Mithras. In J. R. Hinnells (ed.), *Studies in Mithraism*, pp. 51–60. Rome: L'Erma di Bretschneider.

Bey, H. 2003. *T.A.Z. Temporary Autonomous Zone, Ontological Anarchy, Poetic Terrorism.* 2nd edn. Brooklyn, NY: Autonomedia.

Bjørnebye, J. 2002. *The Multivalent Symbol: A Preliminary Study of the Meanings and Functions of the Symbol of the Sacred Meal in Roman Mithraism.* Master's thesis. Oslo: University of Oslo.

Black, J. A. et al. 2006. *The Electronic Text Corpus of Sumerian Literature,* text 1.7.1 (http://etcsl.orinst.ox.ac.uk/), Oxford.

Bloch, M. 1999. Commensality and Poisoning. *Social Research* 66(1): 133–49.

Borowski, O. 1998. *Every Living Thing: Daily Use of Animals in Ancient Israel.* Walnut Creek, CA: AltaMira.

Bott. E. 2003. The Kava Ceremonial as a Dream Structure. In M. Douglas (ed.), *Constructive Drinking*, pp. 182–204. Cambridge: Cambridge University Press.

Bottéro, J. 1995. *Textes culinaires Mésopotamiens* (Mesopotamian Civilization 6). Winona Lake, IN: Eisenbrauns.

—2004. *The Oldest Cuisine in the World: Cooking in Mesopotamia*, trans. T. L. Fagan. Chicago, IL: University of Chicago Press.

Bourdieu, Pierre. 1972. *Esquisse d'une théorie de la pratique, précédé de trois études d'éthnologie kabyle.* Geneva: Droz.

—. 1984. *Distinction: A Social Critique of the Judgment of Taste.* Cambridge, MA: Harvard University Press.

—1984. *Distinction: A Social Critique of the Judgment of Taste*, trans. Richard Nice. Cambridge, MA: Harvard University Press.

Bourke S. J. 2001. "The Chalcolithic Period." In B. McDonald, R. Adams, and P. Bienkowski (eds), *The Archaeology of Jordan*, pp. 107–62. Sheffield: Academic Press.

Bourque, N. 2001. "Eating your Words: Communicating with Food in the Ecuadorian Andes." In J. Hendry and C. W. Watson (eds), *An Anthropology of Indirect Communication*, pp. 85–100. London: Routledge.

Bradley, R. 2003. A life less ordinary: the ritualization of the domestic sphere in later prehistoric Europe. *Cambridge Archaeological Journal* 13(1): 5–23.

—2005. *Ritual and Domestic Life in Prehistoric Europe*. London: Routledge.

Braidwood, R. J. 1953. Symposium: did man once live by beer alone? *American Anthropologist* 55(4): 515–26.

Bray, T. (ed.). 2003a. *The Archaeology and Politics of Food and Feasting in Early States and Empires*. New York: Kluwer Academic/Plenum Publishers.

—2003b. "To Dine Splendidly: Imperial Pottery, Commensal Politics, and the Inca State." In T. Bray (ed.), *The Archaeology and Politics of Food and Feasting in Early States and Empires*, pp. 93–142. New York: Kluwer Academic/Plenum Publishers.

Brembeck, H. and Johansson, B. 2010. "Foodscapes and Children's Bodies." *Culture Unbound* 2: 798–818.

Breniquet, C. 1992. "A propos du vase halafien de la tombe G2 de Tell Arpachiyah." *Iraq* 54: 69–78.

Brown, P. 1995. *Authority and the Sacred. Aspects of the Christianization of the Roman World*. Cambridge: Cambridge University Press.

Bruce, N., Perez Padilla, R., and Albafak, R. 2002. *The Health Effect of Indoor Pollution Exposure in Developing Countries*. Geneva: World Health Organization.

Brück, J. 1999. Ritual and Rationality: Some Problems of Interpretation in European Archaeology. *European Journal of Archaeology* 2(3): 313–44.

Brunke, H. 2011. Feasts for the Living, the Dead, and the Goods. In K. Radner and E. Robson (eds), *The Oxford Handbook of Cuneiform Culture*, pp. 167–83. Oxford: Oxford University Press.

Burckhardt, J. L. 1822. *Travels in Syria and in the Holy Land*. London: J. Murray.

Burgoine, T., Lake, A. A., Stampe, E., Alvanides, S., Mathers. J. C., and Adamson, A. J. 2009. "Changing Foodscapes 1980–000, Using the ASH30 Study." *Appetite* 53(2): 157–65.

Burton, M. McD. 2004. *Collapse, Continuity and Transformation: Tracking Protohistoric Social Change Through Ceramic Analysis. Case Studies of 5th-Earlz 4th Millennium Societies in the Southern Levant*. Unpublished Ph.D. thesis. ProQuest.

Butler, J. 1990. *Gender Trouble*. London: Routledge.

Buxó, R. and Principal, J. 2011. "Consumption Relations in the Northern Iberian Household." In G. Aranda Jiménez, S. Montón-Subías, and M. Sánchez-Romero (eds) *Guess Who's Coming to Dinner: Feasting Rituals in the Prehistoric Societies of Europe and the Near East*, pp. 204–23. Oxford: Oxbow.

CAD Oppenheim, A. L. (ed.) 1958. *Chicago Assyrian Dictionary, Volume 4: E*. Chicago, IL: Oriental Institute.

—(ed.) 1971. *Chicago Assyrian Dictionary, Volume 8: K*. Chicago, IL: Oriental Institute.

Callon, M. and Latour, B. 1992. "Don't Throw the Baby Out With the Bath School! A Reply to Collins and Yearly." In A. Pickering (ed.), *Science as Practice and Culture*, pp. 343–68. Chicago, IL and London: University of Chicago Press.

Camacho, J. 2006. "Bueno para comer, bueno para pensar." In R. Rhodes (ed.), *Desarollo con identidad: Comunidad, cultura y sustentabilidad en los Andes*. Quito: Abya-Yala.

Cameron, A. 2011. *The Last Pagans of Rome*. Oxford: Oxford University Press.

Cameron, C. 2006. "Ethnoarchaeology and Contextual Studies." In D. Papconstantinou (ed.), *Deconstructing Context: A Critical Approach to Archaeological Practice*, pp. 22–33. Oxford: Oxbow.

Cameron, J. 1865. *Our Tropical Possessions in Malayan India: Being a Descriptive Account of Singapore, Penang, Province Wellesley, and Malacca; Their Peoples, Products, Commerce, and Government*. London: Smith, Elder and Co. [Reprinted 1965, Kuala Lumpur: Oxford University Press.]

Campbell, S. 1999. "Archaeological Constructs and Past Reality on the Upper Euphrates." In G. d. O. Lete and J. L. M. Fenollos (eds), *Archaeology of the Upper Syrian Euphrates: The Tishrin Dam Area*, pp. 573–83. Barcelona: Editorial Ausa.

—2004. "Domuztepe 2004 Excavation Season." *Anatolian Archaeology* 10: 4–6.

—2005. "Domuztepe 2005." *Anatolian Archaeology* 11: 4–7.

—2007. "Rethinking Halaf chronologies." *Paléorient* 33(1): 101–34.

—2007–8. "The Dead and the Living in Late Neolithic Mesopotamia." In G. Bartoloni and M. G. Benedettini (eds), *Sepolti tra i vivi. Evidenza ed interpretazione di contesti funerari in abitato*, pp. 125–40. Rome: Atti del Convegno Internazionale, Università degli Studi di Roma "La Sapienza."

—and Carter, E., Healey, E., Anderson, S., Kennedy, A., and Whitcher, S. 1999. "Emerging complexity on the Kahramanmaras Plain, Turkey: The Domuztepe Project 1995–1997." *American Journal of Archaeology* 103: 395–418.

—and Fletcher, A. Forthcoming. "Round the Houses: New Perspectives on Halaf Buildings." *Antiquity*.

—and Healey, E. 2011. "Stones of the Living and Bones of the Dead? Contextualising the Lithics in the Death Pit at Domuztepe." In E. Healey, S. Campbell, and O. Maeda (eds), *The State of the Stone: Terminologies, Continuities and Contexts in Near Eastern Lithics. Studies in Early Near Eastern Production, Subsistence, and Environment* 13, pp. 327–42. Berlin: Ex oriente.

Capatti, A., Montanari, M., and O'Healy, A. 2003. *Italian Cuisine: A Cultural History*. New York: Columbia University Press.

Caplan, P. 1994. *Feasts, Fasts, Famine: Food for Thought*. Oxford: Berg.

Carter, E., Campbell, S., and Gauld, S. 2003. "Elusive Complexity: New Data From late Halaf Domuztepe in South Central Turkey." *Paléorient* 29(2): 117–33.

Carton, P. 1912. *Les Trois Aliments Meurtriers. La Viande, l'Alcool, le Sucre.* Paris: Maloine.

Chan, K S. 2007. Poonchoi: "The Production and Popularity of a Rural Festive Cuisine in Urban and Modern Hong Kong." In S. C.H. Cheung and T. Chee-Beng (eds), *Food and Foodways in Asia: Resource, Tradition and Cooking*, pp. 53–66. London: Routledge.

Chan, S. C. 2010. "Food, Memories, and Identities in Hong Kong." *Identities: Global Studies in Culture and Power* 17(2): 204–27.

Chang, K. C. 1977. *Food in Chinese Culture: Anthropological and Historical Perspectives.* New Haven, CT: Yale University Press.

Chapman, J. 1996. "Enchainment, Commodification and Gender in the Balkan Neolithic and Copper Age." *Journal of European Archaeology* 4: 203–42.

—2000a. *Fragmentation in Archaeology. People Places and Broken Objects in the Prehistory of South Eastern Europe.* London: Routledge.

—2000b. "Pit digging and structured deposition in the Neolithic and Copper Age." *Proceedings of the Prehistoric Society* 66: 61–87.

Chesson, M. S. 2000. "Ceramics and Daily Life in the EBA Household: Form, Function and Action in Residential Compounts at Tell el-Handaquq South, Jordan." In G. Philip and D. Baird (eds), *Ceramics and Change in the EBA of the Southern Levant*, pp. 365–78. Sheffield: Sheffield Academic Press.

Cheung, S. C. H. 2005. "Consuming 'low' cuisine after Hong Kong's handover: village banquets and private kitchens. *Asian Studies Review* 29: 249–63.

Chiera, E. 1934. *Sumerian Texts of Varied Contents.* Chicago, IL.

Chiquart. 1986. *Chiquart's "On Cookery": A Fifteenth-Century Savoyard Culinary Treatise.* T. Scully (ed. and trans.). New York: P. Lang.

Chou, C. 2003. *Indonesian Sea Nomads: Money, Magic, and Fear of the Orang Suku Laut.* London and New York: RoutledgeCurzon.

—2010. *The Orang Suku Laut of Riau, Indonesia: The Inalienable Gift of Territory.* London and New York: Routledge.

Choy, H. Y. F. 2008. *Remapping the Past: Fictions of History in Deng's China, 1979–1997.* Leiden: Brill.

Clarke, G. 2004. *Christianity and Roman Society.* Cambridge: Cambridge University Press.

Clarke, M. J. 2001. "Akha Feasting: An Ethnoarchaeological Perspective." In M. Dietler and B. Hayden (eds), *Feasts: Archaeological and Ethnographic Perspectives on Food, Politics, and Power*, pp. 144–67. Washington, DC: Smithsonian Institution Press.

Clarkson, J. 2009. *Menus from History: Historical Meals and Recipes for Every Day of the Year* (2 vols). Santa Barbara, CA: Greenwood Press.

Clauss, M. 1986. "Mithras und Christus." *Historische Zeitschrift* 243(2): 265–85.

—2000. *The Roman Cult of Mithras: The God and his Mysteries*. R. Gordon (trans.). Edinburgh: Edinburgh University Press.

Cohn, B. and Dirks, N. 1988. "Beyond the Fringe: The Nation State, Colonialism, and the Technologies of Power." *Journal of Historical Sociology* 12: 224–29.

Cologne Mani Codex. 1979. R. Cameron and A. J. Dewey (trans.). Missoula, MT: Scholars Press.

Colson, F. H. 1939. *Philo*. Vol. 8. LCL. Cambridge, MA: Harvard University Press.

Commenge, C. 2006. Gilat's Ceramics: Cognitive Dimensions of Pottery Production. In T. E. Levy (ed.), *Archaeology, Anthropology and Cult*, pp. 394–506. London: Equinox.

Commenge-Pellerin, C. 1987. *La Poterie d'Abou Matar et de l'Ouadi Zoumeili (Beershéva) au IVe millénaire avant l'ère chrétienne*. Les Cahiers du Centre de Recherche Française de Jérusalem 3. Paris: Association Paléorient.

—1990. *La Poterie du Safadi (Beershéva) au IVe millénaire avant l'ère chrétienne*. Les Cahiers du Centre de Recherche Française de Jérusalem 5. Paris: Association Paléorient.

Corley, K. E. 1993. *Private Women, Public Meals: Social Conflict in the Synoptic Tradition*. Peabody, MA: Hendrickson Publishers.

Counihan. C. 1999. *The Anthropology of Food and Body: Gender, Meaning and Power*. New York: Routledge.

—2004. *Around the Tuscan Table: Food, Family, and Gender in Twentieth-Century Florence*. New York andLondon: Routledge.

Crossan, J. D. 1995. *Jesus: A Revolutionary Biography*. New York: HarperCollins.

Crowder, L. S. 2005. "The Chinese Mortuary Tradition in San Francisco Chinatown." In Sue Fawn Chung and Priscilla Wegars (eds), *Chinese American Death Rituals: Respecting the Ancestors*, pp. 195–240. Lanham, MD: AltaMira Press.

Crowley, J. W. 1994. *The White Logic: Alcoholism and Gender in American Modernist Fiction*. Amherst, MA: University of Massachusetts Press.

Curet, L. A. and Pestle, W. J. 2010. Identifying High-Status Foods in the Archeological Record. *Journal of Anthropological Archaeology* 29: 413–31.

D'Anna, M. B. 2010. "The Ceramic Containers of Period VI A. Food Control at the Time of Centralisation." In M. Frangipane (ed.), *Economic Centralisation in Formative States. The Archaeological Reconstruction of the Economic System in 4th Millennium Arslantepe*. Studi di Preistoria Orientale 3, pp. 167–91. Rome: Sapienza Università di Roma.

—2012. "Between Inclusion and Exclusion. Feasting and Redistribution of Meals at Late Chalcolithic Arslantepe (Malatya, Turkey)." In S. Pollock (ed.), *Between Feasts and Daily Meals. Towards an Archaeology of Commensal Spaces, eTopoi, Journal for Ancient Studies*, Special Volume 2, pp. 97–123. Available from http://journal.topoi.org

—and Piccione, P. 2010. "Food Circulation and Management in Public and Domestic Spheres during the Periods VI A and VI B2. A Comparative Perspective." In M. Frangipane (ed.), *Economic Centralisation in Formative States. The Archaeological Reconstruction of the Economic System in 4th Millennium Arslantepe*. Studi di Preistoria Orientale 3, pp. 231–40. Rome: Sapienza Università di Roma.

Dahl, J. 2005. Animal Husbandry in Susa During the Proto Elamite Period. *SMEA* 47: 81–134.

Dalley, S. 1984. *Mari and Karana: Two Old Babylonian Cities*. London and New York: Longman.

Damerow, P. 1998. "Food Production and Social Status as Documented in Proto-Cuneiform Texts." In P. Wiessner and K. Schiefenhövel (eds), *Food and the Status Quest: An Interdisciplinary Perspective. The Anthropology of Food and Nutrition 1*, pp. 149–69. Providence, RI: Berghan Books.

Daróczi-Szabó, L. 2004. "Animal Bones as Indicators of *Kosher* Food Refuse From 14th Century AD Buda, Hungary." In S. J. O'Day W. van Neer, and A. Ervynck (eds), *Behaviour Behind Bones: The Zooarchaeology of Religion, Ritual, Status, and Identity*, pp. 252–61. Oxford: Oxbow.

Davies, R. W. 1971. "The Roman military diet." *Britannica* 2: 122–42.

Davies, S. J. 2008. *Coptic Christology in Practice: Incarnation and Divine Participation in Late Antiquity and Medieval Egypt*. Oxford: Oxford University Press.

Davis, M. 2004. "Power Meal: Craig Claiborne's Last Supper for the *New York Times*." *Gastronomica* 4(3): 60–72.

Dawson, M. 2008. "Changing Tastes in Sixteenth-century England: Evidence from the Household Accounts of the Willoughby Family." In S. Baker, M. Allen, S. Middle, and K. Poole (eds), *Food and Drink in Archaeology I: University of Nottingham Postgraduate Conference 2007*, pp. 20–7. Trowbridge: Prospect Books.

Delgado, A. and Ferrer, M. 2011. "Representing Communities in Heterogeneous Worlds: Staple Foods and Ritual Practices in the Phoenician Diaspora." In G. Aranda Jiménez, S. Montón-Subías, and M. Sánchez-Romero (eds), *Guess Who's Coming to Dinner: Feasting Rituals in the Prehistoric Societies of Europe and the Near East*, pp. 184–203. Oxford: Oxbow.

Delgado, C. L., Rosegrant, M., Steinfeld, H., Ehui, S., and Courbois, C. 1999a. "The Coming Livestock Revolution." *Background Paper* No. 6. June. FAO Department of Economic and Social Affairs—Commission on Sustainable Development. Available from http://www.un.org/esa/sustdev/csd/ecn172000-bp6.pdf

—1999b. *Livestock to 2020, The Next Food Revolution: A 2020 Vision for Food, Agriculture, and the Environment*. October. Washington, DC: IFPRI, Washington (EEUU).

Delougaz, P., Kantor, H. J., and Alizadeh, A. 1996. *Chogha Mish. The First Five Seasons of Excavations 1961–1971*. Oriental Institute Publications 101. Chicago, IL: Oriental Institute of the University of Chicago.

Detienne, M. 1981 "Between Beasts and Gods." In R. Gordon (ed.), *Myth, Religion and Society: Structural Essays by M. Detienne, L. Gernet, J. P. Vernant and P. Vidal-Naquet*, pp. 215–28. Cambridge and Paris: Cambridge University Press/ Editions de la Maison des sciences d l'homme.

Detienne, M. and J. P. Vernant. 1989. *The Cuisine of Sacrifice among the Greeks*. Chicago, IL: University of Chicago Press.

Dietler, M. 1990. "Driven by drink: the role of drinking in the political economy and the case of early Iron Age France." *Journal of Anthropological Archaeology* 9: 352–406.

—1996. "Feasts and Commensal Politics in the Political Economy: Food, Power and Status in Prehistoric Europe." In P. Weissner and W. Schiefenhovel (eds), *Food and the Status Quest: An Interdisciplinary Perspective*, pp. 87–125. Oxford: Berghahn Books.

—2001. "Theorizing the feast: rituals of consumption, commensal politics, and power in African contexts." In M. Dietler and B. Hayden (eds), *Feasts: Archaeological and Ethnographic Perspectives on Food, Politics, and Power*, pp. 65–114. Smithsonian Institution Press: Washington, DC.

—2003. "Clearing the Table: Some Concluding Reflections on Commensal Politics and Imperial States." In T. L. Bray (ed.), *The Archaeology and Politics of Food and Feasting in Early States and Empires*, pp. 271–84. New York: Kluwer Academic/Plenum.

—2006. "Alcohol: anthropological/archaeological perspectives." *Annual Review of Anthropology* 35: 229–49.

—2007. Culinary Encounters: Food, Identity, and Colonialism. In K. Twiss (ed.), *The Archaeology of Food and Identity*, pp. 218–42. Carbondale: Southern Illinois University Press.

—and Hayden, B. (eds). 2001a. *Feasts: Archaeological and Ethnographic Perspectives on Food, Politics, and Power*. Washington DC and London: Smithsonian Institution Press.

—and Hayden, B. 2001b. "Digesting the Feast—Good to Eat, Good to Drink, Good to Think: An Introduction." In M. Dietler and B. Hayden (eds), *Feasts: Archaeological and Ethnographic Perspectives on Food, Politics, and Power*, pp. 1–22. Washington, DC: Smithsonian Institution Press.

Dio Chrysostom. 1932–51. In five volumes with an English translation by J. W. Cohoon and H. Lamar. (Loeb Classical Library). London: Heinemann.

Douglas, M. 1996. *Purity and Danger*. New York: Routledge.

—1975. "Deciphering a Meal." In *Implicit Meanings: Essays in Anthropology*, pp. 249–75. Boston, MA: Routledge & Kegan Paul.

—1984. "Standard Social Uses of Food: Introduction." In M. Douglas (ed.), *Food in the Social Order: Studies of Food and Festivities in Three American Communities*. New York: Russell Sage Foundation.

—(ed.) 2003. *Constructive Drinking*. Abingdon: Routledge.

Drewnowski, A. 1999. "Fat and Sugar in the Global Diet." In R. Grew (ed.), *Food in Global History*, pp. 194–206. Boulder, CO: Westview Press.

Driver, T. 1991. *The Magic of Ritual: Our Need for Liberating Rites that Transform our Lives and our Communities*. San Francisco, CA: Harper San Francisco.

Drouard, A. 2007. "Reforming Diet at the End of the Nineteenth Century in Europe." In P. J. Atkins, P. Lummel, and D. J. Oddy (eds), *Food and the City in Europe since 1800*, pp. 215–26. Aldershot: Ashgate Publishing.

Duncan, W. N. 2005. "Understanding Veneration and Violation in the Archaeological Record." In G. F. M. Rakita, J. E.Buikstra, L. A. Beck, and S. R. Williams (eds), *Interacting with the Dead: Perspectives on Mortuary Archaeology for the New Millennium*, pp. 207–27. Gainesville, FL: University of Florida Press.

Durkheim, E. 1981 [1894]. *The Gift: Forms and Funcitons of Exchange in Archaic Societies [Essai sur le don]*. I. Cunnison (trans.). London: Cohen.

Elias, N. 2000. *The Civilizing Process: Sociogenetic and Psychogenetic Investigations*. Rev. edn. E. Jephcott (trans.) with some notes and corrections by the author; J. Eric Dunning, J. Goudsblom, and S. Mennell (eds). Oxford: Blackwell.

Elsner, J. 1991. "Cult and sculpture: sacrifice in the Ara Pacis Augustae." *The Journal of Roman Studies* LXXXI: 50–61.

Engholm, M. 2010. *2009-boligundersøgelsen. Slutrapport fra undersøgelse af elever og studerendes boligvilkår I Hovedstadsområdet og Århus*. Danske elever og Studerendes Kollegieråd. Hellerup.

Englund, R. K. 1995a. "There's a rat in my soup!" *AltorientalischeForschungen* 22: 37–55.

—1995b. "Late Uruk Period Cattle and Dairy Products: Evidence from Proto-cuneiform Sources." *Bulletin on Sumerian Agriculture* 8: 33–48.

Epiphanius. 1987–94. *The Panarion of Epiphanius of Salamis*. F. Williams (trans.). Nag Hammadi Studies 35. Leiden: Brill.

Eshel, G. and Martin, P. A. 2006. "Diet, Energy, and Global Warming." *Earth Interactions* 10(9): 1–17. FAO Newsroom.

Eusebius, *The Church History*: A new translation and commentary by Paul L. Maier, Grand Rapids: Kregel Publications, 2007.

Farb, P. and Armelagos, G. 1980. *Consuming Passion: The Anthropology of Eating*. Boston, MA: Houghton Miffin Company.

Farquhar, J. 2002. *Appetites: Food and Sex in Post-socialist China*. Durham, NC: Duke University Press.

Felix, M. M. 1996. "Octavius." In *Tertullian: Apology and De Spectaculis. Minucius Felix: Ocatvius*. T. R. Glover and G. H. Rendall (trans.). Loeb

Classical Library. Cambridge, MA. and London: Harvard University Press & William Heinemann.

Ferraro, E. 2008. "Kneading Life: Women and the Celebration of the Dead in the Ecuadorian Andes." *Journal of the Royal Anthropological Institute* 14: 262–77.

Fiddes, N. 1991. *Meat: A Natural Symbol.* London: Routledge.

Fine, G. A. 1996. *Kitchens: The Culture of Restaurant Work.* Berkeley, CA: University of California Press.

Fischler, C. 1988. "Food, Self and Identity." *Social Science Information* 27: 275–92.

—2008. "France, Europe, the United States: What Eating Means to Us: An Interview with Claude Fischler and Estelle Masson, About the New Volume Published by Odile Jacob." OCHA (January 16). Available from http://www. le-mangeur-ocha.com/france-europe-the-united-states-what-eating-means-to-us-an-interview-with-claude-fischler-   and-estelle-masson-about-the-new-volume-published-by-odile-jacob/

—2011. Commensality, Society and Culture. *Social Science Information* 50: 528–49.

Flandrin, J. 2007. *Arranging the Meal: A History of Table Service in France.* J. Johnson (trans.). Berkeley, CA: University of California Press.

Fleming, D. E. 2004. *Democracy's Early Ancestors, Mari and Early Collective Governance.* Cambridge: Cambridge University Press.

—2009. "Kingship of City and Tribe Conjoined: Zimri-Lim at Mari." In J. Szuchman (ed.), *Nomads, Tribes, and the State in the Ancient Near East*, pp. 227–40. Chicago, IL: University of Chicago Press.

Foer, J. S. 2010. *Eating Animals.* New York: Back Bay Books.

Follieri, M. and Coccolini, G. B. L. 1983. "Palaeoethnobotanical Study of the VI A and VI B Periods of Arslantepe (Malatya, Turkey). Preliminary report." *Origini* XII/2: 599–662.

Forbrugerådet. 2010. *Unge om deres spisevaner og interesse for madlavning.* Forbrugerrådet/ YouGov. Available from http://www.taenk.dk/search/node/unge/om/deres/madvaner/og/ interesse/for/madlavning

Foster, R. J. 1991. "Making National Cultures in the Global Ecumene." *Annual Reviews of Anthropology* 20: 235–60.

Foucault, M. 1997. "The Birth of Biopolitics." In M. Foucault, *Ethics: Subjectivity and Truth*, 73–9, P. Rabinow (ed.). New York: The New Press.

Fowler, C. 2003. "Rates of (Ex)change. Decay and Growth, Memory and the Transformation of the Dead in Early Neolithic Southern Britain." In H. Williams (ed.), *Archaeologies of Remembrance*, pp. 45–63. New York: Kluwer Academic, Plenum Publishers.

Fox, R. and Harrell, K. 2008. "An Invitation to War: Constructing Alliances and Allegiances through Mycenean Palatial Feasts." In S. Baker, M. Allen, S. Middle, and K. Poole (eds), *Food and Drink in Archaeology I: University of Nottingham Postgraduate Conference 2007*, pp. 28–35. Trowbridge; Prospect Books.

Frangipane, M. (ed.). 2010. *Economic Centralisation in Formative States. The Archaeological Reconstruction of the Economic System in 4th Millennium Arslantepe*, Studi di Preistoria Orientale 3. Rome: Sapienza Università di Roma.

Frangipane, M. and Palmieri A., 1983. "A protourban centre of the Late Uruk Period." *Origini* XII/2: 287–454.

—1986. "Assetto redistributivo di una società protourbana della fine del IV millennio." *Dialoghi di Archeologia* IV/1: 35–44.

Franklin, B. 2005. *The Autobiography of Benjamin Franklin*. P. Conn (ed.). Philadelphia, PA: University of Pennsylvania Press.

Franzen, J. 2001. *The Corrections*. New York: Farrar, Strauss and Giroux.

Freedman, P. 2007. *Food: The History of Taste*. London: Thames and Hudson.

Freeman, M. 1977. "Sung." In K. C. Chang (ed.), *Food in Chinese Culture: Anthropological and Historical Perspectives*, pp. 141–62. New Haven, CT and London: Yale University Press.

Freiberger, O. 2009. *Der Askesediskurs in der Religionsgeschichte: eine vergleichende Untersuchung brahmanisher und frühchristlicher Texte*. Wiesbaden: Harrassowitz.

Freud, S. 1918. *Totem and Taboo*. New York: Vintage.

Friedberg, S. 2003. "Not all sweetness and light: new cultural geographies of food." *Social and Cultural Geography* 4(1): 3–6.

Garfinkel, Y. 1999. *Neolithic and Chalcolithic Pottery of the Southern Levant*. Jerusalem: Institute of Archaeology, The Hebrew University of Jerusalem (Qedem 39).

Garine, I. de. 2001. "Drinking in Northern Cameroon among the Masa and Muzey." In I. de Garine and V. de Garine (eds), *Drinking: Anthropological Approaches*, pp. 51–65. New York: Berghahn.

Garnsey, P. 1983. "Famine in Rome." In P. Garnsey and C. R. Whittaker (eds), *Trade and Famine in Classical Antiquity*, pp. 56–65. Cambridge: Cambridge Philological Society.

—1999. *Food and Society in Classical Antiquity*. Cambridge: Cambridge University Press.

Garrow, D., Beadsmoore, E., and Knight, M. 2005. "Pit clusters and the temporality of occupation: an earlier Neolithic site at Kilverstone, Thetford, Norfolk." *Proceedings of the Prehistoric Society* 71: 139–57.

Gates, M.-H. 1984. "Zimri-Lim's Palace at Mari." *Biblical Archaeologist* 47: 70–87.

Gearey, B. R., Fletcher, A., Fletcher, W. G., Campbell, S., Boomer, I., Keen, D., and Tetlow, E. 2011. "From Site to Landscape: Assessing the Value of Geoarchaeological Data in Understanding the Archaeological Record of Domuztepe, Eastern Mediterranean, Turkey." *American Journal of Archaeology* 115(3): 465–82.

Geertz, C. 1960. *The Religion of Java*. New York: The Free Press.

Giddens, A. 1984. *The Constitution of Society.* Berkeley and Los Angeles, CA: University of California Press.

—2009. *Sociology.* 6th edn. Cambridge: Polity Press.

Gilead, I. and Goren, Y. 1995. "Pottery Assemblages from Grar." In I. Gilead (ed.), *Grar: A Chalcolithic Site in the Northern Negev,* pp. 137–222. Beersheba: Ben Gurion University in the Negev Press.

Gilhus, I. S. 2006. *Animals Gods and Humans: Changing Attitudes to Animals in Greek, Roman and Early Christian Ideas.* London and New York: Routledge.

Glaeseman, R. R. 1978. *The Practice of the King's Meal at Mari: A System of Food Distribution in the 2nd Millennium B.C.,* Ph.D. dissertation, UCLA.

Goldblatt, H. 2000. "Forbidden food: the 'saturnicon' of Mo Yan." *World Literature Today* 74(3), 477–85.

Goldman, L. R. 1999. *The Anthropology of Cannibalism.* Westport, CT: Bergin and Garvey.

Goldstein, D. J., Coleman, R. C. and Williams, P. R. 2009. "You Are What You Drink: A Sociocultural Reconstruction of Pre-Hispanic Fermented Beverages Use at Cerro Baul, Moquegua, Peru." In J. Jennings and B. Bower (eds), *Drink, Power and Society in the Andes*, pp. 133–66. Gainesville, FL: University Press of Florida.

Goldstein, P. S. 2003. "From Stew-Eaters to Maize-Drinkers. The Chicha Economy and the Tiwanaku Expansion." In T. Bray (ed.), *The Archaeology and Politics of Food and Feasting in Early States and Empires,* pp. 143–72. New York: Kluwer Academic, Plenum Publishers.

Gong, W. 1993. "A Historical Survey of Chinese Wine Culture." *Journal of Popular Culture* 27(2), 57–73.

Goodland, R. and Anhang, J. 2009. "Livestock and Climate Change—What if the Key Actors in Climate Change are Cows, Pigs and Chicken?" *World Watch Magazine* 22(6): 10–19.

Goody, J. 1982. *Cooking, Cuisine and Class: A Study in Comparative Sociology.* Cambridge: Cambridge University Press.

Gordon, R. 1990. "The Veil of Power: Emperors, Sacrificers and Benefactors." In M. Beard and J. North (eds), *Pagan Priests*, pp. 199–231. London: Duckworth.

Goren, Y. and Fabian, P. 2002. *Kissufim Road, A Chalcolithic Mortuary Site.* Israel Antiquities Authority. Jerusalem. Vol. 16.

Gray, A. 2009. "'A Moveable Feast': Negotiating Gender at the Middle-class Tea-table in Eighteenth- and Nineteenth- century England." In S. Baker, A. Gray, K. Lakin, R. Madgwick, K. Poole, and M. Sandias (eds), *Food and Drink in Archaeology 2: University of Nottingham Postgraduate Conference 2008*, pp. 46–56. Trowbridge: Prospect Books.

Green, M. W. 1980. "Animal husbandry at Uruk in the Archaic Period." *Journal of Near Eastern Stidies* 39/1: 1–35.

Grignon, C. 2001. "Commensality and Social Morphology: An Essay of Typology." In P. Scholliers (ed.), *Food, Drink and Identity: Cooking, Eating and Drinking in Europe since the Middle Ages*, pp. 23–36. Oxford and New York: Berg.

Grumett, D. and Muers, R. 2010. *Theology on the Menu: Asceticism, Meat and Christian Diet*. London and New York: Routledge.

Gudeman, S. and Rivera, A. 1990. *Conversations in Colombia: The Domestic Economy in Life and Text*. Cambridge: Cambridge University Press.

Gusfield, J. R. 2003. "Passage to Play: Rituals of Drinking Time in American Society." In M. Douglas (ed.), *Constructive Drinking*, pp. 73–90. Abingdon: Routledge.

Haaland, R. 2007. "Porridge and Pot, Bread and Oven: Food Ways and Symbolism in Africa and the Near East from the Neolithic to the Present." *Cambridge Archaeological Journal* 17: 165–82.

Halstead, P. 2007. "Carcasses and Commensality: Investigating the Social Context of Meat Consumption in Neolithic and Early Bronze Age Greece." In C. Mee and J. Renard (eds), *Cooking up the Past: Food and Culinary Practices in the Neolithic and Bronze Age Aegean*, pp. 25–48. Oxford: Oxbow.

—2012. Feast, Food and Fodder in Neolithic-Bronze Age Greece: Commensality and the Construction of Value. In S. Pollock (ed.), *Between Feasts and Daily Meals: Toward an Archaeology of Commensal Spaces. eTopoi, Journal for Ancient Studies*, Special Volume 2: 21–51. Available from, http://journal.topoi. org (accessed April 2014).

Hamilakis, Y. and Konsolaki, E. 2004. "Pigs for the Gods: Burnt Animal Sacrifices as Embodied Rituals at a Mycenean Sanctuary." *Oxford Journal of Archaeology* 23: 135–51.

Harris, M. 1989. *Cows, Pigs, Wars and Witches: The Riddles of Culture*. New York: Vintage Books.

Harris, O. 1989. "The Earth and the State: The Sources and Meanings of Money in Northern Potosí, Bolivia." In J. Parry and M. Bloch (eds), *Money and the Morality of Exchange*. Cambridge: Cambridge University Press.

Harrison, R. K. 1980. *Leviticus: An Introduction and Commentary*. Downers Grove, IL: Inter-Varsity.

Hastorf, C. A. 1991. "Gender, Space, and Food in Prehistory." In J. Gero and M. Conkey (eds), *Engendering Archaeology*, pp. 132–59. Oxford: Blackwell.

Hastorf, C. A. and Weismantel, M. 2007. "Food: Where Opposites Meet." In K. C. Twiss (ed.), *The Archaeology of Food and Identity*, pp. 308–33. Center for Archaeological Investigations, Southern Illinois University Carbondale, Occasional Paper no. 34, Carbondale, IL.

Hausner, H., Bredie, W., Molgaard, C., Petersen, M. and Moller, P. 2008. "Differential Transfer of Dietary Flavour Compounds into Human Breast Milk." *Physiology and Behavior* 95: 118–24.

Hausner, H., Nicklaus, S., Issanchou, S., Molgaard, C. and Moller, P. 2010. "Breastfeeding Facilitates Acceptance of a Novel Dietary Flavour Compound." *Clinical Nutrition* 29: 141–8.

Hayden, B. 2001. "Fabulous Feasts: A Prolegomenon to the Importance of Feasting." In M. Dietler and B. Hayden (eds), *Feasts: Archaeological and Ethnographic Perspectives on Food, Politics, and Power*, pp. 23–64. Washington, DC: Smithsonian Institution Press.

Hayes, C. E. 2007. "The 'Other' in Rabbinic Literature." In C. E. Fonroebert and M. S. Jaffee (eds), *The Cambridge Companion to the Talmud and Rabbinic Literature*, pp. 243–69. New York: Cambridge University Press.

Hazan, H. 2003. "Holding Time Still With Cups of Tea." In M. Douglas (ed.), *Constructive Drinking*, pp. 205–19. Abingdon: Routledge.

Heimpel, W. 1996. "Moroccan locusts in Qattunan." *Revue d'Assyriologie et d'Archéologie Orientale* 90: 101–20.

—2003. *Letters to the King of Mari. A New Translation with Historical Introduction, Notes, and Commentary*. Winona Lake, IN: Eisenbrauns.

Heinz, B. and Lee, R. 1998. "Getting Down to the Meat: The Symbolic Construction of Meat Consumption." *Communication Studies* 49(1): 86–99.

Helwing, B. 2003. "Feasts as a Social Dynamic in Prehistoric Western Asia: Three Case Studies from Syria and Anatolia." *Paléorient* 29/2: 63–85.

Henrickson, E. F. and McDonald, M. M. A. 1983. "Ceramic Form and Function: An Ethnographic Search and an Archeological Application." *American Anthropologist*, 85/3: 630–43.

Hijara, I. 1978. "Three New Graves at Arpachiyah." *World Archaeology* 10: 125–8.

Hill, J. D. 1995. *Ritual and Rubbish in the Iron Age of Wessex*. Oxford: British Archaeological Reports 242.

Hines. M., Marshall, G., and Weaver, W. 1987. *The Larder Invaded: Reflections on Three Centuries of Philadelphia Food and Drink*. Philadelphia: The Library Company of Philadelphia.

Hirschman, A. 1996. "Melding the Public and Private Spheres: Taking Commensality Seriously." *Critical Review* 10(4): 533–50.

Hobsbawm, E. and Ranger, T. (eds). 1983. *The Invention of Tradition*. Cambridge: Cambridge University Press. http://chutzpah.typepad.com/slow-movement/2009/09/st-can-you-copyright-food-.html (accessed October 13, 2010). http://www.makansutra.com/Makanzine/aug00/national_day.html (accessed October 13, 2010). http://wwwstraitstimes.com/STI/STIMEDIA/pdfs/budget_speech_by_baey_keng.pdf (accessed October 13, 2010).

Hodder, I. 1987. "The Meaning of Discard: Ash and Domestic Space in Baringo." In S. Kent (ed.), *Method and Theory for Activity Area Research: An Ethnoarchaeological Approach*, pp. 424–48. New York: Columbia University Press.

—2004. "Neo-thingness." In J. Cherry, C. Scarre and S. Shennan (eds), *Explaining Social Change: Studies in Honour of Colin Renfrew*, pp. 45–52. Cambridge: McDonald Institute for Archaeological Research.

—2011. "Human-thing Entanglement: Towards an Integrated Archaeological Perspective." *Journal of the Royal Anthropological Institute* 17/1: 154–77.

Hofmann, K. P. and Schreiber, S. 2011. "Mit Lanzetten durch den practical turn: Zum Wechselspiel zwischen Mensch und Ding aus archäologischer Perspektive." *Ethnographisch-Archäologische Zeitschrift* 52(2): 163–87

Holm, L. and Kristensen, S. (eds) 2012. *Mad, mennesker og måltider.* Munksgaard. København.

—and Iversen, T. 1999. "Måltider som familie-skabelse og frisættelse." *Tidsskriftet Antropologi* 39: 53–64.

Holtzman, J. D. 2006. "Food and memory." *Annual Review of Anthropology* 35: 361–78.

Homan, M. M. 2004. "Beer and Its Drinkers: An Ancient Near Eastern Love Story." *Near Eastern Archaeology* 67: 84–95.

Hörning, K. H. 2001. *Experten des Alltags: Die Wiederentdeckung des praktischen Wissens.* 1. Aufl. Weilerswist: Velbrück Wiss.

—and Reuter, J. 2004. "Doing Culture: Kultur als Praxis." In K. H. Hörning and J. Reuter (eds), *Doing Culture. Neue Positionen zum Verhältnis von Kultur und sozialer Praxis*, pp. 9–15. Bielefeld: Transcript.

Howie, L., White, C. D., and Longstaffe, F. J. 2010. "Potographies and Biographies: The Role of Food in Ritual and Identity as Seen through Life Histories of Selected Maya Pots and People." In J. E. Staller and M. D. Carrasco (eds), *Pre-Columbian Foodways: Interdisciplinary Approaches to Food, Culture, and Markets in Mesoamerica*, pp. 369–98. New York: Springer.

Huizinga, J. 1949. *The Waning of the Middle Ages.* New York: Doubleday.

Ibrahim, F. 2001. "The Drinking Ritual among the Maasai." In I. de Garine and V. de Garine (ed.), *Drinking. AnthropologicalApproaches,* pp. 87–95. New York: Berghahn.

Ilan, D. and Rowan, Y. M. 2012. "Deconstructing and recomposing the narrative of spiritual life in the chalcolithic of the southern levant (4500–3600 B.C.E.)." *Archaeological Papers of the American Anthropological Association* 21(1): 89–113.

Irving, A. 2001. *A Contextual Study of Ceramic Evidence for Social Relations and Change During the Halaf-Ubaid Transition.* Unpublished Ph.D. thesis, University of Manchester.

—and Heywood, C. 2004. "The ceramics in the death pit at Domuztepe: conservation and analysis." *Anatolian Archaeology* 10: 6.

Isbell, B. J. 1985. *To Defend Ourselves: Ecology and Ritual in an Andean Village.* Prospect Heights, IL: Waveland Press.

Jamieson, R. W. and Sayre, M. B. 2010. "Barley and Identity in the Spanish Colonial Audiencia of Quito: Archaeobotany of the 18th Century San Blas Neighborhood in Riobamba." *Journal of Anthropological Archaeology* 29: 208–18.

Janowski, M. 2007. "Introduction: Feeding the Right Food: The Flow of Life and the Construction of Kinship in Southeast Asia." In M. Janowski and F. Kerlogue (eds), *Kinship and Food in South East Asia*. Copenhagen: Nordic Institute of Asian Studies Press.

Jauss, C. 2013. "Keramiknutzung in der späten Uruk-Zeit." In *Uruk. 5000 Jahre Megacity (Exhibition Catalogue, Pergamonmuseum, Berlin and Reiss-Engelhorn-Museen, Mannheim)*, pp. 24–5. Petersberg: Imhof-Verlag.

—submitted. "Cooking Techniques and the Role of Cooks in an Early Urban Society. Vessel Analysis, Experiment, Archaeological Context and Texts." To appear in S. Strak and M. Uckelmann (eds), *Proceedings of the Workshop Craft and People. Agents of Skilled Labour in the Archaeological Record, London 01–02.11.2012*. Technology and Change in History. Leiden: Brill.

Jay, N. 1993. *Throughout Your Generation Forever. Sacrifice, Religion, and Paternity*. Chicago, IL. and London: University of Chicago Press.

Jayapal, M. 1992. *Old Singapore*. Kuala Lumpur: Oxford University Press.

Jenkins, R. 2008 *Social Identity*. New York and London Routledge.

Jennings, J., Antrobus, K. L., Atencio, S. J., Glavich, E., Johnson, R., Loffler, G., Luu, C., Dietler, M., Hastorf, C. A., Hayden, B., Ikram, S., Le Count, L. J., McGovern, P. E., Samuel, D., Sigaut, F., Smalley, J. D., and Stika, H.-P. 2005. "'Drinking Beer in a Blissful Mood': Alcohol Production, Operational Chains, and Feasting in the Ancient World." *Current Anthropology* 46: 275–303.

—and Bowser, B. 2009. *Drink, Power and Society in the Andes*. Gainesville, FL: University Press of Florida.

Jennings, M. 2009. *Business Ethics: Case Studies and Selected Readings*. Mason, OH: Southwestern.

Joffee, A., Dessel. J., and Hallote, R. 2001. "The Gilat woman. female iconography, chalcolithic cult, and the end of the southern levantine prehistory." *Near Eastern Archaeology* 64: 9–23.

Johnston, J., Biro, A. and MacKendrick, N. 2009. "Lost in the supermarket: the corporate-organic foodscape and the struggle for food democracy." *Antipode* 41(3): 509–32.

Jones, M. 2007. *Feast: Why Humans Share Food*. New York: Oxford University Press.

—2007. "Food Choice, Symbolism, and Identity: Bread-and-butter Issues for Folklorists and Nutrition Studies." *Journal of American Folklore* 120(476): 129–77.

Joyce, A. A. 2010. "Expanding the Feast: Food Preparation, Feasting, and the Social Negotiation of Gender and Power." In E. A. Klarich (ed.), *Inside Ancient*

Kitchens: New Directions in the Study of Daily Meals and Feasts, pp. 221–39. Boulder, CO: University Press of Colorado.

Joyce, J. 1993. *A Portrait of the Artist as a Young Man*. New York: Penguin.

Joyce, R. A. 2008. "Practice in and as Deposition." In B. J. Mills and W. H. Walker (eds), *Memory Work. Archaeologies of Material Practices*, pp. 25–39. Santa Fe, NM: School for Advanced Research Press.

Junker, L. L. and Niziolek, L. 2010. "Food Preparation and Feasting in the Household and Political Economic of Pre- Hispanic Philippine Chiefdoms." In E. A. Klarich (ed.), *Inside Ancient Kitchens: New Directions in the Study of Daily Meals and Feasts*, pp. 17–53. Boulder, CO: University Press of Colorado.

Justin. 1993. "Apology." Revised by A. C. Coxe. In A. Roberts and J. Donaldson (eds), *The Ante-Nicene Fathers*. Vol. 1. Edinburgh: T&T Clark.

Kane, J. P. 1975. "The Mithraic Cult Meal in its Greek and Roman Environment." In J. R. Hinnells (ed.), *Mithraic Studies*. Proceedings of the First International Congress of Mithraic Studies. Vol. 2, pp. 313–51. Manchester: Manchester University Press.

Kansa, S. W., and Campbell, S. 2002. "Feasting With the Dead? A Ritual Bone Deposit at Domuztepe, South Eastern Turkey (c. 5550 cal. B.C.)." In S. J. O'Day, W. Van Neer and A. Ervynck (eds), *Behaviour Behind Bones: The Zooarchaeology of Religion, Ritual, Status and Identity*, pp. 2–13. Oxford: Oxbow.

—and Kennedy, A., Campbell, S. and Carter, E. 2009a. "Resource exploitation at late Neolithic Domuztepe: faunal and botanical evidence." *Current Anthropology* 50(6): 897–914.

—and Kennedy, A., Campbell, S. and Carter, E. 2009b. "Whose bones are those? comparative analysis of fragmented human and animal bones in the 'death pit' at Domuztepe, a late Neolithic settlement in southeastern Turkey." *Anthropozoologica* 44(1): 159–72.

Katz, S. H. and Voigt, M. M. 1986. "Bread and beer. the early use of cereals in the human diet." *Expedition* 28(2): 23–34.

Kelhoffer, J. A. 2004. "Did John the Baptist eat like a former essene? locust-eating in the ancient near east and at Qumran." *Dead Sea Discoveries*, 11: 293–314.

Kelly, I. 2003. *Cooking for Kings: The Life of Antonin Carême, the First Celebrity Chef*. New York: Walker.

Kennedy, J. R. 2012. "Commensality and Labor in Terminal Ubaid Northern Mesopotamia." In S. Pollock (ed.), *Between Feasts and Daily Meals: Towards Archaeology of Commensal Spaces. e-Topoi. Journal for Ancient Studies* 2: 125–56. Available from http://journal.topoi.org

Kerner, S. 2001. "Das Chalkolitikum in der südlichen Levante. Die Entwicklung handwerklicher Spezialisierung und ihre Beziehung zu gesellschaftlicher Komplexität." Orient Archäologie 8. Rahden/Westf: VML.

—2010. "Craft Specialisation and its Relation with Social Organisation in the Late 6th to Early 4th Millennium B.C.E. of the Southern Levant." *Paléorient* 36(1): 179–98.

Kieburg, A. 2008. "The Distribution of the Catering Trade in Ostia Antica." In S. Baker, M. Allen, S. Middle and K. Poole (eds), *Food and Drink in Archaeology I: University of Nottingham Postgraduate Conference 2007*, pp. 57–64. Trowbridge: Prospect Books.

Klarich, E. A. (ed.) 2010. *Inside Ancient Kitchens: New Directions in the Study of Daily Meals and Feasts*. Boulder, CO: University Press of Colorado.

Knechtges, D. R. "Literary Feast: Food in Early Chinese Literature." *Journal of the American Oriental Society* 106(1), 49–63.

Knipp, P., Cameron, C., Tan, H., Tettoni, H., and Chi, L. Tong. 1995. *The Raffles Hotel Cookbook*. Singapore: Editions Didier Millet.

Kobayashi, M. 1994. "Use-Alteration Analysis of Kalinga Pottery. Interior Carbon Deposit of Cooking Pots." In W. A. Longacre and J. M. Skibo (eds), *Kalinga Ethnoarchaeology. Expanding Archaeological Method and Theory*, pp. 127–68. Washington, DC: Smithsonian Institution Press.

Koentjaraningrat, R. M. 1985. *Javanese Culture*. Singapore: Oxford University Press.

Koeppel, R. 1940. *"Teleilat Ghassul II: compte rendu des fouilles de l'Institut Biblique Pontifical 1932–1936."* Rome: Institut Biblique Pontifical.

Kong, Lily. 2007. *Singapore Hawker Centres: People, Places, Food*. Singapore: National Environment Agency.

Koppen, F. van. 2006. "Miscellaneous Old Babylonian Period Documents." In M. W. Chavalas (ed.), *The Ancient Near East: Historical Sources in Translation*, pp. 107–33. Oxford: Blackwell.

Kyle, D. G. 1995. "Animal spectacles in ancient Rome." *Nikephoros* 7: 181–205.

Lactantius. 1970. *Of the Manner in which the Persecutors Died*. Revised by A. C. Coxe. In A. Roberts and J. Donaldson (eds), *The Ante-Nicene Fathers*. Vol. 7. Edinburgh: T&T Clark.

Lai, A. E. 2010. "The Kopitiam in Singapore: An Evolving Story about Migration and Cultural Diversity." Asia Research Institute Working Paper Series 132. Singapore: Asia Research Institute, National University of Singapore.

Lair, A. 2011. "The Ceremony of Dining at Napoleon III's Court Between 1852 and 1870." In D. De Vooght (ed.), *Royal Taste: Food, Power and Status at the European Courts after 1789*, pp. 143–69. Farnham and Burlington, VT: Ashgate.

Lampe, P. 2003. *Christians at Rome in the First Two Centuries: From Paul to Valentinus*. London and New York: Continuum.

Last, J. 2006. "Potted Histories. Towards an Understanding of Potsherds and their Contexts." In D. Papconstantinou (ed.), *Deconstructing Context, A Critical Approach to Archaeological Practice*, pp 120–37. Oxford: Oxbow.

LeCount, L. J. 2010. "Maya Palace Kitchens: Suprahousehold Food Preparation at the Late and Terminal Classic Site of Xunantunich, Belize." In E. A. Klarich (ed.), *Inside Ancient Kitchens: New Directions in the Study of Daily Meals and Feasts*, pp. 133–59. Boulder, CO: University Press of Colorado.

Lee, E. 2008. *Singapore: The Unexpected Nation*. Singapore: Institute of Southeast Asian Studies.

Legge, James (ed.) 2005. *The Chinese Classics: Volume 1*. London: Elibron Classics.

Leitzman, C. 2003. "Nutrition ecology: The contribution of vegetarian diets." *American Journal of Clinical Nutrition* 78 (sup.): 657S–9S.

Lepp, H. 2009. Desert truffles—Middle East and Mediterranean. http://www.anbg.gov.au/fungi/case-studies/desert-truffles.html (Accessed 1 October 2012).

Lévy-Strauss, C. 1963. *Totemism*. Rodney Needham (trans.). Boston, MA: Beacon Press.

—2008 [1966]. "The Culinary Triangle." Peter Brooks (trans.) In C. Counihan and P. van Esterik (eds), *Food and Culture: A Reader*, pp. 36–43. New York and London: Routledge.

Levy, T. E. (ed.). 2006. *Gilat. Archaeology, Anthropology and Cult*. London: Equinox.

Lewis, K. A. 2007. "Fields and Tables of Sheba: Food, Identity and Politics in Ancient Southern Arabia." In K. C. Twiss (ed.), *The Archaeology of Food and Identity*, pp. 192–217. Center for Archaeological Investigations, Southern Illinois University Carbondale, Occasional Paper no. 34: Carbondale, IL.

Lieber, A. 2006. "From symbolism to eucharist: the banquet in the early Christian world, by Dennis E. Smith." *The Jewish Quarterly Review* 96(2): 263–7.

Li, Z. 1996. *The Private Life of Chairman Mao*. London: Arrow Books.

Lii, H. "Down the Hatch." *Beijing Review* 48(8).

Lin, Q. 2005. *Brushing History Against the Grain: Reading the Chinese New Historical Fiction (1986–1999)*. Hong Kong: University of Hong Kong Press.

Lin, Y. 1938. *My Country and My People*. New York: Halcyon House.

Lindenbaum, S. 2004. "Thinking about Cannibalism." *Annual Review of Anthropology* 33: 475–98.

London, G. 2008. "Why Milk and Meat Don't Mix: A New Explanation for a Puzzling Kosher Law." *Biblical Archaeology Review* 34: 66–9.

Lucian. 1913–67. *On Salaried Posts in Great Houses*. In Complete Works. A. M. Harmon, K. Kilburn and M. D. MacLeod (trans.). (Loeb Classical Library) 8 vols. London: Heinemann.

Malalasekera, G. P. and Jayatilleke, K. N. 1958. *Buddhism and the Race Question*. Paris: UNESCO.

Malmberg, S. 2003. *Dazzling Dining. Banquets as an Expression of Imperial Legitimacy*. Uppsala University: Department of Archaeology and Ancient History.

Mandaville, J. P. 2011. *Bedouin Ethnobotany.Plant Concepts and Uses in a Desert Pastoral World*. Tuscon, AZ: University of Arizona Press.

Margomenou, D. 2008. "Food Storage in Prehistoric Northern Greece: Interrogating Complexity at the Margins of the 'Mycenaean World.'" *Journal of Mediterranean Archaeology* 21: 191–212.

Margueron, J.-C. 2004. *Mari: métropole de l'Euphrate au IIIe et au début du IIe millénaire av. J.-C.* Paris: ERC.

Marom, N., Raban-Gerstel, N., Mazar, A., and Bar-Oz, G. 2009. "Backbone of society: evidence for social and economic status of the Iron Age population of Tel Rehov, Beth Shean Valley, Israel." *Bulletin—American Schools of Oriental Research* 354: 55–75.

Martial. 1961. *Epigrams*. W. C. A. Ker (trans.). Loeb Classical Library. 2 vols. London: Heinemann.

Martin, L., Russell, N., Uluceviz, M. A., Baysal, A., Bredenbert, J., Cessford, C., Conolly, J., Farid, S., Hamilton, N., Last, J., Matthews, W., and Near, J. 2000. "Trashing Rubbish." In I. Hodder (ed.), *Towards Reflexive Method in Archaeology: The Example at Çatalhöyük*, pp. 57–69. Cambridge: McDonald Institute for Archaeological Research.

Matthews, C. 2006. "Livestock a Major Threat to Environment—Remedies Urgently Needed. November. Available from http://www.fao.org/newsroom/en/news/2006/1000448/index.html

Mauss, M. 1954. *The Gift: Forms and Functions of Exchange in Archaic Societies* [Essai sur le don, Paris, 1925]. Glencoe, IL: Free Press.

Mayer, E. 2002. *The Articulated Peasant: Household Economics in the Andes*. Boulder, CO. and Oxford: Westview Press.

McGovern, P. E. 2010. *Uncorking the Past: The Quest for Wine, Beer, and other Alcoholic Beverages*. Berkeley, CA: University of California Press.

McGowan, A. 1994. "Eating people: accusations of cannibalism against Christians in the second century." *Journal of Early Christian Studies* 2–3: 413–42.

—2010. "Rethinking eucharist origins." *Pacifica* 23: 173–91.

McOmish, D. 1996. "East Chisenbury: ritual and rubbish at the British Bronze Age–Iron Age transition. *Antiquity* 70: 68–76.

Meeks, W. A. 1983. *The First Urban Christians. The Social World of the Apostle Paul*. Binghamton, NY: Yale University Press.

Merriam-Webster's Dictionary and Thesaurus. 2014. Springfield, MA: Merriam Webster.

Mieroop. M. van de. 1999. *Cuneiform Texts and the Writing of History*, London: Routledge.

Miksic, J. N. and Low, C.-A. (eds). 2004. *Early Singapore 1300s–1819: Evidence in Maps, Text and Artifacts*. Singapore: Singapore History Museum.

Milano, L. 2004. "Food and Identity in Mesopotamia: A New Look at the Aluzinnu's Recipes." In C. Grottanelli and L. Milano (eds), *Food and Identity in the Ancient World*. History of the Ancient Near East, Studies 9, pp. 243–56. S.A.R.G.O.N. Editrice e Libreria.

Mills, B. (ed.). 2004. *Identity, Feasting, and the Archaeology of the Greater Southwest: Proceedings of the 2002 Southwest Symposium.* Colorado: University Press of Colorado.

—2007. "Performing the feast: visual display and suprahousehold commensalism in the Puebloan Southwest." *American Antiquity* 72: 210–39.

Millstone, E. and Lang, T. 2008. *The Atlas of Food—Who Eats What, Where, and Why.* Berkeley and Los Angeles, CA: University of California Press.

Minucius F. 1984. *Octavius.* G. H. Rendall (trans.). Loeb Classical Library. London: Heinemann.

Mitchell, S. 2007. *A History of the Later Roman Empire, AD 284–641. The Transformation of the Ancient World.* Oxford: Wiley-Blackwell.

Mo, Y. 1992. *Jiu Guo.* Beijing: Dangdai Shijie Chubanshe.

—2000. *The Republic of Wine.* H. Goldblatt (trans.). London: Hamish Hamilton.

Møller-Olsen, A. 2011. "Det Menneskeædende Samfund: Lu Xuns brug af kannibalisme som litterært motiv." *Trappe Tusind—Tidsskrift for litteraturvidenskab* 6: pp. 26–34.

Montefiore, S. 2003. *Stalin: In the Court of the Red Tsar.* New York: Knopf.

Moxey, K. 1989. "Festive Peasants and the Social Order." In K. Moxey (ed.), *Peasants, Warriors and Wives: Popular Imagery in the Reformation*, pp. 35–66. Chicago, IL: University of Chicago Press.

Mrozowski, S. A., Franklin, M., and Hunt, L. 2008. "Archaeobotanical analysis and interpretations of enslaved Virginian plant use at Rich Neck Plantation (44wb52). *American Antiquity* 73: 699–728.

Murdock, G. P. and Provost, C. 1973. "Factors in the division of labor by sex: a cross-cultural analysis." *Ethnology* 12(2): 203–25.

Myers, N. and Kent, J. 2003. "New Consumers: The Influence of Affluence on the Environment." *PNAS* 100(8): 4963–8. Available from http://www.pnas.org/content/100/8/4963

Mylona, D. 2008. *Fish-Eating in Greece from the Fifth Century B.C. to the Seventh Century A.D.: A Story of Impoverished Fishermen or Luxurious Fish Banquets?* Oxford: Archaeopress, BAR International Series S1754.

Namdar, D., Neumann, R., Goren, Y., and Weiner, S. 2008. "The content of unusual cone-shaped vessels (cornets) from the chalcolithic of the southern levant." *Journal of Archaeological Science* 36: 629–36.

National Museum Food Gallery, Exhibit. National Museum of Singapore.

Ng, A. 2009. "A Meal Fit for Royalty: When Chatterbox Presented It as a Premium Dish, It Changed the Way Chicken Rice was Eaten." *Today* 9 August, p. 8.

Niewenhuyse, O. 2007. *Plain and Painted Pottery. The Rise of Late Neolithic Ceramic Styles on the Syrian Plains.*Brussels: Brepols.

Nissen, H. J., Damerow, P., and Englund, R. K. 1990. *Frühe Schrift und Techniken der Wirtschaftsverwal- tung im alten Vorderen Orient: Informationsspeicherung und verarbeitung vor 5000 Jahren [Ausstellung frühe Schrift und Techniken der Wirtschaftsverwaltung im alten Vorderen Orient des Seminars für vorderasi- atische Altertumskunde der Freien Universität Berlin im Museum für Vor- und Frühgeschichte, Berlin-Charlottenburg, vom 16. Mai bis 29. Juli 1990].* Bad Salzdetfurth: Franzbecker.

Ogden, D. 2001. *Greek and Roman Necromancy.* Princeton, NJ and Oxford: Princeton University Press.

Otnes, C. C. 2007. "Consumption Rituals." In George Ritzer (ed.), *The Blackwell Encyclopedia of Sociology*, pp. 753–4. Oxford: Wiley-Blackwell.

Otto, A. 2012. "Defining and Transgressing the Boundaries between Ritual Commensality and Daily Commensal Practices: The Case of Late Bronze Age Tall Bazi." In S. Pollock (ed.), *Between Feasts and Daily Meals: Toward an Archaeology of Commensal Spaces. eTopoi, Journal for Ancient Studies*, Special Volume 2, 179–95.Available from: http://journal.topoi.org

Outram, A. K., Knüsel, C. J., Knight, S., and Harding, A. F. 2005. "Understanding Complex Fragmented Assemblages of Human and Animal Remains: A fully Integrated Approach." *Journal of Archaeological Science* 32(12): 1699–710.

Painchaud, L. 2008. "Polemical Aspects of the Gospel of Judas." In M. Scopello (ed.), *The Gospel of Judas in Context. Proceedings of the First International Conference on the Gospel of Judas.* Nag Hammadi Studies, 62, pp. 171–86. Leiden and Boston, MA: Brill.

Palmer, C. 1998. "From theory to practice: experiencing the nation in everyday life." *Journal of Material Culture* 3(2): 175–99.

—2002. "Milk and cereals: identifying food and food identity among Fallalhin and Bedouin in Jordan." *Levant* 34: 173–95.

Palumbi, G. 2010. "Pastoral Models and Centralised Animal Husbandry: The Case of Arslantepe." In M. Frangipane (ed.), *Economic Centralisation in Formative States. The Archaeological Reconstruction of the Economic System in 4th Millennium Arslantepe*, Studi di Preistoria Orientale 3, pp. 149–63. Rome: Sapienza Università di Roma.

Papaconstantinou, D. 2006. "Archaeological Context as a Unifying Process." In D. Papconstantinou (ed.), *Deconstructing Context, a Critical Approach to Archaeological Practice*, pp. 1–21. Oxford: Oxbow.

Papaefthymiou, A., Pilali, A., and Papadopoulou, E. 2007. "Les installations culinaires dans un village du Bronze Ancien en Grèce du nord: Archontiko Giannitson." In C. Mee and J. Renard (eds), *Cooking Up the Past: Food and*

Culinary Practices in the Neolithic and Bronze Age Aegean, pp. 136–47. Oxford: Oxbow.

Pappi, C. 2006. "The Jebel Bisri in the Physical and Cultural Landscape of the Ancient Near East." *Kaskal. Rivista di storia, ambienti e culture del Vicino Oriente Antico* 3: 241–56.

Parasecoli, F. 1999. "Food and Men in Cinema: An Exploration of Gender in BlockbusterMovies"(Doctoraldissertation).Hohenheim: UniversitätHohenheim. Available from http://opus.ub.uni-hohenheim.de/volltexte/2010/438/pdf/Diss_Food_and_Men_Parasecoli_Fabio.pdf

Parkinson. J. 1874. *American Dishes at the Centennial*. Philadelphia: King and Baird.

Paulos. "To the Corinthians, First." In Nestle-Aland (eds), *Novum Testamentum Graece*. Stuttgart 1981 [1. 1898]: Deutsche Bibelstiftung.

Pedersen, N. A. 1996. *Studies in the Sermon of the Great War: Investigations of a Manichean-Coptic text from the Fourth Century*. Århus: Århus University Press.

Pelto, G., Zhang. Y. and Habicht, J.-P. 2010. "Premastication: the second arm of infant and young child feeding for health and survival? *Maternal and Child Nutrition* 6(1): 4–18.

Petersen, A. K. 2012. "The Gospel of Judas: A Scriptural Amplification or Canonical Encroachment." In E. E. Popkes and G. Wurst (eds), *Judaevangelium und Codex Tchacos: Studien zur religionsgeschichtlichen Verortung einer gnostischen Schriftsammlung*. Tübingen: Mohr Siebeck, 245–82.

Pierce, E. 2008. "Dinner at the Edge of the World: Why the Greenland Norse Tried to Keep a European Diet in an Unforgiving Landscape." In S. Baker, M. Allen, S. Middle, and K. Poole (eds), *Food and Drink in Archaeology I: University of Nottingham Postgraduate Conference 2007*, pp. 96–105. Trowbridge: Prospect Books.

Pimentel, D. and Pimentel, M. 2003. "Sustainability of Meat-based an Plant-based Diets and the Environment." *American Journal of Clinical Nutrition* 78 (sup.): 660S–3S.

—Westra, L., and Noss, R. F. (eds). 2000. *Ecological Integrity: Integrating Environment, Conservation and Health*. Washington, DC: Island Press.

Pinkard, S. 2009. *A Revolution in Taste: The Rise of French Cooking*. Cambridge: Cambridge University Press.

Plinius Caecilius Secundus, C. 1997. C. "Plinius Traiano Imperatori." In *Pliny: Letters, Books VII–X. Panegyricus*. B. Radice (trans.). Loeb Classical Library. Cambridge, MA and London: Harvard University Press.

Pollan, M. 2006. *The Omnivore's Dilemma: A Natural History of Four Meals*. New York: Penguin Press.

—2008. *In Defense of Food: An Eater's Manifesto*. New York: Penguin Press.

Pollard, J. 2001. "The Aesthetics of Depositional Practice." *World Archeology* 33(2): 315–33.

Pollock, S. 2003. "Feasts, Funerals, and Fast-Food in Early Mesopotamian State." In T. Bray (ed.), *The Archaeology and Politics of Food and Feasting in Early States and Empires*, pp. 17–38. New York: Kluwer Academic.

—2012a. Commensality, social relations and ritual: between feasts and daily meals." In S. Pollock (ed.), *eTopoi, Journal for Ancient Studies* Special Volume 2. Available from http://journal.topoi.org

—2012b. "Towards Archaeology of Commensal Spaces. An Introduction." In S. Pollock (ed.), *Between Feasts and Daily Meals: Toward an Archaeology of Commensal Spaces. e-Topoi, Journal for Ancient Studies*, Special Volume 2, 1–20. Available from http://journal.topoi.org

—2012c. "Politics of food in early centralized societies." *Origini* 34: 153–68.

Porter, A. 2012. *Mobile Pastoralism and the Formation of Near Eastern Civilizations. Weaving Together Society*. Cambridge: Cambridge University Press.

Putnam, R. 2000. *Bowling Alone: The Collapse and Revival of American Community*. New York: Simon and Schuster.

Rapp, C. 2005. *Holy Bishops in Late Antiquity. The Nature of Christian Leadership in an Age of Transition*. Berkeley, CA: University of California Press.

Radner. 2004. "Fressen und gefressen warden. Heuschrecken als Katastrophe und Delikatesse im Alten Vorderen Orient." *Die Welt des Orient* 34: 7–22.

—2008. "Food and Diet: The Middle East." In P. Bogucki (ed.), *Encyclopedia of Society and Culture in the Ancient World*, pp. 475–6. New York: Facts on File.

Reckwitz, A. 2000. *Die Transformation der Kulturtheorien: Zur Entwicklung eines Theorieprogramms*. Weilerswist: Velbrück Wissenschaft.

—2002a. "Toward a theory of social practices. a development in culturalist theorizing." *European Journal of Social Theory* 5: 243–63.

—2002b. "Toward a theory of social practices: a development in culturalist theorizing." *European Journal of Social Theory* 5(2): 243–63.

—2002c. "The status of the 'material' in theories of culture: from 'social structure' to 'artifacts'." *Journal for the Theory of Social Behaviour* 32(2): 195–217.

—2003. "Grundelemente einer Theorie sozialer Praktiken: Eine sozialtheoretische Perspektive." *Zeitschrift für Soziologie* 32(4): 282–301.

Reynolds, F. 2007. "Food and Drink in Babylonia." In G. Leick (ed.), *The Babylonian World*, pp. 71–84. New York and London: Routledge.

Rice, P. M. 1987. *Pottery Analysis: A Sourcebook*. Chicago, IL: University of Chicago Press.

Richards, A. I. 1939. *Land, Labour and Diet in Northern Rhodesia*. London: Oxford University Press.

—2004 [1932]. *Hunger and Work in a Savage Tribe: A Functional Study of Nutrition among the Southern Bantu.* London: Routledge.

—and Thomas, J., 1984. "Ritual Activity and Structured Deposition in Later Neolithic Wessex." In R. Bradley and J. Gardiner (eds), *Neolithic Studies,* pp. 189–218. Oxford: British Archaeological Reports.

Riehl, S. 2006. "Nomadism, Pastoralism and Transhumance in the Archaeobotanical Record—Examples and Methodological Problems." In S. R. Hauser (ed.), *Die Sichtbarkeit von Nomaden und saisonaler Besiedlung in der Archäologie. Multidisziplinäre Annäherungen an ein methodisches Problem.* Orientwissenschaftliche Hefte 21, pp. 105–25. Halle.

Rippetoe, R. 2004. *Booze and the Private Eye: Alcohol in the Hard-boiled Novel.* Jefferson: McFarland & Company.

Rives, J. B. 2011. "The Theology of Animal Sacrifice in the Ancient Greek World: Origins and Development." In J. W. Knust and Z. Vérhelyi (eds), *Ancient Mediterranean Sacrifice,* pp. 187–202. Oxford and New York: Oxford University Press.

Robertson-Smith, W. 1889. *The Religion of the Semites.* London: Adair and Charles Black.

Rosenblum, J. D. 2010a. *Food and Identit in Early Rabbinic Judaism.* Cambridge and New York: Cambridge University Press.

—2010b. From Their Bread to Their Bed: Commensality, Intermarriage, and Idolatry in Tannaitic Literature. *Journal of Jewish Studies* 61/1: 18–29.

—Forthcoming. Jewish Meals in Antiquity. In J. M. Wilkins (ed.), *A Companion to Food in the Ancient World.* Malden, MA: Wiley-Blackwell.

Roux V. and Courty, M. A. 1998. "Les Bols élabores au tour d'Abu Hamid: Rupture techniqué au 4e millenaire avant J.C. dans le Levant Sud." *Paléorient* 23(1): 24–43.

Rowan, Y. M. and Golden, J. 2009. "The chalcolithic period of the southern levant: a synthetic review. *Journal of World Prehistory* 22: 1–92.

Roy, P. 2010. *Alimentary Tracts: Appetites, Aversions, and the Postcolonial.* Durham, NC: Duke University Press.

Rozin, P. 1998. "Food is fundamental, fun, frightening, and far-reaching." *Social Research* 66: 9–30.

Rüpke, J. 2010. "Hellenistic and Roman empires and Euro-mediterranean religion." *Journal of Religion in Europe* 3: 197–214.

Rutgers, L.V., van Strydonck, M., Boudin, M., and van der Linde, C. 2009. "Stable Isotope Data from the Early Christian Catacombs of Ancient Rome: New Insights into the Dietary Habits of Rome's Early Christians." *Journal of Archaeological Science* 36(5): 1127–34.

Samuel, D. 2000. "Brewing and Baking." In P. T. Nicholson and I. Shaw (eds), *Ancient Egyptian Materials and Technology,* pp. 537–76. Cambridge: Cambridge University Press.

Sanchez-Romero, M. 2011. "Commensality Rituals: Feeding Identities in Prehistory." In G. A. Jimenez et al. (eds), *Guess Who's Coming to Dinner,* pp. 8–29. Oxford, Oxbow.

Sande, S. 2011. "Smuler fra de rikes bord: antikviteten." *Klassisk Forum* 1: 10–26.

Sartore, R. L. 1994. *Humans Eating Humans.The Dark Shadow of Cannibalism.* Notre Dame: Cross Cultural Publications.

Sasson, J. M. 1984. "Thoughts of Zimri-Lim." *Biblical Archaeologist* 47: 110–20.

—1998. "The king and I: a Mari king in changing perceptions." *Journal of the American Oriental Society* 118: 453–70.

—2004. "The King's Table: Food and Fealty in Old Babylonian Mari." In C. Grottanelli and L. Milano (eds), *Food and Identity in the Ancient World.* History of the Ancient Near East, Studies 9, pp. 179–215. Padua: S.A.R.G.O.N. Editrice e Libreria.

Schafer, E. H. 1977. "T'ang." In K. C. Chang (ed.), *Food in Chinese Culture: Anthropological and Historical Perspectives.* New Haven, CT and London: Yale University Press.

Schatzki, T. R. 1996. *Social Practices: A Wittgensteinian Approach to Human Activity and the Social.* New York: Cambridge University Press.

—2002. *Site of the Social: A Philosophical Account of the Constitution of Social Life and Change.* University Park, PA: Pennsylvania State University Press.

—2006 [2001]. "Introduction. Practice Theory." In T. R. Schatzki et al. (eds), *The Practice Turn in Contemporary Theory,* pp. 1–14. London: Routledge.

—Knorr Cetina, K., and von Savigny, E. (eds). 2006. *The Practice Turn in Contemporary Theory.* London: Routledge.

Scheftelowitz, N. 2004. "The Pottery Assemblage." In N. Scheftelowitz and R. Oren (eds), *Giv'at Ha-Oranim,* pp. 37–58. Tel Aviv: Institute of Archaeology, Tel Aviv University.

Schiffer, M. B. 1987. *Formation Processes of the Archaeological Record.* Albuquerque, NM: University of New Mexico Press.

—1995. *Behavioral Archaeology. First Principles.* Salt Lake City, UT: University of Utah Press.

Scholliers, P. (ed.). 2001. *Food, Drink and Identity: Cooking, Eating and Drinking in Europe since the Middle Ages.* New York: Berg.

Scott, J. C. 1990. *Domination and the Arts of Resistance: Hidden Transcripts.* New Haven, CT: Yale University Press.

Scully, T. and Scully, E. 2002. *Early French Cookery: Original Recipes and Modern Adaptations.* Ann Arbor, MI: University of Michigan Press.

Seaton, P. 2008. *Chalcolithic Cult and Risk Management at Tuleilat Ghassul. The Area E Sanctuary.* Oxford: BAR IS 1864.

Shavit, E. 2008. "Truffles roasting in the evening fires: pages from the history of desert truffles." *Fungi* 1: 3.

Shaw, T. M. 1998. *The Burden of the Flesh. Fasting and Sexuality in Early Christianity*. Minneapolis, MN: Fortress Press.

Sherratt, A. 1981. "Plough and Pastoralism: Aspects of the Secondary Products Revolution." In I. Hodder, G. Isaac, and N. Hammond (eds), *Pattern of the Past: Studies in Honour of David Clarke*, pp. 261–305. Cambridge: Cambridge University Press.

—2007. "Alcohol and its Alternatives: Symbol and Substance in Pre-industrial Cultures." In J. Goodman, P. E. Lovejoy, and A. Sherratt (eds), *Consuming Habits*, pp. 11–46. London: Routledge.

Simmel, G. 1997a. "The Sociology of the Meal." In G. Simmel (ed.), *Simmel on Culture: Selected Writings*, pp. 130–6. London: Sage.

—1997b. *Simmel on Culture: Selected Writings by Georg Simmel*. D. Frisby and M. Featherstone (eds). London: Sage Publications.

—1997c [1910]. "Soziologie der Mahlzeit." In M. Landmann (ed.), *Brücke und Tür. Essays des Philosophischen zur Geschichte, Religion, Kunst und Gesellschaft*, 243–50. Stuttgart: K. F. Koehler.

Simoons, F. J. 1991. *Food in China: A Cultural and Historical Inquiry.* Boston, MA: CRC Press.

Singapore Infopedia. (2010). "Hainanse Chicken Rice." Available from http://infopedia.nl.sg/articles/SIP_910_2005–01–11.html (accessed October 13, 2010).

Singapore: The Encyclopedia. 2006. Singapore: Editions Didier Millet.

Siskind, J. 1973. *To Hunt in the Morning*. Oxford: Oxford University Press.

Skibo, J. M. 1992. *Pottery Function. A Use-Alteration Perspective*. New York: Plenum Press.

Smith, A. and Munro, N. D. 2009. "A Holistic Approach to Examining Ancient Agriculture." *Current Anthropology* 50: 925–36.

Smith, D. E. 2003. *From Symposium to Eucharist. The Banquet in the Early Christian World*. Minneapolis, MN: Fortress Press.

Smith, J. Z. 1998. Religion, Religions, Religious. In M. C. Taylor (ed.), *Critical Terms for Religious Studies*, pp. 269–84. Chicago, IL: University of Chicago Press.

Smith, M. L. 1985. Toward an Economic Interpretation of Ceramics: Relating Vessel Size and Shape to Use. In B. A. Nelson (ed.), *Decoding Prehistoric Ceramics*, pp. 254–309. Carbondale, IL: Southern Illinois University Press.

Smith, W. Robertson. 1889. *Lectures on the Religion of the Semites*. Edinburgh: Black.

—1957 [1889]. *The Religion of the Semites*. New York: Meridian Books.

—1997 [1889] Lectures on the Religion of the Semites. In *The Early Sociology of Religion*, pp. 244–68. London: Routledge/Thoemmes Press.

Sobal, J. 2000. "Sociability and Meals: Facilitation, Commensality, and Interaction." In Herbert L. Meiselman (ed.), *Dimensions of the Meal: The Science, Culture, Business, and Art of Eating*, pp. 119–33. Gaithersburg, MD: Aspen.

—and Wasink, B. 2007. Kitchenscapes, Tablescapes, Platescapes, and Foodscapes. *Environments and Behavior* 39: 124–42.

Sorabji, R. 1993. *Animal Minds and Human Morals: The Origins of the Western Debate*. London: Duckworth.

Spedding, P. A. 1998. "Contra-afinidad: algunos comentarios sobre el compadrazgo andino." In Denise Y. Arnold (ed.), *Gente de carne y hueso: las tramas de parentesco en los Andes*. La Paz: ILCA/CIASE.

Spielmann, K A. 2002. "Feasting, craft specialization, and the ritual mode of production in small-scale societies." *American Anthropologist* 104(1): 195–207.

—Clark, T., Hawkey, D., Rainey, K., and Fish, S. K. 2009. "'… Being weary, they had rebelled': Pueblo subsistence and labor under Spanish colonialism." *Journal of Anthropological Archaeology* 28: 102–25.

Steinfeld, H., Gerber, P., Wassenaar, T., Castel, V., Rosales, M., de Haan, C. 2006. "Livestock's Long Shadow— Environmental Issues and Options." FAO/LEAD Report 2006. Available from http://www.fao.org/newsroom/en/news/2006/10004

Stobart, H. 2006. *Music and the Poetics of Production in the Bolivian Andes*. Aldershot and Burlington, NH: Ashgate.

Stocks, P. 1970. "Cancer mortality in relation to national consumption of cigarettes, solid fuel, tea and coffee. *British Journal of Cancer* 24(2): 215–25.

Stowers, S. K. 1995. "Greeks Who Sacrifice and Those Who Do Not: Towards an Anthropology of Greek Religion." In L. M. White and O. L. Yarsbrough (eds), *The Social World of the First Christians. Essays in Honor of Wayne A. Meeks*, pp. 293–333. Minneapolis, MN: Fortress Press.

Strack, H. L. and G. Stemberger. 1996. *Introduction to the Talmud and Midrash*. M. Bockmuehl (ed. and trans.). Minneapolis, MN: Fortress Press.

Strong, R. 2002. *Feast: A History of Grand Eating*. London: Jonathan Cape.

Stross, B. 2010. "This World and Beyond: Food Practices and the Social Order in Mayan Religion." In J. E. Staller and M. D. Carrasco (eds), *Pre-Columbian Foodways: Interdisciplinary Approaches to Food, Culture, and Markets in Mesoamerica*, pp. 553–76. New York: Springer.

Sunseri, K. U. 2009. "Nowhere to Run, Everywhere to Hide: Multi-scalar Identity Practices at Casitas Viejas," Ph.D. dissertation, Department of Anthropology, University of California, Santa Cruz, CA.

Sykes, N. 2005. "Hunting for the Anglo-Normans: Zooarchaeological Evidence for Medieval Identity." In A. Pluskowski (ed.), *Just Skin and Bones? New Perspectives on Animal-Human Relations in the Historic Past*, pp. 73–80. Oxford: Archaeopress, BAR International Series 1410.

—2006. "The Impact of the Normans on Hunting Practices in England." In C. Woolgar, D. Serjeantson, and T. Waldron (eds), *Food in Medieval England: History and Archaeology*, pp. 162–75. Oxford: Oxford University Press.

Szuchman, J. (ed.). 2009. "Integrating Approaches to Nomads, Tribes, and the State in the Ancient Near East." In J. Szuchman (ed.), *Nomads, Tribes, and the State in the Ancient Near East*, pp. 1–14. Chicago, IL: University of Chicago Press.

Tallon, P. 1997. "Old Babylonian texts from Chagar Bazar." *Akkadica Supplementum* 10.

Tam, S. M. 2001. "Lost and Found? Reconstructing Hong Kong Identity in the Idiosyncrasy and Syncretism of *Yumcha*." In D. Y. H. Wu and C.-B. Tan (eds), *Changing Chinese Foodways in Asia*, pp. 49–69. Hong Kong: Hong Kong University Press.

Tan, C.-B. 2003. "Family Meals in Rural Fujian: Aspects of Yongchun Village Life." *Taiwan Journal of Anthropology* 1(1): 179–95.

Tan, S. 2004. *Singapore Heritage Food: Yesterday's Recipes for Today's Cook*. Singapore: Landmark Books.

Tani, M. 1995. "Beyond the Identification of Formation Processes: Behavioural Inference Based on Traces Left by Cultural Formation Processes." *Journal of Archaeological Method and Theory* 2(3): 231–52.

Tannahill, R. 1988. *Food in History*. New York: Three Rivers Press.

Tertullian. 1993. "Ad nationes." Dr. Holmes (trans). In A. Roberts and J. Donaldson (eds), *The Ante-Nicene Fathers*. Vol. 3. Edinburgh: T&T Clark.

—1966. *Apologeticus*. T. R. Glover (trans.). Loeb Classical Library. London: Heinemann.

—"The Prescription against Heretics." Revised by A. C. Coxe. In A. Roberts and J. Donaldson (eds), *The Ante-Nicene Fathers*. Vol. 3. Edinburgh: T&T Clark.

Thomas, J. 1996. *Time, Culture and Identity: An Interpretative Archaeology*. London: Routledge.

—1999. *Understanding the Neolithic*. London: Routledge.

Thomas, R. 2007. "They Were What They Ate: Maintaining Social Boundaries through the Consumption of Food in Medieval England." In K. C. Twiss (ed.), *The Archaeology of Food and Identity* pp. 130–51. Center for Archaeological Investigations, Southern Illinois University Carbondale. Occasional Paper no. 34: Carbondale, IL.

Thomassen, E. 2004. "Orthodoxy and Heresy in Second-century Rome." *Harvard Theological Review* 97(3): 241–56.

Thoreau, H. D. 2008 [1854]. *Walden (or Life in the Woods)*. Radfod, VA: Wilder Publications.

Tilman, D., Fargione, J., Wolff, B., D'Antonio, C., Dobson, A., Howarth, R., Schindler, D., Schlesinger, W. H., Simberloff, D., and Swackhamer, D. 2001. "Forecasting Agriculturally Driven Global Environmental Change." *Science* 292: 281–4.

Tomkins, P. 2007. "Communality and Competition: The Social Life of Food and Containers at Aceramic and Early Neolithic Knossos, Crete." In C. Mee and J. Renard (eds), *Cooking Up the Past: Food and Culinary Practices in the Neolithic and Bronze Age Aegean*, pp. 174–99. Oxford: Oxbow.

Troubleyn, L., Kinnaer, F., Ervynck, A., Beeckmans, L., Caluwé, D., Cooremans, B., Buyser, F. D., Deforce, K., Desender, K., Lentacker, A., Moens, J., Bulck, G. V., Dijck, M. V., Van Neer, W., and Wouters, W. 2009. "Consumption Patterns and Living Conditions inside *Het Steen*, The Late Medieval Prison of Malines (Mechelen, Belgium)." *Journal of the Archaeology of the Low Countries* 1–2: 5–47.

Turkon, P. 2004. "Food and Status in the Prehispanic Malpaso Valley, Zacatecas, Mexico." *Journal of Anthropological Archaeology* 23: 225–51.

Turnbull, M. C. 1989. *A History of Singapore 1819–1988*. Singapore, Oxford, New York: Oxford University Press.

Turner, V. 1969. *The Ritual Process: Structure and Anti-structure*. Chicago, IL: Aldine.

—1988. *The Anthropology of Performance*. New York: PAJ Publications.

—1997 [1969]. *The Ritual Process: Structure and Anti-structure*. Hawthorne, NY: Aldine de Gruyter.

—and Bruner, E. M. (eds). 1986. *The Anthropology of Experience*. Urbana and Chicago, IL: University of Illinois Press.

Twiss, K. C. (ed.). 2007a. *The Archaeology of Food and Identity*. Carbondale, IL: Center for Archaeological Investigations.

—2007b. "Home is Where the Hearth Is: Food and Identity in the Neolithic Levant." In K. Twiss (ed.), *The Archaeology of Food and Identity*, pp. 50–68. Center for Archaeological Investigations, Southern Illinois University Carbondale, Occasional Papers 34.

—2008. "Transformations in an early agricultural society: feasting in the southern levantine pre-pottery Neolithic." *Journal of Anthropological Archaeology* 27: 418–42.

—Bogaard, A., Charles, M. P., Henecke, J., Russell, N., Martin, L., and Jones, G. 2009. "Plants and animals together: interpreting organic remains from building 52 at Çatalhöyük." *Current Anthropology* 5: 885–95.

Ullén, I. 1994. "The power of case studies: interpretation of a late Bronze Age settlement in central Sweden." *Journal of European Archaeology* 2(2): 249–62.

Urem-Kotsou, D. and Kotsakis, K. 2007. "Pottery, Cuisine and Community in the Neolithic of North Greece." In C. Mee and J. Renard (eds), *Cooking Up the Past: Food and Culinary Practices in the Neolithic and Bronze Age Aegean*, pp. 225–46. Oxford: Oxbow.

Ussishkin, D. 1971. "The 'Ghassulian' temple in Ein Gedi and the origin of the hoard from Nahal Mishmar." *The Biblical Archaeologist* 34(1): 23–39.

Valantasis, R. 1995. "A Theory of the Social Function of Asceticism." In V. L. Wimbush and R. Valantasis (eds), *Asceticism*, pp. 544–2. Oxford and New York: Oxford University Press.

Van Esterik, P. 1995. "Care, caregiving and caretakers." *Food and Nutrition Bulletin* 16(4): 378–8).

—"Anna and the king: digesting difference." *Southeast Asian Research* 14(2): 289–307.

—"Revisiting Lao Food: Pain and Commensality." In L. Coleman (ed.), *Food: Ethnographic Encounters*, pp. 59–68. London: Berg Press.

—"Right to food; right to feed; right to be fed: the intersection of women's rights and the right to food." *Agriculture and Human Values* 16: 225–32.

Vandenbroeck, P. 1984. "Verbeeck's peasant weddings: a study of iconography and social function. *Simiolus* 14: 79–124.

Veen, M. van der. 2007. "Luxury Foods: Their Nature and Role in Iron Age and Early Roman Southern Britain." In K. C. Twiss (ed.), *The Archaeology of Food and Identity*, pp. 112–29. Center for Archaeological Investigations, Southern Illinois University: Carbondale, IL.

Vencl, S. 1994. "The archaeology of thirst." *Journal of European Archaeology* 2(2): 299–326.

Vermaseren, M. J. 1965. *Mithras. Geschichte eines Kultes*. Stuttgart: Kohlhammer Verlag.

Vernant, J. P. 1981. "Sacrificial and Alimentary Codes in Hesiod's Myth." In R. Gordon (ed.), *Myth, Religion and Society. Structural Essays by M. Detienne, L. Gernet, J. P. Vernant and P. Vidal-Naquet*, pp. 57–79. Cambridge and Paris: Cambridge University Press/Editions de la Maison des sciences de l'homme.

Vogel, H. 2009. *Wie man Macht macht: Eine macht- und genderkritische Untersuchung der frühesten Repräsentationen von Staatlichkeit*. Ph.D. Dissertation. Freie Universität Berlin 2008. Available from http://www.diss. fu-berlin.de/diss/receive/FUDISS_thesis_000000008148

Vooght, D. de. (ed.). 2011. *Royal Taste: Food, Power and Status at the European Courts after 1789*. Farnham and Burlington, VA: Ashgate.

Wagensonner, K. 2010. "Early Lexical Lists Revisited: Structures and Classification as a Mnemonic Device." In L. Kogan and N. V. Koslova (eds), *Language in the Ancient Near East: Proceedings of the 53e Rencontre Assyriologique Internationale*, pp. 285–310. Winona Lake, IN: Eisenbrauns.

Wagner, R. 1991. "The Fractal Person." In M. Godelier and M. Strathern (eds), *Big Men and Great Men. Personifica- tions of Power in Melanesia*, pp. 159–73. Cambridge, Paris: Cambridge University Press, Éditions de la Maison des Sciences de l'Homme.

Warner, D. X. 1998. *Mr. Five Dippers of Drunkenville: The Representation of Enlightenment in Wang Ji's Drinking Poems*. The Journal of American Oriental Society 118(3): 247–356.

Watson, J. L. 1987. "From the Common Pot: Feasting with Equals in Chinese Society." *Anthropos* 82: 389–461.

—2011. "Feeding the Revolution: Public Mess Halls and Coercive Commensality in Maoist China." In Everett Zhang, A. Kleinman and W. Tu (eds), *Governance of Life in Chinese Moral Experience*, pp. 33–46. London: Routledge

Wei, H., Chen, H., and Zu, S. 2005. "China: alcohol today." *Addiction* 100(6), 737–41.

Weiner, A. 1992. *Inalienable Possessions. The Paradox of Keeping-While Giving.* Berkeley, CA: University of California Press.

Weismantel, M. J. 1988. *Food Gender, and Poverty in the Ecuadorian Andes.* Philadelphia, PA: University of Pennsylvania Press.

Wenger, E. 1999. *Communities of Practice: Learning, Meaning, and Identity.* Learning in Doing: Social, Cognitive, and Computational Perspectives. Cambridge: Cambridge University Press.

Wharton, E. 1996. *The Age of Innocence.* New York: Penguin.

White, C. 2005. "Gendered Food Behaviour among the Maya." *Journal of Social Archaeology* 5: 356–82.

Whiting, R. M. 1995." Amorite Tribes and Nations." In J. Sasson (ed.), *Civilizations of the Ancient Near East*, pp. 1231–42. New York: Scribner.

Whittle A., Pollard, J., and Grigson, C. 1999. *The Harmony of Symbols: The Windmill Hill Causewayed Enclosure, Wiltshire.* Oxford: Oxbow.

Wilk, R. R. 1999. "Real Belizean food: Building Local Identity in the Transnational Caribbean." *American Anthropologist* 101(2): 244–55.

Williams, A. 2009. "Lifecycle Influences and Opportunities for Change." In F. Dykes and V. Moran (eds), *Infant and Young Child Feeding: Challenges to Implementing a Global Strategy.* Oxford: Wiley-Blackwell.

Williams, S. and Friell, G. 1995. *Theodosius. The Empire at Bay.* New Haven, CT: Yale University Press.

Wilson, D. C. 1994. "Identification and assessment of secondary refuse aggregates. *Journal of Archaeological Method and Theory* 1(1): 41–68.

Winston, A. 2004. "Bringing political economy into the debate on the obesity epidemic. *Agriculture and Human Values* 21: 299–312.

Wise, M. 1996. *Travellers' Tales of Old Singapore.* Singapore: Times Book International.

Wong, H. S. 2009. *Wartime Kitchen: Food and Eating in Singapore.* Singapore: National Museum of Singapore and Editions Didier Millet.

Woolf, A. and Eldridge, R. 1994. "Sharing a drink with Marcel Mauss: the uses and abuses of alcohol in early medieval Europe. *Journal of European Archaeology* 2(2): 327–40.

Woolgar, C. 1999. *The Great Household in Late Medieval England.* New Haven, CT: Yale University Press.

World Health Organization [WHO]. 2011a. *Regional Strategy on Nutrition 2010–2019 and Plan of Action.* Available from http://applications.emro.who. int/dsaf/dsa1230.pdf

—2011b. "Pollution Sources and Levels." January 21. Available from: http:// www.who.int/indoorair/health_impacts/exposure/en/index.html (accessed July 14, 2014).

—2011c. "Household Air Pollution and Health." Fact sheet No. 294. January 21. Available from: http://www.who.int/mediacentre/factsheets/fs292/en/index. html#.TxwWR7Y-y1A (accessed July 14, 2014).

—2011d. "Indoor Air Pollution. Broader Impacts of Household Energy." January 21. Available from: http://www.who.int/indoorair/impacts/en/ (accessed July 14, 2014).

Wright, J. C. 2004. "A Survey of Evidence for Feasting in Mycenaean Society." In J. C. Wright (ed.), *The Mycenaean Feast*, pp. 13–58. Princeton, NJ: American School of Classical Studies at Athens.

—2010a. "Commensal politics in ancient Western Asia: the background to Nehemiah's feasting (Part I)." *Zeitschrift für Alttestamentliche Wissenschaft* 122: 212–33.

—2010b. "Commensal politics in ancient Western Asia: the background to Nehemiah's feasting (Part II). *Zeitschrift für Alttestamentliche Wissenschaft* 122: 333–52.

Yü, Y. S. 1977. "Han." In K. C. Chang (ed.), *Food in Chinese Culture: Anthropological and Historical Perspectives*, New Haven, CT and London: Yale University Press.

Yue, G. 1999. *The Mouth That Begs: Hunger, Cannibalism and the Politics of Eating in Modern China*. Durham, NC: Duke University Press.

Index